W9-AMV-669

AFRICANS ON AFRICAN-AMERICANS

Also by Yekutiel Gershoni

BLACK COLONIALISM: The Americo-Liberian Scramble for the Hinterland

Africans on African-Americans

The Creation and Uses of an African-American Myth

Yekutiel Gershoni
Tel Aviv University

NEW YORK UNIVERSITY PRESS
Washington Square, New York

© Yekutiel Gershoni 1997

All rights reserved

First published in the U.S.A. in 1997 by
NEW YORK UNIVERSITY PRESS
Washington Square
New York, N.Y. 10003

This book is printed on paper suitable for recycling and
made from fully managed and sustained forest sources.

Library of Congress Cataloging-in-Publication Data
Gershoni, Yekutiel, 1943–
Africans on African-Americans : the creation and uses of an
African-American myth / Yekutiel Gershoni.
p. cm.
Includes bibliographical references and index.
ISBN 0–8147–3082–5
1. Africa—Civilization—Afro-American influences. I. Title.
DT14.G47 1996
305.896'07306—dc20   96–9222
                                                            CIP

Printed in Great Britain

I dedicate this book to my very dear friend, the late Simcha Holtzberg, a Holocaust survivor who devoted his life to helping others.

Contents

Preface

The idea for a comprehensive study of the image of African-Americans in Africa came to me in the course of my research on Liberia, which has been the subject of most of my historical investigations. While exploring the history of the black republic, I wondered whether Liberia was the only country in Africa where African-Americans lived. Gradually, I found out that while their physical presence was restricted almost exclusively to Liberia, their image pervaded the entire continent. Ironically, though, Liberia is the only place in Africa where the Americo-Liberians or Congos – as the black Americans who settled there were termed – were feared and hated. The colonial-like administration which they established for the African population and their oppressive rule inspired resentment and violent reactions. In the rest of the continent, as will be shown, many Africans greatly admired African-Americans, to the point of creating a whole mythology around them.

This study would never have been completed without the help of many friends and colleagues, who are too numerous to name. I would, however, like to express my gratitude to my family – to my sons, Arik, Kobi and Maor, and especially to my wife Ruth – who gave unstinting encouragement and support during the long years of research and writing. I would also like to thank Miriam Greenfield for her wonderful work as my research assistant and typist. Finally, I would like to thank Toby Mostysser, whose editing ability made writing this manuscript a far less plodding affair.

Introduction

Ever since the fifteenth century, when European traders first established trading posts along the coasts of Africa, the black continent has had strong economic, cultural and political ties to Europe. The traders were followed by missionaries who labored to spread Christianity and European culture. They, in turn, were followed by European settlers and, in the nineteenth century, by the colonial authorities. The overall outcome was that generations of Africans, especially in the western and southern parts of the continent, absorbed European values. Western-educated Africans strove to become black Frenchmen and black Englishmen. America, whose lifestyle, cultural values and political system were all so different from those of Europe, seemed far away from Africa and alien to most Africans.

On the other side of the Atlantic, few African-Americans found Africa appealing or attractive. While there were black Americans who emigrated to their motherland, the back-to-Africa movement never developed into a mass exodus. Most African descendants preferred to remain in the New World. St Clair Drake, a major scholar who analyzes the relationship between African-Americans and Africans, emphasizes the lack of contact:

> Despite the ever-present consciousness of Africa, very few American Negroes since the Civil War have had any face-to-face contact with Africans. From Emancipation until the close of World War II, the primary type of contact between Africans and Negro Americans on American soil was that which took place upon the campuses of Negro educational institutions between the few African students who happened to be in the United States and Negro students and teachers. . . . Within Africa itself, the primary type of contact was that of a few Negro missionaries interacting with varied categories of Africans, these, too, being relatively few in number.[1]

Nevertheless, the physical and cultural distance between the two continents did not entirely cut them off from one another. The slave trade and the facts it created had a decisive impact on the relationship between Africa and the New World. In the Caribbean, South America and North America, communities of Africans were established. These Africans retained their ties with their motherland. A small number of them made their way back to Africa, some of them intent on settling permanently in their ancient homeland, others as explorers, missionaries and seamen. George Shepperson points out that there was 'a commerce of ideas and politics between the descendants of the slaves in the West Indies and North America and their ancestral continent'.[2] The most obvious example is Liberia, established in 1822 as a colony by free blacks and ex-slaves from the southern United States and the West Indies, and made the first black republic in Africa in 1847. From its inception, small numbers of blacks from the western hemisphere returned and settled there.

Not only people, but also information traveled from the New World to Africa. Throughout the nineteenth century, information about America, and especially about the social, economic and political situation of African-Americans, reached Africa via New World blacks who returned to Africa, whether to visit or settle, and via the written word: newspapers, pamphlets and books. The main attraction of America for Africans was the simple fact that millions of African descendants lived there, which could not be said of any European country. This attraction overcame the geographical and cultural distances as well as the relative indifference of American blacks toward their African brethren.

During the colonial period between the late nineteenth century and the outbreak of World War II, Africans' generally moderate interest in the black communities in the New World was greatly intensified. The expansion of colonial rule and white settlement caused massive disorientation among both traditional and western-educated Africans. Traditional Africans suddenly found their cultural institutions and mores, which had stood them in good stead for centuries, utterly ineffective in the face of the new political, cultural and economic realities. Western-educated Africans, who had enjoyed elite status in the small European enclaves along the coast, found themselves displaced in favor of traditional tribal chiefs, as the Europeans pushed into the interior of the continent, and spurned under the rationale of the then fashionable social Darwinism. In their efforts to deal with these upheavals, many Africans, traditional no less than westernized, sought succor in images of America and black Americans.

America became a reference point. Africans could compare the social, economic and political status of African-Americans with their own status under white colonial rule. They could contrast the racial equality guaranteed by the United States Constitution with the colonial governments' legal discrimination against blacks. In these comparisons, the United States emerged as powerful, progressive and humanitarian, 'God's country', as the Nigerian national leader Nnamdi Azikiwe called it.[3] The positive perception of the United States flowed into a positive perception of the black community. As many Africans saw it, American blacks enjoyed all the advantages of the country's free market economy and freedom of expression, movement and association. Black Americans were considered a highly advanced and privileged group who had attained financial and social status far above that of Africans in their own continent.

The more frustrated Africans became with the limitations imposed on them by colonial rule, the greater their drive to look to America for solutions to their cultural, social and political dilemmas. In their search, many of them mythologized the black American experience, idealizing black Americans' accomplishments and well-being, downplaying their miseries, and creating what in this book is termed the African-American myth. This was a myth in the sense of the term as explained by Mark Schorer: 'A myth is a large, controlling image that gives philosophical meaning to the facts of ordinary life; that is, which has organizing value for experience.'[4]

Myth, to be sure, is a complex phenomenon which scholars in many disciplines have struggled to comprehend.[5] It is open to many interpretations, many definitions. Though this study borrows freely from the insights of scholars in the field, it does not enter into the depths or complexities of the concept or into the scholarly debates that surround it. Such a journey would take us far beyond the scope of the book, which is, first of all, to show that there was in fact an African-American myth in many parts of Africa and, secondly, to indicate at least some of the ways in which it was used by Africans. For these purposes, the concept of myth is treated rather loosely. It is applied without philosophical rigor, in the layman's sense or senses of the term, sometimes in the singular, when the global concept is meant, sometimes in the plural, when the reference is to the various images, components, or versions of the larger myth, each of which can be considered a myth on its own.

Roughly, the term as it is employed in this study refers to a commonly held set of images and convictions, uncritically accepted and used for a variety of social and political purposes. As distinct from Christianity and other religions, the convictions were in no way codified or formalized. Nor did they exist apart from the uses that Africans made of them. They were developed in Africa itself and varied from one part of the continent to another. What holds them together as myth for this study is the commonality and aggrandizement inherent in the beliefs. This book thus speaks of a multifaceted myth that provided Africans with a point of reference and an imaginary world that had just enough relation to the real one to make it alluring and convincing, and which could be used for many far-ranging purposes.

Because the myth had so many permutations and uses, any single definition, as desirable as it might seem, could not but be a Procrustean bed. In the late nineteenth century, the myth was espoused in West Africa by some of the cultural nationalists, who aspired to revitalize Africa with the active participation of their brethren from the New World. In East-Central, Central and Southern Africa, the myth was embodied in the various millenarian movements, whose leaders drew on it for evidence for their eschatological prophecies and exploited it to consolidate their influence over their adherents. Throughout the continent, the myth was the force behind the tremendous attraction to Booker T. Washington's educational philosophy of self-help through vocational training. Supported by the myth, the Booker T. Washington educational approach became a magic formula by which Africans hoped to bridge the gap between themselves and technologically advanced Europeans. The myth also lent credence to political ideas originating with black American leaders. It was part of what led African delegates from British and French colonies to participate in the pan-African congresses organized by William Edward Burghardt Du Bois, and some Anglophone and Francophone Africans to adopt Marcus Garvey's militant political ideas.

While some Africans believed that the African-American model would help them resolve their social, political and cultural problems, others rejected the model and the myth that underpinned it. Some cultural nationalists rejected the idea of regenerating Africa by the active help of African-Americans, claiming that Africans could carry out the task independently. They repudiated all political ideas imported from the United States and instead promoted African-led organizations. African-American educational models also came under fire from Africans who advocated the development of curricula based on European or Japanese models. In short, in the fifty or so years between about 1890 and 1940, America and the black community there were either emulated or rejected. With very few exceptions, they evoked a stark either/or response.

The six chapters of this book attempt to trace African responses to the United States and the black community there. There is already a hefty body of research on the relationship between Africans and African-Americans. But most of the literature is written from the African-American point of view.[6] Only a few studies approach the relationship from the African perspective. Among them are publications by George Shepperson, which emphasize the impact of African-American thinking on African political thought, especially in East-Central Africa.[7] Shepperson's joint study with Thomas Price – *Independent African*, on Chilembwe's 1915 Uprising in Nyasaland – is a landmark in the research of African-American political influence in Africa.[8] Edward H. Berman, J. Ayodele Langley, John W. Cell, Kenneth King and others analyzed the social, educational and political impact of the African-American experience in various regions of Africa.[9] Their studies serve as valuable secondary sources and are liberally cited where relevant.

However, neither these nor almost any other sources deal directly with the development and dissemination of the African-American myth, or with the purposes it served in Africa.[10] This is a problematic subject because the myth is not discussed in the existing corpus of scholarly literature on Africa. Discussing the myth in this book thus necessitated, first of all, establishing that there was an African-American myth – evidence for which is largely indirect and difficult to come by. Not surprisingly, the evidence was not found in the archives of the colonial powers or other official reports. There are few, if any, written documents that refer to the myth or even give indirect confirmation of it. Nor could I find anthropological or sociological documentation that would support it. Much of the evidence for the myth is oral. For example, I was told by the historian L. H. Gann that most popular movies for Africans in the Copperbelt of Northern Rhodesia were American westerns and that a favorite recreation was playing cowboys. But this and similar information is not the type of material that is reported in official documents. Oral evidence of the myth, such as rumors and stories spread by word of mouth in places where people congregate, such as churches and bars, is difficult to obtain. Most of it passes unrecorded and without trace.

As a result, this study does not presume to be a classical history, constructed on the firm foundation of written primary sources. Rather, it was necessary to ferret out the elusive data from between the lines of an extensive range of documentation, including both primary sources, such as personal memoirs, African newspapers and some archival material, and many secondary sources, including unpublished doctoral dissertations along with books and articles. In all cases, it was necessary to carefully glean the material for the hints and clues that would make it possible to interpret Africans' views of African-Americans.

The availability of written material was uneven. The western and southern regions of the continent, where a relatively large stratum of western-educated Africans lived, yielded a relatively fair amount of written evidence from which the African response to black Americans could be extracted. In the eastern parts of the continent, written documentation was more scarce. This made it impossible to trace the evidence of the myth there in as much detail as one would have liked.

Some of the topics in the book, namely cultural nationalism, pan-Africanism, and African education, have already been dealt with by other scholars and will doubtless be investigated by yet others in the future. This study analyzes these topics from a new perspective – the African view of black Americans. Focusing on the creation and application of the African-American myth, it attempts to synthesize in one volume the various sources relating to the African-American role in Africa, embracing the whole of black Africa and concentrating on the African point of view. The effort to write a comprehensive volume entails a certain organizational dilemma. The myth was played out differently in different regions of Africa; at the same time, certain key elements of the myth appear in more than one place. This made it necessary to write separate chapters on East-Central Africa (Chapter 2), West Africa (Chapter 3), and South Africa (Chapter 6), as well as on general themes, namely the dissemination of the myth (Chapter 1), the political uses of the myth (Chapter 4), and the educational model to which the myth gave rise (Chapter 5). This, in turn, results in a certain amount of overlap, most notably in the treatment of the African-American educational model. Chapter 5 discusses how this model was implemented in most parts of Africa, while Chapter 6 deals with it as a key item on the agenda of the South African liberal movement. The educational model could not be discussed in a single chapter without short-changing the liberal movement, which developed this model and other aspects of the myth in its own unique way, in keeping with the specific situation in South Africa in the early part of the twentieth century.

Similarly, there is an overlap in dealing with key black Americans, namely Booker T. Washington, W. E. B. Du Bois and Marcus Garvey, as well as with the American-educated African, James D. Kwegyir Aggrey. Each of these men contributed to shaping the myth, yet the myth existed apart from them. They themselves were mythologized, their lives and achievements were incorporated into the myth, and their careers provided proof of the myth's validity. At the same time, the myth enhanced the prestige of their ideas in Africa, making their disparate and even contradictory philosophies attractive models for African educational and political activities. Because of their wide-ranging influence and various roles, these figures are presented numerous times, woven into the fabric of the various chapters.

The following pages should convey something of the wide scope and multitudinous expressions of the African-American myth in Africa. They are only a beginning, however. The rich findings suggest that the subject can be mined more deeply. There are reasons to believe that Africans took a lively interest in the black communities of the Caribbean and South America, for example, and that exploration in this vein would yield much interesting material. Similarly, further permutations of the myth may well be found in such cultural expressions as music, art, literature and even dress, which are beyond the scope of this book, as well as in oral history. Hopefully, the inevitably incomplete account that follows will stimulate scholars to look further.

1 The Shape and Shaping of the African-American Myth

Africans throughout the continent had access to information about their brethren in the New World. Distance, geographical barriers, illiteracy and the lack of efficient means of communication never prevented the flow of information from America to Africa. Though the distribution was uneven, information about America and African-Americans reached Africans even in the remotest parts of the continent. Beginning in the last quarter of the nineteenth century, Africa was recipient of a steady stream of correspondence, newspapers, periodicals and books from and about the New World, sent from America or brought in by visitors, seamen, churchmen, agents of African-American organizations, and others. To the written documentation were added oral reports, spread by African and foreign sailors who stopped at the ports and by migrant laborers and peddlers who traveled from village to village, region to region. In the twentieth century, these sources of information were supplemented by films. Africans who traveled to America or read about African-Americans were better informed; those who received information second and third-hand were less accurately informed.

Africans in West and some parts of Southern Africa met black Americans who arrived as missionaries, teachers, seamen or adventurers, bringing, in addition to oral and written information about America and the black community there, their own persons and personal examples. In East, East-Central, Central and most of Southern Africa, direct contact was less extensive. Nevertheless, Africans there had a chance to meet black representatives of the New World, especially during World War I, when West Indian troops and African-American members of the Young Men's Christian Association (YMCA) were stationed in East Africa. These arrivals provided a steady source of information on the black community in America.

The information that thus reached Africa through the written and spoken word and through visitors from the New World was the basis of the creation of the African-American myth – a myth made in Africa out of American material. Without that information, there would have been no African-American myth. This does not mean that a clear connection can always be traced between text – whether written, oral, or behavioral, to use the term in its widest application – and tenets. It cannot. It is known that certain Africans read or heard certain material coming from America, and in some cases their responses to the material were also a matter of record;

and African newspaper articles on the United States can be cited in abundance. For the most part, though, the information served as a kind of pool from which Africans picked and chose at will, with Africans in different parts of the continent and with different needs selecting different bits and pieces and interpreting them in different ways to make their own distinct versions of the myth.

This chapter describes the many sources of information that reached Africa from America, the variety of agents who conveyed it, the emotional impact it had on Africans, and, above all, the general outlines of the myth itself. To do justice to the numerous sources and components of the myth, it is necessary to distinguish between the various sources of information. In actual fact, the sources mix, mingle and overlap and the myth owes its shape to all of them, and sometimes even the sources and components of the myth are inseparable from one another.

THE WRITTEN WORD AND WORD OF MOUTH

Africans who studied in the United States became a powerful source of information. In East Africa, Daniel Kato of the Ganda ethnic group, the first African from Uganda to study at the Tuskegee Institute of Alabama, wrote of his experiences to his friends and family in Africa. His letters began a chain of events when they aroused the interest, among many others, of Joseph R. Kamulegeya, secretary of the Young Baganda Association, which operated among the Ganda people in the 1920s and 1930s.[1] Kamulegeya learned from those letters about the activities of the National Association for the Advancement of Colored People (NAACP) and, in consequence, started his own correspondence, first with the NAACP's research director, W. E. B. Du Bois, then with other African-American organizations. Among the outcomes was a significant expansion of Kamulegeya's and other Africans' knowledge of life in the New World.[2]

In East-Central Africa as well, letters between Africans and American blacks also proved to be an important source of information about the black community in the New World. African students at the Livingstonia Overtoun Institute in Nyasaland, now Malawi, a leading school in East-Central Africa, became acquainted with black American life by way of correspondence with two teachers at the Tuskegee Institute. Reverend Hanock Phiri, who was a student at Livingstonia from 1903 to 1910, recalled: 'While there, I learned a great deal about the education provided by the American Negroes from Mr. Edward Boti Manda who was a teacher from Tongaland. Mr. Manda used to receive letters from two teachers at

Tuskegee.'[3] Much like Kamulegeya's correspondence, the Livingstonia students' correspondence also soon expanded. The letters they received led them to African-American newspapers, among them the *Negro World*, the organ of the Universal Negro Improvement Association (UNIA) headed by Marcus Garvey. These letters and newspapers made an enormous impact and created a strong sense of identification with blacks in America. Something of this is suggested in the following excerpt from a 1920 letter by the Livingstonia student, Charles Chidongo Chinula, who wrote that 'in those days, we read Marcus Garvey's newspapers and learned that many American Negroes would be carried back to Africa in ships. We believed that Garvey was a great man and that he was there to help all of us.'[4]

In Southern Africa, Charlotte Manye, a young woman from the Cape Colony who was studying at the black college in Wilberforce, Ohio, affiliated with the African Methodist Episcopal (AME) Church, the largest black church in the United States, wrote of her experiences to her family back home in 1895, and they in turn passed on the information. One of her letters reached Reverend Mangena Maake Makone, the founder of the Ethiopian Church in the Cape Colony, who was so impressed by the large, independent black church thriving in the United States that he wrote to one of the church leaders, Bishop Henry McNeal Turner.[5] Their correspondence soon led to the temporary amalgamation of the African church and the black American church. More will be said of this shortly.

To remote parts of Africa, information about the New World passed by word of mouth. A British district commissioner in an out-of-the-way area of Nigeria recalled how in 1921 Africans in his district were excited by rumors that a black king was bringing a big iron ship full of black American soldiers to expel all the whites from Africa. These rumors were a distortion of information about Marcus Garvey's establishment of the Black Star Line shipping company. The British administrator was not surprised by the Africans' interpretation of this event, but wondered how news of Garvey's activities had reached the district, which was four days' journey from the nearest telegraph office and eight days from the nearest railroad.[6] The answer can be found in Kenyan leader Jomo Kenyatta's recollections of how illiterate young Africans used to gather around someone reading the *Negro World*, listen to the articles being read several times, and later make their way by foot to distant villages and repeat what they had memorized.[7]

Information was borne through many channels. Black seamen were the major bearers of newspapers and oral information about America in general and Garveyism in particular. They distributed issues of the *Negro World* and other literature in basic English at African ports where their ships anchored, and from there the news found its way into the interior.[8]

The UNIA appointed special envoys to spread their messages and carry information about blacks in the United States. It is known, for example, that in 1920 UNIA headquarters in New York appointed the Sierra Leonean, John Kamara, as a 'travelling commissioner' for West Africa.[9] In the same year, Ernest S. Ikoli, secretary of the Lagos UNIA branch, ordered 200 copies a week of the *Negro World* and hundreds of copies of the organization's constitution for distribution in the British colonies in West Africa.[10] In 1921 a Sierra Leonean informed the editor of the *Negro World*, 'We have been reading the *Negro World* for about two years . . .'[11] In July 1922 six Sierra Leoneans were deported from Rufisque and Dakar by the French authorities in Senegal when copies of the *Negro World* and UNIA leaflets were found in their possession. In addition, Sierra Leone merchants who traveled to the neighboring French colonies also bore information about their brethren in the New World.[12]

Labor migrancy added its contribution to the spread of information. By 1910 almost all of East-Central and Central Africa was connected by webs of wandering laborers going to and from the mines and industrializing cities. Africans from East-Central Africa who completed their labor contracts in the gold and diamond mines of the Union of South Africa and returned home became carriers of American and African-American writings. In September 1926 a laborer who returned to the Nyasaland Protectorate was sentenced to three years' hard labor for smuggling unauthorized literature, including six copies of the *Negro World*.[13]

The variety and wide distribution of American literature in Africa can be illustrated by the following examples. Reverend Pambani Jeremiah Mzimba, a minister of the Free Church of Scotland in Lovedale, South Africa, up to 1898, and founder of an independent African church, acknowledged his intellectual debt to the writings of the black American historian George Washington Williams.[14] In September 1921 Harry Thuku, leader of the anti-colonial movement in Kenya, wrote that information about vocational education for African-Americans had reached him through books and articles.[15] The source was probably Robert Russa Moton, the President of Tuskegee Institute, who received requests from Uganda for African-American literature and in early 1920 sent copies of black American newspapers and magazines, including *Crisis* and *New York Age* and even black fashion magazines.[16] The *Crisis* and *New York Age*, along with other black newspapers, such as *Washington Bee*, *Colored American* and *Crusader*, were in demand in West Africa as well. The editor of *Crusader* pointed out that his newspaper reached 'the coastal districts of West, East and South Africa, penetrating Kano on the Nigerian railway, as far as Coquithatville on the Congo river, and in South Africa as far as Pretoria'.[17]

In 1925 Clemens Kadalie, the leader of the South African Industrial and Commercial Workers' Union, informed his uncle in Lusaka, Northern Rhodesia, now Zambia, that he had received a copy from New York of the book *From Superman to Man* by the African-American author J. A. Rogers, and that the book was selling in South Africa as well.[18] Even a less well-known black American periodical such as *International African Opinion* was in circulation among western-educated Africans in West Africa in the late 1930s.[19] This sample is only a fraction of the probably thousands of pieces of literature ranging from pamphlets through history, philosophy and fiction by Americans or about America that reached the African continent.

During the 1920s and 1930s, a new medium reached Africa's bigger cities – American film. Going to the movies became fashionable among Africans. America's buildings, streets, people, fashion, scenery and history were all brought before African audiences. Tom Mboya, one of the Kenyan national leaders, wrote how the 'African reads of the fabulous riches of America and the wealth of its people. He sees the movies portraying the extent of these riches, and others showing the Wild West, cowboy, gun-slinging life.'[20] Ezekiel Mphahlele, an African writer from South Africa, describes pictures from African-American life brought to South Africa by Hollywood movies.[21] The films, which were accessible to the continent's many illiterate, had an even more extensive impact on Africans than the written word.

IN GOD'S COUNTRY

Information covering the whole range of life in America was absorbed by Africans from different regions, with different cultural backgrounds and different religions. Each group created its own image of America. Varied as these images were, however, certain basic motives recurred. Running through most of the images was intense admiration for American achievements, often accompanied by the conviction that America was unique among western countries. The United States was perceived as a power whose intellectual and economic strength enabled it to make a significant impact on other parts of the world. For example, in 1900 a West African newspaper credited the United States with the will and ability to spread fraternity and western culture: 'For next to Europe (we were going to say England) America can boast of her Christianity and civilization. Indeed she has gone to the extent of charging herself with the duty and responsibility of evangelizing and civilizing the dark places of the earth.'[22] Thirteen years later, the *Lagos Weekly Record* described the openness and democratic proclivities of Americans who visited the British colony, which set them apart from Europeans there. The newspaper stated that the colonial authorities feared that American democratic ideas and manners would spread among colonial subjects and 'interfere with European policies of political and social control'.[23]

The quality of life in the United States drew the interest of many Africans who believed that America was the land of unlimited opportunity. People in America could achieve status and wealth more easily than in Africa. Reverend John Langalibalele Dube from the British colony Natal, who visited and studied in the United States in the last decades of the nineteenth century, summed up the impression of his Zulu brethren when he stated, 'Most of the Zulus think that if they can only come to America, they can acquire in two or three years what takes us ten years.'[24] The picture of America as a success story bored so deeply into the African mind that any outstanding achievement was identified with the United States.

Africans were convinced that Americans were wealthier than other white people. That belief was cemented when American missions paid higher wages to their African employees than either European churches or European farmers. Moreover, the American Christian missions that Africans came across seemed to be financially better off than most of the European missions.[25] America's perceived wealth was probably the reason that when, in 1911, the African members of the Seventh Day Baptist Church in Nyasaland asked to be sent a resident missionary, they specifically requested a 'white man, not Scotch, not English, but American'.[26]

Africans were also taken with white America's apparent generosity to blacks. In particular, they were moved by the support whites gave to African-American educational institutions. A Lagos newspaper, for example, noted that the State of Alabama paid the salaries of African-American instructors at the all-black Tuskegee Institute. Describing the variety of academic and vocational activities at the college, the paper stated: 'All this has been made possible through the liberality and generosity of liberal-minded white men, North and South, who have given generously to the work of Tuskegee in donations and endowment funds.' It also noted a £4,000 philanthropic contribution towards building a library at Tuskegee.[27]

Information about American society made many Africans want to go to that magic country and see it for themselves. Americans and Africans who had been to America were often approached by Africans eager for assistance, information and advice that would help them reach that wonderful country. Reverend W. C. Wilcox, a white missionary of the American Board of Commissioners for Foreign Missions who served among the Zulu people in Natal for seven years, tells that on one occasion when he spoke to his students about his native land, 'Every one came and begged to go with me to that wonderful land of liberty and light.'[28] Orishatukeh Faduma, a Sierra Leonean who studied in the United States and worked there for more than twenty years as a pastor, delivered a lecture in Freetown on the life of African-Americans. His lecture was published in local newspapers and Faduma was surprised at how many Africans from town and hinterland made their way to him for advice on how they might travel to America.[29] The urge to live in America is clearly expressed by George Mwase in his account of American-educated John Chilembwe's uprising against the British authorities in Nyasaland in 1915. Mwase was more impressed by Chilembwe's willingness to leave the United States after having lived there than by his being leader of the uprising. As Mwase put it: 'He [Chilembwe] then determined to return back to his country, leaving pleasures of all sorts in America, coming back to a poor country as this. America as far as I am aware is the best country, where a Negro of Africa, such as John was, would permanently settle there, and enjoy the beauty of the country with his fellow Negroes.' As for himself, Mwase tells: 'If I were I [*sic*], surely I could never dream, after having a big fortune of reaching America, of returning to this country.'[30]

America provided Africans with a rich historical analogy for their own aspirations. A clear example can be found in South Africa, where Africans who struggled for equality drew parallels with the struggle of the American colonists against the British authorities. For example, Professor Davidson Don Tengo Jabavu, an African from the Cape who had been to America, clinched his argument before the Natal missionary conference against generous government spending on white education while 'it provides next to nothing for black people who pay much of the taxes and stand in sorest need of this training' with the assertion: 'In politics the black people are in the predicament of the American colonists who were taxed without representation.'[31]

Africans saw Americans as fearless guardians of freedom and equality, who had created an egalitarian, non-hierarchical society and who served as the 'conscience of the world' – a western power which was not involved in the scramble for and colonialization of Africa. Nnamdi Azikiwe, a prominent Nigerian leader, called the United States 'God's country' and confided that 'deep in my heart I can honestly confess that the United States of America impressed me as a haven of refuge for the oppressed sections of humanity in Europe, Africa, Asia and the rest of the world'.[32]

American leaders were portrayed as wise, brave and generous even where the facts did not entirely support the picture. A story published by a West African newspaper in 1908 is a case in point:

When an old slave took off his hat and said to George Washington, the first President, 'Good morning massa,' the first president took off his hat. The President's attendant was surprised by this condescension and told the President so. The President said 'I would not have my slave to have better manners than his master.' That was and represents the true American gentleman.

The African newspaper chose to downplay the fact that the first President of the United States was a slave-holder, to 'judge of a people by its best', and to proclaim that George Washington 'represents the true American gentleman'.[33] In a similar vein, Thomas Jefferson, also a slave-holder, was presented as the American leader who predicted that the emancipation of the slaves was inevitable.[34] Africans deliberately attributed virtues to American leaders which elevated them above the average person. For example, the *Lagos Standard* waxed enthusiastic over the courage and determination of Theodore Roosevelt before he became President, telling how bravely he fought as a cavalry officer in the glorious Rough Riders during the Spanish American War.[35]

The idealization of American leaders, government and society sometimes approached Utopian proportions. The idealization was extended to the life of black Americans, who, being of African descent, were naturally the main focus of African attention and an obvious reference for comparison. Concrete evidence of black–white cooperation was present in organizations such as the National Urban League and the NAACP.[36] In the African mind, American blacks were full partners in the wealth, efficiency and good fortune of the country, working side by side with whites in a joint enterprise. Something of this thinking may be illustrated by D. D. T. Jabavu's account of how he 'discovered that progress there [in the United States] was due to the fact that the entire population, black and white, was inured to the habit of work. Nobody shirked work as so many people here, both black and white, seek to do.'[37] African farmers in the Luapula valley of Northern Rhodesia believed that the large African-American community in the United States lived in perfect harmony with the white population.[38]

To support their sanguine views, Africans avidly sought out black American accomplishments. An African newspaper claimed that blacks in America were economically and politically equal, and in some cases even superior, to many whites. They were entrepreneurs in banks and insurance companies, owned beauty parlors, and a quarter of a million blacks were freeholder farmers in the American South. In romance, black men vied with whites and many white ladies were willing to 'give their hands and hearts' to blacks.[39] According to an article published in 1932 in a West African newspaper, eminent African-American personalities, such as Paul Robeson, Roland Hayes, W. E. B. Du Bois, Alain Locke and R. R. Moton, were 'almost as widely known in this country as in America'.[40] These and other African-Americans of renown aroused great enthusiasm among Africans, who were thrilled by the social and economic opportunities apparently open to them and the respect with which they were treated, and who sought to emulate them. For example, Wulf Sachs tells of a South African *nganga* (medicine man) who, upon coming across a magazine showing a picture of a 'Bantu Man' wearing European clothes and surrounded by white people, and learning that he was Paul Robeson: 'For days afterwards, lived in a world of fantasy. He would go to America. He would sing the Manyika songs. His voice was good and he could master the language. He would acquire great wealth, open a shop. He would buy a gramophone, a house, furniture, a motorcycle. No – a car!'[41]

A seemingly fantastic but not unrepresentative image of the high level that African-Americans attained in the New World despite their history of slavery may be seen in a legend prevalent in the lower Congo. As Kimpianga Mahania records the story:

> The white men dumped these Africans on a big island where they abandoned them. After many centuries of isolation, the African descendants, who came to be called black Americans, developed a prosperous industrial country with a strong army. When the white men came back, they were surprised to see that the black Americans had developed an industrialized society. Before such a reality the white men were forced to accept them as equals.[42]

As these examples show, Africans created a mythical vision of America and the black community there. They attributed to their brethren in the New World not only opportunities but also attainments which did not reflect their true situation. In the words of a white missionary who worked in the Union of South Africa, 'Natives received impressions of an idealized America, which they took to be almost entirely peopled by blacks.'[43]

The myth was reinforced by the apparently positive attitude of some American presidents toward the black community. It was fed by President Theodore Roosevelt's appointment of two blacks to federal posts despite wide-ranging criticism by leading American newspapers such as the *New York Times* and the *New York Herald*. The papers pointed out that even before these appointments, the American President had already braved waves of unpopularity when he invited Booker T. Washington to the White

House. The *Sierra Leone Weekly News* brought that information to its African readers and exclaimed that in standing firmly behind his appointment, 'President Roosevelt is doing his best to remove the reproach against America that the freed slaves have never been free men.'[44] The same newspaper asserted that President Roosevelt's actions proved that he was President of all Americans, including black Americans, and went on to affirm that 'one cannot help but admire the firmness and determination which ... has kept the President in maintaining his bold stand for the right, unmoved alike by the solicitation of friends and the clamour of enemies'.[45] Moreover, Africans who came across Roosevelt's book *American Ideals and Other Essays, Social and Political* were no doubt impressed by his anti-colonial stand and encouraged by his prediction that Africans would eventually 'cast off the yoke of their European conquerors sooner or later, and will become independent nations once more'.[46] They were undeterred by the fact that he put the date off for centuries, as well as by his colonial ambitions in the Far East and South America. The myth was also fed by President William Howard Taft, who declared that the United States needed educated blacks and should provide better education for its black citizens. The *Sierra Leone Weekly News* quoted his assertion that 'The Negro race is a great and growing race ... a race ... with whose progress and improvement this country must always be bound and united. ... [T]he white race and the Negro race live contentedly together ...'[47] The newspaper's relish in the idea and the man behind it is obvious.

Africans saw in the attitudes of these presidents the promise of black integration and advancement in American society, ignoring the inherent contradiction that if progress were required, the present state of affairs was not what it should be. Thus the *Sierra Leone Weekly News* stated in 1909: 'The new doctrine is that the Negro in America is an American and being no more an African his work lies in the land of his birth.'[48] Imbued with the vision of black Americans' future prosperity, the article conjured up a fanciful prophecy foretelling a new 'Negro empire': 'There looms up before us now in the future, AFRICA IN AMERICA. It is not impossible that in the Southern States, especially in the Black Belt – there may arise an *imperium in imperio* – a Negro empire separate and distinct ...'[49] Twenty-one years later, in the same spirit of enthusiasm, the same newspaper boasted that 'Already Chicago has one Negro Senator, and in the next decade or so there are prospects of Negro Congressmen from New York, Chicago and similar centres. Ultimately the Negro will gain full and unhampered civil states [rights] throughout the entire country.'[50] African-American personalities were also mythologized. During the centennial celebration in 1916 of the AME Church, the *Sierra Leone Weekly News* described its founder Richard Allen in the following superlatives: 'For his manly stand, we are met, not only to do him honor, and transmit his name to the coming generations, as a leader worthy of the highest rank in the temple of fame, but to mark the hundredth milestone of our existence as a branch of the Christian Church.' Describing Allen's ideas of racial equality and his courage in forming a separate church for blacks when he was denied 'his liberty as a Christian', the article placed Allen grandly in the tradition of the American Revolution: 'Richard Allen, the hero of manhood Christianity, was in the war; and he marched to the music of the band, led by the immortal George Washington.'[51]

The image of America and the African-American was not only unrealistic, it was outright grandiose and fantastic. It was a myth which, in the definition of Raffaele Pettazzoni, 'belongs to the realm of the imagination, which as such is distinct from, even opposed to, the world of reality'.[52] The mythical image cannot be put down to any lack of accurate information. The true picture of African-American life in America was amply available. African reporters and writers described and vigorously condemned racial segregation and the ugly side of black life in the United States. In British West Africa, the *Lagos Standard* reported in 1903 that shooting and lynching blacks had become more frequent and that the political status of African-Americans was much worse than it had been immediately after the Civil War, noting that there was not a single 'Negro congressman' and only a few blacks in any of the state legislatures.[53] In 1908 the *Sierra Leone Weekly News* quoted a racial slur by Governor Smith of Mississippi, that 'I am just as much opposed to Booker Washington, with all his Anglo-Saxon reinforcement, voting as I am to the voting by the coconut headed, chocolate coloured, typical coon who blacks my boots.'[54] In 1911 the paper published a strong condemnation of racial discrimination as a practice which 'merely shows a spirit of segregation on the part of the white Americans based on selfishness, race-prejudice and dread of absolute tolerance to the descendants of a race of people once looked upon and used as serfs, than on any laxity or deficiency on the part of the American Negro'.[55] Similarly, the book *As Seen Through African Eyes*, published in 1903 by the Nigerian writer Esien Ukpabio under the pseudonym Esere, roundly criticized discrimination against blacks in the United States and South Africa.[56]

Francophone African novelists and poets joined their Anglophone brethren in criticism of Jim Crow. Bernard Dadie from Cote d'Ivoire described Harlem as 'the camp of the shipwrecked, of orphans mistreated by a stepmother, the camp of men to be integrated but for the time being wrapped up in jazz as in an iron corset. Each night Harlem blows its trumpet of

Jericho at the feet of Wall Street. Harlem, funeral home of America where
Negro tears are taken for cries of joy.'[57] Similarly, the Senegalese poet
Assane Diallo wrote of the 'Alabama Negro, whose meat tastes sweet to
police dogs'.[58]

In East and East-Central Africa, the negative side of the life of American
blacks was also known, even though there were no African newspapers or
other sources of regular information. Information about the negative aspects
of the life of American blacks was spread by word of mouth and reshaped
in accord with traditional beliefs and customs. For example, the people in
Nyasaland believed that the Africans who had been shipped to America as
slaves never returned because they had been eaten there by white men.[59]
How seriously Africans took this most unflattering legend is indicated in
the biography of the African-born, American-educated James D. Kwegyir
Aggrey, who visited Nyasaland in 1924 as the only black member of the
American Phelps-Stokes Education Commission. Because he traveled with
whites on equal footing, there were Africans who believed that Aggrey was
actually white and had merely been painted black. A servant boy who was
asked to look after him refused to be alone with him in his room, explaining
that his teacher at school had told the class that Aggrey's people, the
Americans, had at one time been cannibals, so he wanted a witness in case
he disappeared.[60] The harsh reality of African-Americans' lives during the
depression was also reported. The *Lagos Daily News* quoted the African-
American leader, W. E. B. Du Bois, warning that, 'Economically weak,
the Negro is put to test to keep his head above the starvation line.'[61] News
of segregation and discrimination against blacks in America and criticism
of the white community which allowed lynching continued in the African
press up to the eve of World War II.

Africans did not have to read newspapers or books to know that white
Americans were not always fair or benevolent toward blacks. Most of the
missions established by white Americans in the black continent pursued a
policy of discrimination. For example, the American Zulu Mission operating in Natal since 1844 refused to ordain African ministers.[62] In some cases,
Africans took action. In 1888 most of the congregation of the Southern
Baptist Church in Lagos seceded in protest against the segregation practices that the southern white American pastor, W. J. David, had brought
from the American South. Nearly 200 African members followed Moses
Stone and D. B. Vincent, later known as Mojola Agbebi, to establish the
Native Baptist Church; only 24 Africans remained with David.[63]

Similar protests occurred in a Methodist Episcopal Church established
by Americans in Mozambique in 1895. Shortly thereafter three missionary
stations were set up among the Tonga in the area of Inhambane Bay. These

stations were superintended by Erwin H. Richards, a white American who regarded his African converts as a completely inferior breed. On one occasion he went so far as to proclaim that the African 'is stark naked for the most part and full of leecherous [*sic*] sores and his spiritual nature is so very low that his breath would pollute the waters of the Stygian Lake – of which it is said that it stunk so bad the birds were unable to fly over it'.[64] Richards' contempt for the natives set the tone for the entire mission. African employees were grossly underpaid and African preachers and members alike excluded from all church decision making. Thus, in 1907 African Methodist preachers and teachers under the leadership of Muti M. Sikobele organized the Home Mission Society to collect money to support African church workers. This act marked the beginning of the schism in the AME Church in Mozambique, which ended in a final split in 1917, a few years after the white members of the church drew up a detailed set of regulations pertaining to church employment and morality without consulting the Africans. Muti Sikobele and his African followers left the church altogether and established the Mozambique Independent Methodist Episcopal Church.[65]

Given the many clear instances of discrimination against blacks by white American missionaries in Africa and the ample evidence of the inferior status of African-Americans in the United States, one would expect Africans to have had a more balanced and realistic image of America and the black community there. The question that arises is why Africans clung to a vision of the New World that was not only idealized but mythical. To answer this question, one has to remember that, as suggested earlier, the United States provided Africans with an important reference point for their own lives. It gave them grounds for believing that there were white people who treated black people well and it provided proof that blacks were capable of cultural and technological achievements. Up to this point, there were enough facts and no need for myth. There were white Americans who treated African-Americans decently and some black Americans did rise in the system. The myth was created because 'some' was not enough. Africans needed a wholly positive vision of a prosperous and progressing African-American community, stripped of the unpalatable facts, in order to maintain their own hopes of advancing in a world governed by whites. According to Levi-Strauss, 'the purpose of myth is to provide a logical model capable of overcoming a contradiction'.[66] The contradiction that Africans could neither resolve logically nor abide was that in 'God's country', ungodly deeds were done against African-Americans. In the words of G. S. Kirk, 'myth offers an apparent way out of the problem, either by simply obfuscating it, or making it appear abstract and unreal'.[67]

MISSIONS AND MISSIONARIES

The mythical image of the life of African-Americans was enhanced by Africans' face-to-face contact with blacks from the New World. This contact provided Africans with live evidence that African-Americans, although black, enjoyed privileges which were denied to Africans. Colonial regimes and white governors treated black Americans with respect. This was particularly conspicuous in Southern Africa, especially in the Boer republics, where segregation was part of both the legal and social structure. Article 9 of the constitution of the independent Boer state Transvaal, under President Paul Kruger, stated: 'the people will not allow any equalization of the colored inhabitants with the whites'. Nevertheless, African-Americans who resided in Transvaal were granted the status of 'honorary whites', which put them on equal footing with Europeans. They were respected as citizens of a foreign country and were entitled, like white Americans, to all consular services by the American Consul in Johannesburg. They were free to choose what class of car to travel in on trains and could obtain accommodation at any hotel – privileges not enjoyed by the African and colored populations.[68]

Of all the contacts with black Americans, those with the representatives of the all-black American churches perhaps did the most to reinforce the myth. The contact can be traced to the visit in 1890 of the black American gospel choir, the Jubilee Singers, also known as the McAdoo Minstrels, to the Cape Colony on a three-year concert tour. Their tour left a deep impression on the Africans. The black singers' high professional standard demonstrated the attainments blacks could reach when given the opportunity and filled the Africans with pride. In the words of the African newspaper *Imvo Zabantsundu*, 'Their visit will do their countrymen here no end of good. Already it has suggested reflections of many who, without such a demonstration, would have remained skeptical as to the possibility of the natives of this country being raised to anything above perpetual hewers of wood and drawers of water.'[69] The direct contact with these black Americans enhanced Africans' self-confidence and gave them a conception of their own potential. It also showed Africans that the white authorities could be compelled to modify their discriminatory practices. To enable the choir members to reach the places where they performed, the white authorities had to relax the segregation laws. This was so extraordinary that even seven years after the Jubilee Singers' tour, a Cape newspaper noted that Africans were still affected by the visit.[70]

A year after the tour, Africans established a choir of their own, named the African Choir or the Zulu and African Choir, which performed in the

Cape Colony and Natal and then toured Great Britain and later the United States. In Cleveland, Ohio, the group fell short of money and, in 1895, disbanded. One of the members, Charlotte Manye, was taken in by Bishop William B. Derrick of the AME Church, who helped her through the church-affiliated Wilberforce University. As noted above, a letter she wrote to her family was shown to Reverend Mangena Maake Makone, the founder of the Ethiopian Church in the Cape Colony, and he then wrote to Bishop Henry McNeal Turner of the AME Church.[71] As a result of their correspondence, Bishop Turner was sent to visit South Africa in 1898 and for six weeks toured the Cape Colony and the Boer republics, bringing the message of the AME Church to thousands of Africans. For the first time, Africans in those areas saw a black bishop who had the authority to ordain elders, deacons and ministers. They also saw that, once again, whites were compelled to deal differently with African-Americans. President Paul Kruger of Transvaal gave Bishop Turner an audience, telling him, 'You are the first black man whose hand I have ever shaken.'[72] M. T. Steyn, President of the Orange Free State, also received him with cordiality.[73]

The influence of that tour was tremendous. Turner's speeches and sermons moved his African audiences deeply. With his strong presence and the rhetorical techniques adapted from his American experience, he brought his hearers to a state of ecstasy. Basing his presentations on Psalm LXVIII, verse 31: 'Princes shall come out of Egypt; Ethiopia shall soon stretch out her hands to God', he offered the Africans who heard him the proof they sought that those who regarded blacks as a congenitally backward race were wrong. Africans welcomed him with delirious enthusiasm, as if he were the Savior himself, and probably some actually thought he was the Messiah.[74] Charlotte Manye told that 'Bishop H. M. Turner . . . was welcomed as never a man was received before. Some called out "now is the promise fulfilled," others saw him as a Moses to deliver them from chains of sin and superstition.'[75] Under the impact of his visit, AME Church membership increased fourfold in South Africa.[76]

To be sure, there were western-educated Africans who were not so enchanted by Turner, who objected to his imposition of black American separatism on Africa, and argued that his black segregationist message was inconsistent with Christian values and would not help Africans.[77] Nonetheless, his visit opened the way for further contacts between Africans and their brothers in the New World. During his visit to South Africa, Turner established the Fourteenth District of the AME Church there and united the African-American church and the Ethiopian Church. A year later, the two churches split. But though the split was a blow to the black church in general and to Bishop Turner in particular, it did not put an end to AME

Church activities. The church soon extended its operations all over the southern part of the continent. African-American bishops, superintendents, teachers and doctors were stationed in the whole region, exerting an increasing range of influence over Africans.

The impact on the Africans of the encounter with these church emissaries, who were in many cases the first American blacks they saw, is described in several accounts. One is by Amos Jerome White, a doctor of law at Wilberforce University, and his wife Luella Graham White. In 1937 Jerome White was asked by the AME Church resident bishop in the Union of South Africa, Richard R. Wright, to supervise a church school on the outskirts of Johannesburg.[78] In addition to supervising the school, White was required to tour the region on various church tasks. White relates that during a 1938 trip to Southwest Africa, now Namibia, to inspect the AME Church missions there and explore the possibility of erecting new missions in the territory, he met an African from the Ovambo ethnic group who was excited to meet, for first time, an African-American. On the next day, the African came to see White off at the train station, giving him a half-crown coin as a farewell gift and waving his handkerchief at the departing train until it disappeared. This is only one of White's many meetings with Africans who had never before set eyes on black Americans. His description of their reaction when he told them about the church he represented is telling: 'Many questions were asked about the A.M.E. Church, and great surprise was shown when told that there were black bishops. They associate only white people with that office – and didn't know that black people anywhere kenw [*sic*] enough to become bishops.'[79]

Bishop Wright similarly describes the responses of Africans whom he met on the streets of Cape Town: 'In fact I was struck by the unusual courtesy shown to me. Of course, I wore a clergyman's collar, purple rabat, which is worn only by the bishops and indicated that I was, perhaps the only colored bishop in town.'[80] A similar picture of wonder and admiration for black American ministers is painted in the Copperbelt of Northern Rhodesia, where the AME Church set up missions between 1930 and 1940. According to the scholar Walton Johnson, Africans joined the black church, bringing with them a variety of gifts, food, goods, and even cattle. The main attraction was the black minister. 'It was the people's first time to see an African minister. He was like Jesus.'[81]

Another important contact was with the American-based, all-black African Methodist Episcopal Zion Church (AME Zion Church) that was brought to West Africa by the Barbados-born Bishop John Bryan Small. Small first visited the Gold Coast, now Ghana, as a sergeant clerk of the West Indian Regiment, between 1863 and 1866. He studied the Fanti language, visited other British possessions in West Africa, and realized the great potential for missionary work in the region. In 1871 he went to the United States and joined the AME Zion Church. Finally, in 1896 he returned to the Gold Coast, and two years later, in 1898, the Gold Coast branch of the AME Zion Church was established along with two churches, in Keta and Cape Coast.[82] The arrival of a black bishop of a black American church and the subsequent establishment of an independent African church were interpreted by Africans in mythical terms. For them, it was nothing short of the fulfillment of the will of God.[83]

The mythical image grew even stronger as the Africans became more familiar with the AME Zion Church and with what was, in African terms, its remarkable wealth. Though such church wealth was normative for black Americans, Africans were impressed by the various manifestations of the black church's wealth. They marvelled that it had a membership of 550,000 people and was headed by nine bishops, three of whom had completed their master's degrees at the best universities in the United States. They looked with wonder on the publishing house, newspapers and magazines it owned, and with even greater astonishment at the fact that it maintained three colleges, the principal one being Livingstone in Salisbury, North Carolina, with property valued at $150,000.[84] The abundance and precision of details cited are testimony to the extraordinary impression the AME Zion Church's wealth made on Africans.

The Africans' idolization of the black American churches and their leaders is fully understandable. Establishing churches, appointing bishops, and managing one's own affairs were things that, as far as Africans were aware, only whites had done. That American blacks could do these things elevated them, in the African mind, to the level of the white race. The successful struggle of the African-American churches, both the AME Church and the AME Zion Church, against racial discrimination in the United States only strengthened that image. Africans believed that the black American churches proved to white people 'that the black man was not the incapable being he was taken by some to be but that he had something of originality too in him'.[85] Their contact with the black American churches strengthened the Africans' belief in their ability to do things that in Africa were reserved for whites only. The very fact that they, Africans, were members of a church which was founded and run by black people and was recognized by white denominations was crucial to them. David Kimble, in his book *A Political History of Ghana*, noted that 'the point was not so much that it was independent, as that it was wholly a black man's Church'.[86] In the words of a local Gold Coast newspaper article on the AME Zion Church, the great advantage of these churches was that 'no white man has ever been elected to the Bishopric. It is, indeed, an entirely negro church; organized by negroes for negroes, manned, governed, controlled and supported by negro energy, intellect, liberality and contributions.'[87]

But it was not only by their example that these churches spread the myth. The African-American churches that operated in Africa had easier entrance requirements than the European churches, were more willing to promote Africans to positions of authority, and provided them with higher levels of education in both Africa and abroad. Their readiness to advance Africans in areas into which the European churches were loathe to let them go also made the African-American churches natural promulgators of the myth. George Shepperson records, for example, that the relatively easy entry requirements of the African-American missions in Nyasaland, in comparison to those of the European-controlled Presbyterian, Anglican and Catholic missions, contributed to the Africans' view of America 'as a land of liberality'.[88]

The AME Zion Church allowed 'the natives of the soil', as one of the church leaders put it, to manage its Gold Coast branch. Bishop Small appointed Reverend Fyrm Egyir Assam of Kwitta to head the branch, and later another African, Reverend Thomas Birch Freeman Jr, joined the branch leadership.[89] When Bishop Henry McNeal Turner established the Fourteenth District of the AME Church in Cape Colony, he ordained several Africans as ministers; the AME Church also appointed Africans as ministers in its missions in Southern and Northern Rhodesia. The readiness of these churches to promote Africans to positions of responsibility boosted Africans' self-esteem, reinforced the attraction of the churches, and made the Africans that were active in them emissaries of the myth. Not surprisingly, King Lewanika of Barotseland preferred the African missionaries sent by the AME Church to the white missionaries of the Paris Evangelical Mission.[90]

Of all the activities of the African-American churches, it was perhaps their strenuous promotion of African education that did most to bolster, at one and the same time, Africans' self-image and the African-American myth. Although all the church missions operating in Africa embarked on basic educational programs as part of their conversion activities and taught the three R's as a means of spreading the gospel, the African-American churches were the only ones to provide more than a few exceptional Africans with more than the basics.

Africans looked to the African-American churches to meet their educational needs. When Bishop Turner visited the Cape in 1898, the leaders of the Ethiopian Church there brought to his attention the lack of quality higher education for Africans and requested that the AME Church send

African-American missionary teachers to South Africa, provide training for Africans in black church schools in the United States, and establish an African college in the Cape. In a bid for membership, Turner duly promised $10,000 towards building the college.[91] The AME Church purchased twelve acres near Queenstown in the Cape Colony for the college campus and undertook to bring sixteen young Africans to America for training to serve as the core of the college faculty.[92] Such assistance, never offered by the white churches, was enormously valued, as can be seen from the letter to Bishop Turner written by Rev. James M. a leader of the Ethiopian Church and, after the amalgamation, head of the AME Church branch in the Cape Colony: '[P]eople in this country are very anxious about higher education. I hope the AME Church will soon take up this question in earnest. You have not the least idea, my Lord, how much depends on this question. The failure of the white churches to do so is a source of much discontent and our church must take the matter up.'[93]

The AME Church saw to the enrollment of nearly seventy South African students at various black schools in the United States, but, due to a shortage of funds, did not make good on its promise to build a college.[94] The Africans' disappointment, according to the scholar R. Hunt Davis Jr, was one of the main reasons for the split in the AME Church in South Africa in 1899.[95] In February 1901 the AME Church sent Bishop Levi J. Coppin to the Cape Colony to repair the damage to its image there, which he proceeded to do by demonstrating that African education was still top priority for the black American church. At his recommendation, the AME Church acquired a secondary school, the Bethel Institute in Cape Town, which had a multiracial enrollment of about 400 students. The benefits of the policy were quickly realized. Coppin reported that requests from all over the country to 'open new work' among the various ethnic groups arrived 'faster than we can respond to the calls'.[96]

Africans showed similar enthusiasm for the AME Zion Church's educational work. When the AME Zion Church began its operations in Kwitta in 1899, it immediately opened a sabbath and day school. Within about a decade, the school had grown large enough to require a supervisor sent from America. A few years later, under the supervision of the African-American, Reverend W. E. Shaw, M.D., it developed into Kwitt (or Walters) College, an academic institution well-known along the coast of West Africa 'beginning at Dakar and extending south to Nigeria'.[97] These educational efforts, made in the contexts of the AME Zion Church's egalitarianism, created a feeling of kinship and gratitude among West Africans. In the words of Kofi Asaam, a lawyer and church activist in the Gold Coast: 'Our fellow blacks in America . . . have for the first time in the history of our

nation stretched out the hand of kinship to us across the seas, and are ready
to educate and Christianize us and make the land of our common ancestors
a glorious habitation in the eyes of the world.'[98] Like the AME Church,
the AME Zion Church also provided African students with stipends to
study at its colleges in America.[99]

In addition to the representatives of the large and relatively powerful
black American churches, Africans also came to feel strong affinity with
individual African-American missionaries. Samuel B. Coles, a black missionary who served in Angola from 1923 to 1953 as a representative of
the American Board of Congregational Christian Churches, an umbrella
organization for black and white churches, described the enthusiastic
welcome he and his family received upon their arrival at Galangue in
the hinterland of Angola: 'I was thrown onto the shoulders of the men and
my wife and our little daughter Laura were placed in a hammock and
carried all over the place by excited men and women. At long last, they
cried, one of their own had returned to help them.'[100]

Coles attributed the success of African-American missionaries in Africa
both to the knowledge of white ways that American blacks had gained
during their 250 years of slavery and to the egalitarian treatment that
African-American missionaries extended to the Africans. Coles records
that Africans were free to enter his home through the front door and felt
at ease there, which was certainly not the case in the homes of white
missionaries.[101] The African-American Reverend Charles S. Morris of the
Negro Baptists describes similar openness in the home of another black
missionary:

> And as I sat in his house the native men and women came and squatted
> on the floor and perched on the trunks and chairs, and there was such
> a freedom and a lack of formality as would be impossible in the house
> of any other missionary than a black man. Night came on ... this
> missionary's little daughter slept in the middle and those two heathen
> girls on either side. That would be impossible to any other missionary
> than a black man.[102]

The significance of such apparently uncommon openness for Africans
may be understood against the contrasting description of C. C. Boone, a
white American missionary who served from 1901 to 1906 in the Congo
Free State, now Zaire, with the Lott Carey Baptist Foreign Missionary
Convention of the United States and the American Baptist Foreign Mission
Society of Boston. African boys, Boone wrote disparagingly in his autobiography, 'have no standard of right or wrong. The smart boy is the one
that can tell a lie and get out of it. The trials that we have with the native

boys in the home are innumerable.'[103] Africans' gratitude for black missionaries can certainly be appreciated against this suspicion and denigration. African-American churches did not differ in their aims from other churches and missions. The ultimate goal of all Christian denominations operating in Africa was to spread the Gospel among the heathen. As Bishop Alexander Walters put it at the AME Zion Church's East Gold Coast Conference in Kwitta, 'My main object is to have our men help to civilize and Christianize heathen Africa, and this must be done quickly or Mohammedanism will overrun the country.'[104] But, in addition to the Gospel, the black American churches and missionaries brought a unique message: that the black man was capable and able. This was a vital social message for a race which had to deal with theories that placed it on the lowest rung of human development. It was also the main allure of the African-American myth.

BLACK LEADERS IN THE NEW WORLD

Two New World blacks, the American-born Booker T. Washington and the Jamaican-born Marcus Garvey, also played crucial roles in both forming and confirming the myth. Both Washington and Garvey held leadership positions in the black community in the United States, which made them a source of pride and authority in Africa. But they were not representatives of a religious body and not bound to spread Christianity among the heathen. Washington was a leader in African-American education, Garvey an advocate of black nationalism. Though both were devout Christians, their endeavors were emphatically secular. Washington placed his hopes for the advancement of his people not in the Divinity but in the gospel of labor and education. Garvey went to great lengths to keep organized religion out of his political activities.[105] Their secular orientations meant that the myth could spread beyond the religious frameworks and spiritual lives of the Africans to educational and political domains.

Born a slave in about 1859, Booker T. Washington forged his way to become the head of the Tuskegee Institute for vocational education founded in 1880 in Tuskegee, Alabama, and an advisor on African-American affairs to President Theodore Roosevelt. His birth into slavery represented the struggle of all American blacks and his remarkable rise held out for Africans, no less than for African-Americans, the promise that they too could pull themselves up from their lowly position to make a contribution to humanity and attain recognition for their worth.

Washington was best known in Africa for his work in making education available to American blacks and for his Tuskegee philosophy aimed at instilling the virtues of hard work and manual labor. Only by developing these values, Washington held, would blacks be able to find their place in American society. In the American spirit, he argued that 'there is something in human nature which always makes an individual recognize and reward merit, no matter under what colour of skin merit is found'. Washington supported his belief with examples of Tuskegee graduates: 'Wherever one of our brickmakers has gone in the South, we find that he has something to contribute to the well-being of the community into which he has gone; something that has made the community feel that, in a degree, it is indebted to him, and perhaps, to a certain extent, dependent upon him. In this way pleasant relations between the races have been stimulated . . .' The man with Tuskegee training, who knows how 'to build and repair wagons and cart', Washington clinches his argument, 'is regarded as a benefactor' and '[t]he people with whom he lives and works are going to think twice before they part with such a man'.[106] Booker T. Washington's message was accepted by many blacks and whites in the United States, and vocational schools for blacks were opened in the major black communities in the American South.[107] These schools and the philosophy behind them became a model for similar endeavors in Africa, about which more will be said in Chapters 5 and 6.

Washington's main concern was with American blacks. His work focused on helping his people, so recently emancipated from slavery, to integrate into American society. Nonetheless, he also felt an obligation to his brethren in Africa.[108] He believed that his educational philosophy would benefit Africans as much as African-Americans. This view is illustrated in a lecture he delivered in Indianapolis in 1897:

A friend of mine . . . who went to Liberia to study conditions once came upon a negro shut up within a hovel reading Cicero's orations. That was all right. The negro has as much right to read Cicero's orations in Africa as a white man does in America. But the trouble with the colored man was that he had on no pants. I want a tailor shop first so that the negro can sit down and read Cicero's orations like a gentleman with his pants on.[109]

His door was always open to Africans who came to the United States, he carried on long and warm correspondences with Africans, and he avidly promoted the Tuskegee approach in Africa.

Washington's fame soon spread beyond the borders of the United States into Africa. The *Sierra Leone Weekly News* compared him to the greatest of American presidents, noting that 'No man of American descent, outside of

George Washington and Abraham Lincoln, did so much for his country as Booker Washington did.'[110] The *Lagos Weekly Record* extolled his achievements above those of any other black American, writing that 'No other Negro living has made such a record or has been able to surround himself with such influential and powerful friends to sustain a work fraught with so much importance and destined to be of such incalculable value in the uplifting of the submerged half of black and oppressed humanity in the Southern States of America.'[111] Africans credited him with dignifying manual labor. One Sierra Leone newspaper reported: 'Booker T. Washington has died indeed; but this great apostle of the dignity of labor is now living in Freetown – he has been reincarnated here; and has preached even here that no work is below one's dignity.'[112] Harry Thuku, the Kenyan national leader, saw Booker T. Washington and black Americans like him as saviors, noting that 'the Negro race in America has been successful in producing many large-hearted men like Booker T. Washington. . . . We regard such men as our saviours.'[113] D. D. T. Jabavu was convinced that the Africans in the Union of South Africa needed a leader like Booker T. Washington.[114]

The admiration for Booker T. Washington often extended into the realm of the mythical. A representative of the Ethiopian Church at Klipsbruit, Johannesburg, saw 'God's hand' in Booker T. Washington's deeds and believed that he would redeem Africa.[115] In a speech at the 1912 International Conference on the Negro, held in Tuskegee, Alabama, the Reverend Frank Atta Osam Pinanko, an AME Zion Church superintendent in the Gold Coast, described Booker T. Washington as an emissary of God: 'The Lord has not left the Negro without a hope to rise. Here and there, in the wilderness of the Race's struggle for greater heights are found oases refreshing and invigorating and Booker T. Washington is a Moses of his race.'[116] If such biblical appellations sound commonplace, in Africa they were terms of exaltation generally reserved for admired African-Americans.

In contrast to Booker T. Washington, Marcus Garvey stemmed from an aspiring bourgeois family. He received an education in an integrated school and, until he became disillusioned with whites, attended an integrated church. As a young man, he earned his living as a printer and, later on, as a correspondent. Garvey rose to prominence in Africa after World War I, as Africans became increasingly self-conscious and politically aware, and for a period of time he was considered 'the best known figure of African descent in the whole world'.[117] Garvey extended Booker T. Washington's dictum of black self-help from the educational to the political realm. More radical, more militant, and more separatist than Washington and other black American leaders of his time, he rejected the white world with which he had rubbed elbows in his youth. He made his platform 'Africa for the

Africans' and devoted his energies to the idea of expelling the colonialists and turning all of Africa into one huge black state – using force if necessary – where African-Americans would lead their African brethren to freedom and progress.

Garvey's was a global view – in contrast to Washington's focus on the United States – which saw the solution to the problems of blacks in the New World as inextricably intertwined with the elimination of colonialism.[118] An activist from an early age, Garvey was influenced both by the writings of western-educated Africans such as Joseph E. Casely Hayford, John Mensah Sarbah, the Reverend Attoh Ahuma, and the Egyptian-born critic of colonialism, Duse Mohamed Ali, on whose magazine *African Times and Orient Review* he worked while living in London between 1912 and 1914, as well as by Booker T. Washington's educational philosophy, which so impressed him that on his return to Jamaica he tried to set up an industrial school patterned after Tuskegee.[119]

The vehicle for his efforts to transform the lives of blacks was the Universal Negro Improvement and Conservation Association (UNIA), which he founded in Jamaica in 1914 along with the African Communities League. Both organizations had the aim of 'drawing the peoples of the race together' under the banner 'One God! One Aim! One Destiny!'[120] In 1915 Garvey moved to Harlem, New York, and set up his UNIA headquarters there to attract American blacks. At first only a trickle, mainly Jamaicans and other West Indians, joined. But after World War I, when the economic boom ended and many blacks found themselves out of work, UNIA's membership increased rapidly. By the end of 1919, the UNIA publication, the *Negro World*, claimed that the organization had about two million members in thirty separate branches throughout the United States and the West Indies.[121] These claims are exaggerated because the UNIA was in the habit of counting supporters as members.[122] Nonetheless, through the *Negro World* and other publications, Garvey worked to instill race pride and to urge blacks to unite to overthrow white domination. To translate these concepts to material reality, he established the Black Star shipping line, inaugurated on 26 June 1919, both to foster trade between African-Americans and Africa and to transport African-Americans back to their motherland.[123]

For many Africans, both the UNIA and Garvey himself were prodigious phenomena which could arise only in America, where an abundance of amazing things happened. The very fact that the UNIA, like the black American churches, was an all-black organization run for and by blacks was not only a source of amazement and pride; it was also, in the eyes of Africans, a uniquely American phenomenon. Indeed, Africans ignored Garvey's Jamaican origins. In the words of the *Nigerian Pioneer*, 'He is an American. A direct descendant of those who have borne and suffered the horrors of slavery in America.'[124]

Garvey and his organization were regarded by many Africans with the same mixture of realism and fantasy that characterized the African approach to America and the black community there in general. The *Gold Coast Independent* declared that the UNIA was the 'most potent organization in the United States'.[125] Like Booker T. Washington, Garvey too was compared to biblical figures. The *Sierra Leone Weekly News* called him 'a modern Joshua'.[126] Another Sierra Leone newspaper, the *Colonial and Provincial Reporter*, went so far as to describe him as a messenger of the mighty Lord, writing that 'the voice of God now seems to utter through Marcus Garvey'.[127] More moderately, but still in superlative vein, it dubbed him 'Paramount Chief of the Negro Race or, in other words, "His Supreme Highness the Potentate"'.[128] Writing of the first UNIA convention held in New York in August 1920, it hailed him as 'that laurelled champion and leader of freedom's cause – that gifted humanitarian'.[129] The assistant general-secretary of the UNIA branch in Sierra Leone read a report which called upon 'Mr. Marcus Garvey, or as he is commonly known, "The World's Greatest Orator," to come forward like a Moses to show us rightly the method of creating love and unity in our midst as Negroes.'[130] One can see in these statements how praise of Garvey's leadership, audacity, zeal and oratorical skills mingled with an idolization that lifted him above the ordinary run of humanity.

In no small measure, Garvey himself contributed to his larger-than-life image. Garvey waged his campaign on behalf of the black race with bombastic declarations and a great deal of personal aggrandizement. At the First International Convention of the UNIA in 1920, a 'Declaration of Rights of the Negro Peoples of the World' was adopted; Garvey was elected 'Provisional President of the African Republic'; a black, green and red flag was chosen; and a national anthem, 'Ethiopia, Thou Land of Our Fathers', was adopted. Garvey created a nobility with such titles as Earl of the Congo, Viscount of the Niger, and Knight of the Distinguished Service Order of Ashanti.[131] Suitably impressed by such unabashed self-aggrandizement, at least some Africans believed that UNIA had grown within four years from a membership of thirteen persons to four million, with chapters all over the world.[132] When an article in a black South African newspaper pronounced that 'Garvey was only a self-elected and self-styled president', W. O. Jackson, an African from Cape Town, accused the newspaper of 'ignorance and prejudice, for the Hon. Marcus Garvey was elected by representatives of 400,000,000 of the Negro race' – the astronomical figure testifying to Garvey's larger-than-life dimensions in Africa.[133]

More substantially, the myth was reinforced by the reality of Garvey's Black Star Line, the first shipping line established by an African-American organization. The *Times of Nigeria* repeated Garvey's declaration that it was more than just another shipping line owned by a commercial company, but rather the property of the whole black race.[134] In 1920 the UNIA branch in Freetown, Sierra Leone, put on public display what it announced as a 'splendid model' of the first Black Star Line ship, especially sent from New York for the purpose.[135] In 1921, when a ship was added to the growing fleet, the *West Africa Mail and Trade Gazette* wrote that this was 'enough in itself and of itself to thrill the heart of every member and true lover of our race and fill us with the contagious and enkindling power of rapturous enthusiasm'.[136] Feeling was backed by action. According to an AME Church missionary returned from West Africa, 'the young men of Sierra Leone are giving up first-class jobs and waiting for the Black Star Line to touch the shores'.[137] On the Nigerian coast, Africans camped on the beaches and lit bonfires to signal the ships of 'Moses Garvey'.[138]

The hopes Garvey evoked in Africa made his UNIA the only secular African-American organization widely accepted throughout the continent. The *Negro World* and other UNIA publications were disseminated far and wide. African adherents of Garveyism established UNIA chapters in some parts of Africa, while Africans in other parts read or heard of Marcus Garvey. For many Africans Garvey and the Black Star Line were symbols of African pride, freedom and independence.

Garvey never realized his dreams. He never generated a mass back-to-Africa exodus; no black-ruled African republic was established during his lifetime; and the Black Star Line proved an economic disaster. In 1921 he was accused of mail fraud in the United States; two years later he was tried and imprisoned, and in December 1927 he was deported. His political schemes and aspirations, as well as his grandiosity and flamboyance, provoked vigorous opposition among both blacks and whites in the United States and, as we shall see in Chapter 4, among Africans as well.

Nevertheless, Garvey's aura remained strong in Africa and many of his teachings outlived his downfall. Loyal supporters continued to express gratitude for Garvey's message of race consciousness and black pride. In 1921 a Sierra Leonean wrote to the editor of the *Negro World*: 'Some of us Negroes did not know that we have a soul in ourselves, and did not feel that we should be respected as other men as the whites are, until we began to read the sentences of the Honorable Marcus Garvey in the *Negro World*.'[139] In 1927 another African, Benjamin Majafi, from Liddesdaale, Evaton, South Africa, assured a UNIA activist in the United States that 'most of our people who read the *Negro World* are awakened, because your speeches are encouraging us a great deal'.[140] Garvey's opponents also continued to acknowledge the impact of his leadership. In 1923, when Garvey was tried for mail fraud, the *Gold Coast Leader* criticized his separatism and management of the UNIA, but heartily approved his teachings of 'racial unity and cooperation, the reliance of the African upon himself in taking his proper place in the world order, and the doctrine that whatever other men and other races can do . . . the African can do for himself', and concluded that 'it is also true that he has driven these lessons home upon the African mind and sentiment with a vision and a force of character, which his very enemies must, and do, admit'.[141] In 1924 the newspaper quoted one such admission by a strong opponent of Garvey's radicalism, Albert T. Marryshaw: 'His [Garvey's] ways might not be my ways, nor his methods my methods', but 'I returned to Grenada from New York with the newly formed opinion that Marcus Garvey is the greatest black man raised in the world since "Toussaint L'Ouverture!"'[142] According to the South African author Peter Abrahams: 'Marcus Garvey gave to the Negroes of the twentieth century a sense of self-awareness, a sense of pride and dignity that largely overcame the inferiority complex bred by centuries of racial and colour oppression.'[143]

Neither Booker T. Washington nor Marcus Garvey were ever involved with the African masses or even visited the black continent. Although they both played a crucial role in generating and reinforcing the mythical image of America, their only contact with Africans was with the western-educated Africans who visited the United States or who participated in international conferences in Europe.

Very different was James E. Kwegyir Aggrey. Unlike Booker T. Washington and Marcus Garvey, Aggrey was born in Africa – in Anamabo, the Gold Coast, now Ghana, on 18 October 1875. He belonged to a generation of Africans who were educated in church schools in Africa, acquired their higher education in the United States, and returned to Africa eager to improve the lot of their people. This made him one of the people, as Washington and Garvey could never be. It also made him a distinctly African, as opposed to American, success story. Like other Africans with similar careers, he demonstrated in his own person that not only African-Americans could rise up in the world in the United States, but that native born and bred Africans could do so too. Like the other Africans educated in the United States, he provided living proof that the African-American myth could be applied to Africans.

But it so happened that Aggrey returned to Africa not on his own steam, as most of his American-educated contemporaries did, but as the only black delegate on the highly prestigious American Phelps-Stokes Commission.

This commission toured various parts of Africa, first in 1920 and again in 1924, under appointment by the British, Belgian and Portuguese colonial authorities, to investigate African education and to make recommendations for a new approach. More will be said about the commission and Aggrey's role in it in Chapter 5. Here what must be stressed is its eminence at the time. It was an enormously prestigious commission, awaited with high expectations by Africans and Europeans alike, who looked to it to resolve the dilemma of African education which had troubled them for at least two decades. Its activities were closely followed by local newspapers and carried by word of mouth. It commanded the respect of the authorities and drew large native audiences to public lectures in city after city.

Aggrey's participation in the commission thrust him into prominence and had far-reaching impact as far as the African-American myth was concerned. The very fact that an African was invited to participate in such a body on supposedly equal footing with whites was a colossal event bound to endow him with mythical proportions. It was noted above that in some parts of Africa Aggrey was taken as a white man painted black. His participation on the commission gave Aggrey an edge over other Africans educated in the United States. It made him more than a success story and more than proof of the applicability of the myth to Africans. It made him the very embodiment of the myth. Furthermore, the sheer scope of the commission's travels and large number of its public engagements practically guaranteed that the myth he embodied would spread far and wide. During the Phelps-Stokes Commission's travels in West, East, Central and Southern Africa, Aggrey was the keynote speaker at hundreds of public lectures and was seen and heard by thousands of Africans. He thus became a major disseminator of the myth, which Booker T. Washington and Marcus Garvey were not.

Aggrey's personality and talents as a speaker made him particularly fit for the roles of embodiment and disseminator of the myth. Aggrey's physical appearance was not imposing. Africans who heard his name and expected to meet a tall, well-built person with a commanding voice were often disappointed to see an ordinary person of ordinary size: humble, kindly and, some said, even ugly.[144] However, he possessed excellent rhetorical skills and a knack for forming personal relationships. The *Sierra Leone Weekly News* acclaimed his ability to capture audiences, telling that 'he drew audiences of men who had sworn they would never listen to him'.[145] Kwame Nkrumah, who heard Aggrey while a student at Accra Teachers' Training College, said that 'To me he seemed the most remarkable man that I had ever met, and I had the deepest affection for him.'[146] Even after his death in 1927, Godwin A. M. Lewanika, a stepbrother of Paramount Chief Yeta

III of Barotseland in North Rhodesia, now Zambia, named Aggrey, along with Booker T. Washington, as his model.[147]

Aggrey's biographer, Edwin W. Smith, describes the enthusiasm with which Aggrey was greeted during the Phelps-Stokes Commission's tour of West Africa in 1920. Welcoming delegations, congregations in over-crowded churches, and packed audiences – black and white – in public halls all waited to hear Aggrey's speeches. At a public meeting at the Wesleyan Church in Accra, the Gold Coast Governor Sir Gordon Guggisberg would not allow the black chairman to introduce Aggrey, but stood up himself and said, 'Mr. Bannerman, a black man introduced all the white men; now a white man must have the privilege of introduc-ing the black man.' In fact, Aggrey's speech provoked so much excite-ment that he had to stop several times when he was interrupted by loud applause, and the two speeches that were scheduled to follow his were canceled.[148] A West African newspaper, which gave a detailed portrait of the commission members' aims, ideas and qualifications, devoted a long paragraph to Aggrey and summed up the feelings of the people of the Gold Coast by saying, 'But of all facts . . . the Gold Coast is more especially proud of this: that the only black member of the Commission, Prof. Aggrey, M.A., D.D., is a native of that colony' – with clear relish in Aggrey's academic title and degrees.[149]

Aggrey's 1924 visit with the second Phelps-Stokes Commission to the east, central and southern regions of Africa aroused no less enthusiasm. In these parts of the continent, admiration for Aggrey himself was augmented by another factor: that Aggrey traveled on equal terms with whites and was, or seemed to be, respected as their peer. In Kenya, Africans saw him as one of their own but on par with the white colonial rulers. As a group of young Africans said in a welcoming address: 'We are glad to enter-tain the man of our own race who is very greatly honoured by the White races, as well as by the black.'[150] In Nyasaland, the commission's next stop, Aggrey's apparent equality with whites led Christian-educated Africans to compare him to the great explorer and missionary David Livingstone. In Southern Rhodesia, now Zimbabwe, the population was thrilled that an African could reach such a high level of culture and learning.[151]

Aggrey's impact on his African audiences went far beyond the overt message he relayed. Aggrey was appointed to the Phelps-Stokes Commis-sion to preach Washington's Tuskegee philosophy and to provide proof, in his own person, of its success. He carried out the assignment loyally and with deep personal conviction. More will be said of his outlook on education in Chapter 5. Here what is notable is that Aggrey shared Booker T. Washington's deep sense of moderation and readiness to cooperate with whites, even to the point of accepting a degree of discrimination. His overt message was one of patience and compliance. At a meeting of a mixed white and black audience in Johannesburg, for instance, Aggrey called upon whites to have patience with Africans who 'have not the same opportunities as they had' and upon Africans to 'look out for the White people who are interested in us. There are many of them, even right here in the city. Stand by them always.'[152] This is only one of countless examples. In his many speeches, Aggrey never condemned the colonial regimes, not even indirectly. On the contrary, he repeatedly urged Africans to obey the colonial authorities. There is no record of his objecting to the assertion of the British governor, Lieutenant Colonel Sir John Robert Chancelor, during the commission's visit to Southern Rhodesia that 'some measure of segregation is essential to the comfort and happiness of Europeans and natives alike, and to the maintenance of the goodwill between the two races'.[153] When the governor pointedly failed to invite him to a garden party in honor of the members of the commission, Aggrey ignored the slur and spent his time talking to Africans at a site near Salisbury.[154]

Not surprisingly, European settlers and colonial officials saw Aggrey as a reasonable African who served their interests. As the *Rhodesia Herald*, the voice of the white settlers, put it, 'Dr. Aggrey is a black man who is proud of his colour, and who believes that the salvation of the African is through religion, hard work and especially manual work, and co-operation with the whites. He is a remarkable orator and his influence with African natives is very great. One governor said that one Aggrey could be as useful to him as two regiments of soldiers.'[155]

Aggrey's acceptance of colonial rule and Africa's white minority governments stemmed not from sycophancy but from his deep belief that the attainment of western standards by blacks in general, and Africans in particular, depended heavily on the good will of white people. To support his position, Aggrey used a musical image, the black and white keys of the piano, reminding his audience that to play a melody one must strike both the white and black keys.[156] Aggrey urged that cooperation between whites and blacks would benefit both races.

But Aggrey also carried another message: that Africans had it in them to rise up and recover their lost pride and dignity. He conveyed this message using what became his famous parable of the eagle. In this parable, the eagle had been captured and placed in a chicken coop, fed on chicken feed, and came to act just like a chicken. Then one day a naturalist visited the farm where it was held and asked about it. The farmer told him that the bird was no longer an eagle. It had been fed on chicken feed and was a chicken. The naturalist disagreed. 'No, it is an eagle still!' The farmer, to prove his point, lifted the eagle into his hands and spread its wings. The eagle rose into the air for a moment, then descended among the chickens again. The farmer repeated the experiment several times, and each time the eagle merely flew in a small circle only to land again among the chickens. The naturalist remained unconvinced and the next morning took the eagle to the foot of the mountains, picked it up, and told it, 'Eagle, thou art an eagle; thou dost belong to the sky and not to this earth; stretch forth thy wings and fly!' Suddenly the eagle stretched out its wings, and with an eagle's screech, mounted higher and higher and never returned. It was an eagle, though it had been kept and tamed as a chicken! When Aggrey finished his story, he looked at his audience and said 'My people of Africa, we were created in the image of God, but men have made us think that we are chickens, and we still think we are; but we are eagles. Stretch forth your wings and fly! Don't be content with the food of chickens!'[157]

Kwame Nkrumah, who recounts hearing the parable at a mass meeting in Accra, tells that at this point the crowd, which till then had been listening with deepest concentration to Aggrey's every word, broke out in excited talk and cheering.[158] Aggrey repeated this parable hundreds of times during his visits to Africa, and his colleagues on the Phelps-Stokes Commission confirm Nkrumah's account of the audience reaction. Whenever Africans were seen waving their arms wildly and laughing uproariously after hearing Aggrey speak, the commission members would smile and say, 'The Eagle again!'[159]

The parable of the eagle did not contradict the message of cooperation, which is why the whites on the Phelps-Stokes Commission were unperturbed by it. It did, however, provide Africans with a promise of a brighter future, in which they would rise above their present downtrodden condition to heights commensurate with their innate nobility. It is this promise that the African-American myth held out and that Aggrey, as its embodiment, exemplified.

DIFFERENT PLACES, DIFFERENT FORMULATIONS OF THE MYTH

By their very being, African-Americans disproved the racist theories that placed blacks on the lower rungs of the evolutionary ladder. For in America there were blacks who were able to interact freely and on equal terms with whites and who occupied high positions in fields such as literature, education, economics and politics. Bishops Turner, Small and Walters, political leaders Garvey and Du Bois, educators Booker T. Washington and Aggrey were living evidence that refuted the disparagements of social Darwinism. As the *Lagos Weekly Record* put it:

> That a people suddenly emancipated from the shackles of an iron servitude should have been able in less than a century to create such a brilliant record as the Census returns of the United States abundantly demonstrate is not only phenomenal and miraculous but also raises the presumption that such a race is endowed with a high order of biological elasticity or capacity for social expansion.[160]

The African-American myth spread to all parts of the continent. But the shape it took differed from place to place in accordance with cultural, political and economic circumstances. The major differences occurred between West Africa, on the one hand, and East-Central and Southern Africa, on the other.

In West Africa, the myth was largely the province of western-educated Africans who had fairly extensive contact with African-Americans, access to relatively accurate information, and the educational and cultural backgrounds to comprehend that information. While the myth also spread to the rural areas of West Africa and was adapted by traditional natives there, the western-educated Africans were the ones who gave it public articulation and led the efforts to use it in response to the colonial situation. At the same time, the Europeans in West Africa, consisting mainly of traders, missionaries and, during the nineteenth century, colonial officials, enabled this use of the myth, as they were seen in generally positive terms: as agents of an advanced civilization to which Africans could aspire.

For the western-educated elite in West Africa, the African-American myth, with its image of the educated and economically and politically integrated black American, served as an instrument in their self-assumed mission of bringing Africans up to the level of Europeans so that they could take their place alongside the colonial powers in the social, economic and political life of their countries. This elite saw education as the means to that end. The success of Booker T. Washington's educational activities in the United States made them eager to adapt his model to Africa. They saw Aggrey, who achieved equal status with whites by going to the United States and getting an education at black American schools, as a perfect product of western education: a man who combined the virtues of the African with those of the African-American. The *Nigerian Pioneer*, for example, credited Aggrey with 'the intellectual acumen of Du Bois, the common sense of Booker T. Washington, and the peculiar wit of the African'.[161] West Africans expected Aggrey to create an educational system which would bring them up to the same level as whites. When he died in 1927, after only a short term on the staff of Achimota College in the Gold Coast, the *Sierra Leone Weekly News* lamented, 'It is one of the tragedies of Africa that Aggrey's time at Achimota was so short.'[162]

In East-Central and most of Southern Africa, the myth prevailed largely among the traditional rural Africans, who had no direct contact with American blacks, little accurate information, and little ability to comprehend the bits and pieces of fact, fiction and rumor that reached them. In these parts of the continent there were fewer western-educated Africans and those few were less familiar with western life. There was not the same firmly established class of western-educated African intellectuals as in West Africa to sift and filter the information and to rationalize and tone down the more fantastic elements of the myth on which the traditional natives seized. Moreover, the European presence consisted mainly of colonial authorities and privileged white settlers whose heavy-handed oppression of the natives evoked fear and hatred. Here the image that the myth offered was that of the mighty African-American, who in some magical and powerful act would swoop down, expel the European oppressors, and liberate the suffering Africans. Power, rather than education and commerce, was regarded as the magic that would make Africans' lives better. Africans in these parts of the continent aggrandized both Aggrey and Garvey as embodiments of a messianic, metaphysical power, supposedly inherent in the Africans of the New World. This power, in their view, was the only thing which could deal with white rule in Africa and cure the continent's social, economic and political ills.

As a result of differences in both the availability of information and the political situation, the myth assumed fairly rational forms in West Africa, while its more fantastic elements were seized upon in East-Central and most of Southern Africa. The role of knowledge in the promulgation of myth has been suggested by Harry Levin. According to Levin, a myth can be either 'a deviation from fact or an approximation to fact', and 'when the facts are under control, we emphasize the degree of deviation; but when we are out of touch with the facts, we utilize fiction to explain the unexplainable'.[163] The role of the surrounding situation is emphasized by Jerome Bruner, who compares myth to the sound of a conch. Bruner observes that although the sound heard is the sound of the sea, it is produced by the vibration of the hand in the chambers of the shell. 'And so with myth. It is at once an external reality and the resonance of the internal vicissitudes of man.'[164]

The next two chapters discuss the different resonances of the African-American myth in East-Central Africa and in West Africa.

2 African Millenarianism and the African-American Myth

Europeans arrived in significant numbers in East-Central and parts of Southern Africa only in the nineteenth century, about three hundred years later than in West Africa and the Cape. The fertile land, clement climate and relative freedom from disease in Nyasaland and Southern and Northern Rhodesia attracted European farmer-settlers alongside the British colonial authorities. The white settlers formed a privileged class exploiting the African natives. A similar dichotomy between newly arrived, privileged white settlers and exploited natives existed in the Boer republics of Transvaal and Orange Free State, where the settlers formed their own government. In all these places, the white settlers wreaked havoc with the Africans' lives. Riding roughshod over traditional African laws and legal systems, they confiscated Africans' most fertile lands, prohibited African farmers from using modern agricultural methods, restricted the growth of cash crops, imposed forced labor on Africans, and, in general, made every effort to keep Africans down as a permanent class of cheap, subservient labor.

The Africans found themselves helpless before the onslaught, as their traditional institutions, way of life, rituals and religions proved unable to cope with the new social, political and economic realities. The anthropologist William Bascom describes the resulting disorientation and emotional uprooting:

> In the old days there were things to be proud of, even for the humble farmer or herder: the valor of their heroes and the victories that were won, the battles lost with honor, the wealth and power of their kings or of their lineage heads, the shrewdness of their statesmen, the long and honorable line of their family ancestors, the skill of their craftsmen, the miracles of their magicians, the knowledge and wisdom of their priests, and the efficacy of their time honored rituals. But today they live under the rule of white men who tell their chiefs what they can and cannot do; and who can pretend that the heroes of the past could stand up against the modern weapons of the white man?[1]

Yet while the support of their local gods and spirits was pulled out from under them, the new religion, Christianity, did not meet their needs. As in other parts of Africa, colonial rule was accompanied by extensive missionary efforts to Christianize and otherwise civilize the natives. But, unlike in those places, missionary education did not improve the lives or status of its recipients. Few western-educated natives were permitted to advance in commerce or the professions and few, if any, found places in the white governments. The upshot was that while they were deprived of their former religions, the new religion gave them little in compensation. The feeling of loss and embitterment is expressed by a native of Southern Rhodesia, today Zimbabwe: 'We used to pray in olden times to our native god, Mwari, and to the *midzimu*, for rain. It always helped. Now we pray to Jesus and rain never comes. We have no corn, no land, nothing. We all hate the Christians; they talk, talk, and nothing comes to us from it.'[2] Illiterate Africans who accepted Christianity because it was the religion of the ruling whites and hoped to benefit from the Christian God in their everyday affairs were also disappointed. Writing of the Shona in Southern Rhodesia, the historian T. O. Ranger observes that, 'Neither in the urban nor in the rural areas did education and espousal of the Christian values seem likely to lead to security or prosperity.'[3]

To make matters worse, rural Africans also lost their faith in their traditional leaders after the colonial powers divested the once venerated tribal chiefs of their legitimacy by turning them into agents of colonial rule. Chiefs and headmen were ridiculed by their own followers. The historian Robert I. Rotberg tells how in the Fife and Chinsali districts in Northern Rhodesia, today Zambia, the important Chief Kafwimbi was mocked as not being a man but a pregnant woman.[4] In many areas, mainly in East-Central and Southern Africa, it became necessary to invent new codes of behavior, new ceremonies and a new social hierarchy to avoid social anarchy.

Africans in these regions – the farmers in the rural areas and the laborers in the mining and urban centers – tried to cope with their social, religious and economic distress by forming and joining messianic and quasi-messianic sects. The motive for their behavior is aptly described by the concept of 'decremental deprivation' described by Michael Barkun in *Disaster and the Millennium*: 'Millenarian movements seem to result most often from situations of decremental deprivation. Decremental deprivation occurs when the expectations of a group concerning its overall well-being remain basically unchanged, but its perceived capabilities for realizing these expectations decline.'[5]

AFRICAN MILLENARIANISM

Beginning in the first decade of the twentieth century, many messianic and millenarian sects sprung up in various parts of the continent.[6] Some were affiliated with American eschatological movements, such as the Watch Tower and Seventh Day Adventists. Others were local in origin, though they borrowed the American sects' messianic ideology. The Watch Tower and its local versions, Chitawala and Kitawala, along with original African messianic movements – such as Kimbanguism, the Khaki movement, the Tonsi, Mpandism, and others – spread in the British, French, Belgian and Portuguese territories. The movements were syncretic in nature, combining Christian beliefs with local traditions, and they attracted large numbers of Africans. The colonial authorities and established churches regarded them as anarchistic and destructive. But, according to R. Bastide, who studied their social and economic impact, the movements grew out of a rupture with tradition and represented a legitimate attempt to deal with a changing world:

> [M]essianic or millenarian movements are not so much movements of retreat and escape into the imaginary as they are bona fide attempts at a rational solution for problems posed by contact with the whites. They are doubtless syncretistic movements, but this syncretism should be regarded less as a bastardizing of European elements, lost in the flux of traditional elements originating in a remote past, than as an initial movement toward acculturation, toward an acceptance of new values. ... Prophetism, messianism, and millenarianism are indeed actions causing a rupture in the social fabric, but they are not merely a rupture with European society. They also reflect a sharp break, and even more so, with traditional society.[7]

The millenarian movements helped the Africans to interpret their lives under colonialism, gave them ways of expressing their dissatisfaction with their situation, and provided hope of a new society in which the black man would triumph. The appeal of these movements to. African peasants and workers lay in their messianic promise. The Watch Tower, the prototype of these movements, preached the Apocalypse in the current generation.[8] The Kingdom of Evil would be replaced by the Kingdom of God – a material, not a spiritual kingdom, where people would enjoy the goods of the earth and be free of hunger, oppression and suffering in their earthly lives. In one form or another, all the various messianic sects held out similar promises.

The Watch Tower and Seventh Day Adventists made Africans familiar with 'more fundamentalist, egalitarian interpretations of the Scriptures'.[9] Thus, Watch Tower challenged colonial abuses, but even more important, it challenged the ideological structure of colonial rule. 'All governments were regarded as Satanic, and the organized churches were seen as Satan's emissaries.'[10] African millenarian activists followed suit. They made extensive use of the Old Testament not only to comfort and console their followers, but also to express defiance of the white rulers. The story of David and Goliath, with its triumph of the weak over the strong, served both purposes and held particular appeal. Messianic leaders in various parts of Africa tended to use that story to drive home their message of defiance. In Southern Rhodesia, George Kunga, a Watch Tower activist, preached: 'Goliath was a big man . . . David was a small man. The white race are now powerful but it will be the same as happened to Goliath. David the small man rose up and killed him. So it will be with the white and black races. The king of the white man will cease to be king and we shall reign.'[11] Simon Kimbangu, who founded the popular Kimbangu messianic movement in the Belgian Congo, today Zaire, which later spread to the French Congo, today Congo Brazzaville, used the story to deliver a clear political message, both to his followers and to the white authorities. In a telling incident in 1921, the Belgian administrator Morel, accompanied by a party of soldiers, came to Kimbangu's village of Nkamba to investigate rumors about his messianic movement. Kimbangu stepped up to the administrator in full view of his followers, loudly read him the story of David and Goliath, and waved a picture of the defeated giant in his face, then turned away when Morel tried to question him.[12]

In Nyasaland, today Malawi, the beast mentioned in the Book of Revelation was identified with the Europeans. The historians Ian and Jane Linden quote Africans as saying that 'Europeans were zirombo (beasts) from the water which we heard of in Revelations.'[13]

Millenarian ideas also provided an explanation for why Africans were culturally and economically so far behind Europeans. According to millenarian thinking, the mighty Lord did not neglect his black children. Rather, white people deliberately kept God's blessings from the Africans. In the Abercorn district of Northern Rhodesia, Hanoc Sindano, the leader of the Kitawala, as the Watch Tower was called in that area, accused Europeans of defying God's will by deliberately refusing to provide Africans with all the knowledge and skills they themselves possessed.[14] This explanation converged convincingly with current realities.

Of all the foreign millenarian movements, the American-based Watch Tower was probably the best known in Africa. The sect spread the word by disseminating inexpensive literature in various African languages. In the 1920s and 1930s, the Watch Tower was practically the only source of eschatological literature in Africa, and up to World War II its publications constituted the basic reading material for Africans in the rural areas.[15] The eschatological literature combined with the total rejection by the Watch Tower of all church hierarchy made a long-lasting impression mainly on

Christian Africans. Some of these Africans who had graduated from mission schools and were deterred by the racial discrimination they encountered there, decided to defy the church authorities and to establish their own independent messianic sects. While potentially they might have formed or joined separatist black churches that remained affiliated with the established white churches, as did their peers in West Africa, in East-Central Africa messianic sects had more appeal and provided a larger following. One of these leaders was Elliot Kamwana, of the Tonga ethnic group in Nyasaland. Educated by the Scottish Livingstonia Mission, Kamwana joined the Watch Tower when he worked in a mining hospital near Johannesburg, and in October 1908, after returning to his native area, founded a local Watch Tower branch there.[16]

Alongside the Watch Tower affiliated groups, indigenous messianic movements also emerged. While the Watch Tower groups explained Africans' suffering by concepts drawn from their eschatological arsenal, the indigenous movements relied mainly on local, pre-Christian concepts and mythology. Kimbanguism, Mwana Lesa, the Tonsi, and other messianic movements were rooted in local traditions and made ample use of precolonial memories, images, ancestors and culture heroes. One of the most popular of these sects was led by Tomo Nyirenda of Nyasaland who, like Kamwana, was educated at the Scottish Livingstonia Mission. In the mid-1920s, he settled among the Lala people of Northern Rhodesia and became a millenarian prophet there. He called himself Mwana Lesa, meaning the son of god in the Lala language, and was believed by the Lala people to be the resurrection of their traditional god. According to the testimony of one of his followers, telling them that their salvation was at hand, Nyirenda would instruct them to make a fire in the bush 'and watch by it till the evening star set for God Coming. . . . When God came all the dead would rise and all would live happily. The Black man in their part and the white man in theirs.'[17] The anticipation of the second coming and the resurrection of the dead are Christian enough, but the lighting of bush fires and the promise that God would make an appearance on earth take one very far from Scripture. The lack of any boundary in the ceremony between the material and the spiritual worlds, between the present and the afterlife, are characteristic of these atavistic movements and rooted in traditional African perceptions.

The motive of these atavistic messianic movements was to restore the sense of security and wholeness that white colonial rule so badly undermined. To this purpose, merely ousting the Europeans, which was how the Africans interpreted Watch Tower eschatology, was not adequate. Something with deeper roots in the culture and the individual psyche was called for. It is in this context that the avid witch-hunting of these groups is to be understood. The trauma of colonial rule and the missionaries' attempts to wipe out traditional customs were threats which Africans could best understand by equating them with witchcraft, the form of evil most familiar to them.[18] In 1934, for example, the Christian Bemba of North Rhodesia welcomed from Nyasaland an anti-sorcery cult known as *mucapi*. The cult leaders promised to eliminate sorcery from among the Bemba once and for all. Those who were identified as sorcerors were forced to take the *mucapi*, 'a soapy solution of redwood powder which was said to react fatally on those who took it and then relapsed into evil ways'. Some members of the community used the *mucapi* to purify themselves and regain their former social status.[19] The Bemba adopted the cult because their old traditions and previous forms of sorcery control evidently failed them, while neither the Church nor the government, which denied the existence of witches, seemed to provide any substitute.

Fear of witchcraft rose sharply among Africans as a result of the colonial conquest. Africans believed that individuals who carried 'evil spirits' were responsible for the hard times they were having. For them, sorcery stood for 'anti-social employment of mystical power'. Therefore, they gave high priority to the purification of African communities from witchcraft.[20] Tomo Nyirenda, the best known of the witch-hunters, was responsible for the execution of 174 people accused of practicing witchcraft in Northern Rhodesia and the Belgian Congo before he was stopped by the British authorities in 1926.[21] William Wade Harris, a prophet active in the Ivory Coast from 1913 to 1915, destroyed fetishes and offered baptism as protection from evil spirits. Simon Kimbangu tried to defeat the local evil spirits Kindoki and Kundu. In 1953 Alice Lenshina, who started a widespread religious movement in Northern Rhodesia, asked people to leave their instruments of witchcraft with her, and then she cleansed and blessed them and gave them medicine to protect them from witchcraft.[22] These atavistic groups, which were deeply anchored in African tradition, represented a genuine African paradigm of messianic or millenarian movements.

THE AFRICAN-AMERICAN FACTOR

Superficially, it might seem that the indigenous messianic movements, with their emphasis on African values and traditions, would not have been affected by the African-American myth. Moreover, unlike the AME Church and the AME Zion Church, the Seventh Day Adventists and the Watch Tower were not dominated by African-Americans. Nevertheless, the myth

did find its way into the messianic movements. The various messianic movements in the Belgian Congo and the French Congo were influenced not
only by Watch Tower literature, but also by UNIA literature and thinking.

Although the UNIA was not a religious movement, its ideology had
strong messianic elements which African millenarian movements could
adapt to their own needs. Garvey's ideology, with its insistence on a solution to Africa's problems in the present and its call for total war against
the colonial powers, radiated an apocalyptic message, as is eminently clear
in his poem, 'The Tragedy of White Injustice':

> There shall be conquests o'er militant forces;
> For as man proposes, God disposes.
> Signs of retribution are on every hand:
> Be ready, black men, like Gideon's band.
> They may scoff and mock at you today,
> But get you ready for the awful fray.[23]

A recurring motif in UNIA publications was the call for the 'redemption
of Africa'. This redemption was at one and the same time presented as an
eschatological goal to which history would lead and as a here-and-now
aim to be attained by military action, if need be.[24]

The UNIA's militancy was a strong attraction to the millenarian groups.
Its open demand that Africa be returned to the Africans and its call to
blacks to drive out the Europeans were totally consistent with the aspirations of the African millenarian groups. Its militancy was given powerful
symbolic expression in its annual parades featuring uniformed African-
American soldiers. Units of the African Legion, Black Cross nurses, black
pilots who were called Black Eagles, and black motorcar drivers all marched
along the streets of Harlem.[25] Descriptions of the parade published in
the *Negro World* found their way to Africa and seemed to provide visible
proof that the eschatological belief was not just a dream, but a reality
which would soon manifest itself in Africa.

Millenarian movements in Africa were, in a sense, gatherings of powerless people looking for a supernatural force to intervene and alleviate their
suffering. The African-American myth made the black Americans the most
likely candidates. Marcus Garvey was turned into an almighty power who
would sweep away the colonial rulers and the misery they wrought. In the
Transvaal, Africans regarded him as a king with godly authority. They were
ready to follow him through fire and water.[26] In Natal, Garvey's name was
intertwined with the hope of liberation by millenarian means.[27] In Kimberly,
a group of Africans led by Moses Itholing formed the secret House of
Athlyi society dedicated to the Garveyite ideology of the redemption of

Africa. According to the Criminal Investigation Department of the Union of South Africa, the society intended to form a religious movement and to appoint ministers who would 'spread the doctrine of hatred to all Europeans'. The society's one idea was 'that the supreme enemy of the black man is the European. Their watch word is "Oust the white man".'[28]

In East-Central, Central and most of Southern Africa, the myth underpinned the fantasy that African-Americans would swoop down as a supernatural force to liberate the Africans from their European oppressors and deliver a world that was closer to paradise than the one that most people know. Millenarian preachers saw African-Americans as an essential element in the coming of the New Kingdom, who would usher in the Apocalypse and be the rulers in the new era. The Kitawala leader Joseph Sibakwe, a member of the Namwanga ethnic group active in the countryside, promised his followers in the Broken Hill area that the evil government in Northern Rhodesia would be replaced within a year by a government coming from America 'made up of natives only'.[29] A Kitawala preacher from Lusaka proclaimed that 'the negroes of America had heard of their ill-treatment and were coming to drive out their white oppressors, that there would be a fierce war between blacks and whites . . . and they would become rulers of the country'.[30] In the Belgian Congo, rumors spread in 1931 that the African-Americans were due to come shortly and then prices would fall.[31] Kitawala preachers in Northern Rhodesia proclaimed that on the Day of Judgment, Europeans would be cast into a boiling Lake Mweru, and many African-Americans would arrive in Africa with the second coming of Christ.[32] In Cape Town, a clerk by the name of Joel Mnyimba said, 'I waited everyday for those Americans to come to free South Africa.'[33]

The African-Americans' role as all-powerful redeemers was based on their possession of modern technology. In West Africa, the technological know-how of black Americans was understood rationally as something that they learned, could in turn teach their African brothers, and could use to develop the continent. In East-Central and Southern Africa, it seemed a magical attribute. The technological achievements of the modern world were beyond the ken and comprehension of the Africans in these parts of the continent, and certainly beyond their power to emulate. Marcus Garvey's formation of a black mass movement and establishment of a black shipping line were things that African peasants and laborers could hardly grasp. The logical consequence of this was that they saw African-Americans, who could do such things, as supernatural beings of extraordinary and unbounded power. Their identification with their African-American brethren gave these Africans a sorely needed sense of power and helped overcome their feelings of inferiority.

The Africans in these regions were particularly captivated by what they viewed as the African-Americans' possession of modern instruments of power: the gun, the ship and the airplane. These were instruments that could be used to expel the Europeans and they were potent symbols of power, strength and manhood. Kamwana, the Watch Tower activist in Nyasaland, emphasized that after the Battle of Armageddon, Africans would make their own guns and gunpowder, as black Americans supposedly did. Till then, a Watch Tower follower told a group of Shona in Southern Rhodesia, 'We have no guns ... therefore we are as children and must wait for the [supernatural] wind and aeroplanes from America which will rid us of the Europeans who are oppressors.'[34]

As far as Africans were concerned, the ships and airplanes, like the guns, were built and operated by New World blacks. An African who worked in Port Elizabeth in the Union of South Africa said that a ship having eight chimneys and crowded with African-Americans was coming to free Africans from their white rulers.[35] As for the airplane, a song sung in Nyasaland told, 'We went to America / To learn the making of aeroplanes / So as to "fix up" all foreigners.'[36] In May 1929 a Watch Tower preacher informed Shona people in Urungwe that

> In about six months a flight of aeroplanes will come from America – sent by a person who lives under the water there – manned by black people, who will make an aerial reconnaissance of the whole country. These Negroes will recognize their own people and will then return to America. Shortly after this they will return and bring war in their train. The white people will then be driven out of the country and the natives will be freed from all taxes and European control.[37]

Jeremiah Gondwe of the Henga ethnic group in Nyasaland similarly told that 'our elder brothers have made aeroplanes' to come to Africa – to check on rumors in the United States that Africans were monkeys and had tails.[38] In Transkei, millenarian preachers struck the same note, promising that when the day of liberation arrived, Americans would fly over and drop balls of burning charcoal on Europeans and non-believing Africans alike.[39] Africans in Nyasaland associated the commercial flights that were started over the territory in the 1930s with African-Americans who would come to liberate them.[40]

The historian T. O. Ranger has argued that the millenarian groups in East-Central Africa fell back on the African-Americans to rescue their movements when their prophecies of the second coming failed to materialize. In Nyasaland, Kenan Kamwana, adopting the end-of-world prophesies of the Watch Tower founder, John Russel, predicted the second coming would take place in October 1914, and Africans would drive away the Europeans and abolish taxes. At about the same time, in the northern province of Northern Rhodesia, a Watch Tower preacher predicted a millennial transformation in the near future. When these prophesies failed to materialize, people left the messianic movements and went back to their original churches. To control the damage, Watch Tower leaders introduced a new liberator: the African-American.[41] What can be added to Ranger's explanation is that the choice of the new savior rested on the fact that the African-American mythical image was well-entrenched in the above-mentioned regions. In East-Central and Southern Africa, the African-American mythical image served as a kind of steady backdrop to the various millenarian movements without any steadfast opposition. Some leaders relied extensively on the myth, while others simply ignored it. For example, Kamwana and Kimbangu won followers by using local customs and beliefs; they occupied strong positions in their communities and did not need the magic of the African-American to attract believers. On the other hand, they did not object to the African-Americans and even adapted African-American symbols; for example, the Kimbanguist movement borrowed the colors of the UNIA flag.[42] The African-American myth was there to be adapted when needed. John Chilembwe's January 1915 rebellion against British colonial rule in Nyasaland is a case in point.

Born in Nyasaland, Chilembwe was educated in America. On his return, he established the Providence Industrial Mission in Chiradzulu, southern Nyasaland, with the help of the National Baptist Convention.[43] Initially, like western-educated Africans in the western part of the continent, Chilembwe believed that by adopting Christianity and western culture, Africans could elevate themselves and become equals in the modern world. But he soon became disillusioned by the racial discrimination that the white settlers and the colonial regime in Nyasaland practiced against all Africans, Christian and non-Christian alike, and became the local champion for African rights. At some point in this struggle, he abandoned peaceful protest by means of petitions and letters of dissent and turned to armed struggle. In this, some scholars have suggested, he was influenced by the millenarian ideas, even though he himself had established an orthodox, not a millenarian, church and spoke out strongly against messianism.

The outbreak of World War I led to a rise in millennial expectations all over the region. The year the war broke out, 1914, was the same year that Kamwana predicted the Battle of Armageddon would take place. In September of that year, rumors spread throughout Nyasaland that African-American soldiers were fighting in the battle in Karonga.[44] But when the war dragged on and Armageddon did not come, disappointed Africans broke with Kamwana and some of them joined Chilembwe. One of them wrote in January 1915, 'The people will not be saved by you [Kamwana] but here it is possible that we will be saved [because] that John Chilembwe is a real American. Here I am with people that I know and I am not afraid.'[45] Chilembwe's training in the United States and his connections with African-Americans made him a kind of a savior in the eyes of the Africans. Even though he personally rejected millenarian visions, he could not avoid being identified with the American soldiers who allegedly were fighting in Karonga. It is probable that in the beginning of 1915, Chilembwe was 'pushed into inaugurating the millennium by the sword'.[46]

Chilembwe's biographer, George Simeon Mwase, suggests that Chilembwe was inspired by the American folk hero John Brown, who took up arms against slavery and in 1857 raided the US federal arsenal at Harper's Ferry, West Virginia. According to Mwase, Chilembwe borrowed John Brown's battle cry in that raid, 'Let us strike a blow and die.' In his speech on the eve of his own uprising, Chilembwe told the chief headman and elders that 'this case stands the same as that of a Mr. John Brown, I have referred to above. "Let us then strike a blow and die" for our blood will surely mean something at last.'[47] Although scholars have questioned the accuracy of this account, its academic merit is secondary to the fact that Mwase, thus far Chilembwe's only African biographer, presented a genuine African view of the rebellion.[48] Mwase's rendition indicates that the American mythical image provided a point of reference for Africans in Nyasaland. Indeed, though Chilembwe was killed by British troops in 1915, many Africans in Nyasaland believed he did not really die but managed to escape to America, and that one day he would lead African-Americans back to liberate them.[49] The arrival of James Kwegyir Aggrey, like Chilembwe an African educated in America, with the second Phelps-Stokes Commission in 1924, evoked hopes in Nyasaland that Chilembwe would rise again and expel the British from the land. There were even rumors that a telegram had arrived from the United States announcing that Chilembwe was about to come back.[50]

The mythical aura surrounding American blacks was easily translated into millenarian belief. Aggrey himself evoked millenarian expectations in East, Central and Southern Africa. His visit to these regions in 1920 and 1924 aroused strong eschatological feelings among some groups of Africans. For some Africans in Transkei, the fact that Aggrey was an apparently equal member of a commission of whites from America made his visit an omen of the fulfillment of their millenarian expectations. According to his biographer:

Aggrey was supposed by some to be the herald of an invading band of Negroes – they thought all Americans were Negroes – who would drive the Whites of South Africa into the sea. Men came to the meeting in Umtata on horseback, with empty sacks for saddle cloths. He will order the merchants to sell their goods cheaply – he may even compel them to give the goods away for nothing! So they imagined. The empty grain bags under the saddles were to carry away these easily gotten possessions.[51]

Africans from East-Central Africa who worked in the Union of South Africa and had heard Aggrey speak, or heard of him, carried back home the legend of the African-American savior who would put an end to African subjugation.[52] When Aggrey visited East-Central Africa with the second Phelps-Stokes Education Commission, his name was already known, and in some places he was accepted as the Messiah himself. In Nyasaland, a white missionary from the Blantyre Mission, Dr Hetherwick, wrote that to the people of the area, 'he was a new revelation. . . . They flocked around him whenever he was free and his sayings and doings were quoted long after he left.' Dr Hetherwick also reported that common Africans as well as headmen and chiefs walked many miles to meet Aggrey.[53] The idea that Aggrey was the Messiah reached as far as East Africa. Reverend H. D. Hooper, who hosted Aggrey for a weekend at a church missionary station in Kahuhia in the reserve of the Kikuyu ethnic group in Kenya, compared the Africans who were waiting to meet him to Jews awaiting the Messiah, telling that 'there was the same sort of eye lifted to the threshold to see the arrival of the leader'.[54] As in South Africa, millenarian expectations ran high in these regions. Aggrey was again regarded as the forerunner of an invading black army that would drive out the Europeans. This army would drop bombs from airplanes – bombs which would kill only whites.[55] Aggrey never did anything to encourage these millennial expectations. On the contrary, he vigorously spoke out against them. Millenarianism was diametrically opposed to everything he stood for. His message was that blacks and whites should live together harmoniously – like the black and white keys of the piano, as he put it. Some Africans were disappointed with his position. An African chief, a member of the Bunga, the Transkei Legislative Assembly, who took part in a mass meeting with Aggrey, complained that 'he did not say what we expected'.[56] Other Africans simply ignored his denials. For them, Aggrey was living proof of their millennial expectations and they were not ready to relinquish them. One of them, a Zulu named Wellington, who pretended to be an African-American and bestowed on himself the title of doctor, went so far as to offer an explanation for Aggrey's behavior. In 1926 he claimed in Transkei that Aggrey 'had been bought by the Whites – that is why he had talked about co-operation with, and love for, their enemies'.[57]

Aggrey's return to America without fulfilling the Africans' eschatological expectations neither put an end to the millenarian movements nor caused them to abandon their high hopes of the African-American and look for another messiah. On the contrary, Africans in East-Central, Central and most of Southern Africa seem to have had little alternative but to cling tenaciously to the African-American promise. They could see little if any other hope for a better future. Millenarian sects continued to spread the belief that African-Americans would come to liberate their African brethren. In the Belgian Congo, Africans hoped 'that the blacks of America will soon come and conquer the Congo'.[58] In June 1932, in the Gutu region of what was then Southern Rhodesia, a native preacher Luka Jarawani preached that 'The time is at hand, America is coming to rule the country. The white people are going back to their own country. . . . The Americans will soon come and you will be happy when they come because you will be free of all troubles the white people have caused you.'[59] Jarawani's message aroused such enthusiasm that many Africans left their former churches and joined him. The head of the Dutch Reformed Church schools complained to the Superintendent of Natives' Office that: 'at one of the schools forty children are left out of two hundred and at another seven are left out of sixty. The Missionaries are naturally much upset to see the work of twenty-five years swept away in this manner.'[60]

Jarawani's emissaries fanned out to the various villages of the Gutu region and carried the African-American gospel to almost every remote corner. Their message remained constant: Americans are coming to free the Africans and will bring with them wealth and prosperity. Only they offered a new harbinger of salvation: instead of the American-educated African Aggrey, the herald of good tidings was to be the African-American bishop of the AME Church, the only black man who held that important title in all of Southern Africa.[61] According to testimony given to the Superintendent of Natives in the area, Jarawani's emissaries promised the villagers 'that the Bishop was arriving shortly; that on his arrival the Europeans would leave the country; that no tax for either men, dogs or cattle would in future be paid and that registration certificates would not be required' and that 'when the Bishop came there would be a great change as he would release the Natives from bondage'.[62]

World War II reinforced the Africans' millenarian expectations of African-Americans. United States army units, which included black soldiers, were stationed in several African colonies. Many Africans interpreted their arrival as the fulfillment of the millenarian prophecies and regarded the black soldiers as messengers of God come to liberate them.[63] In territories where the US Army was not stationed, rumors that American soldiers were arriving were enough to inflame millenarian expectations. In those territories, African-American soldiers were expected to arrive in ships, airplanes, or miraculously out of the blue and totally change the world in which the Africans were living. Some messianic movements, which originally were not connected with the African-American myth, interpreted the arrival of black American soldiers as harbingers of the reincarnation of local heroes. The arrival of American units in the Belgian Congo in 1940 was taken as proof that two famous African prophets, Simon Kimbangu and Simon Mpandi, would return. Belief had it that the black American soldiers would supply Kimbangu and Mpandi with magical vehicles, including 'a locomotive, a holy truck, a ship and an airplane'. The two prophets would then 'bring the Congolese new arms with terrible effects', including the power to de-rail the trains in which the Belgians traveled. The Bacongo people attributed the de-railment of a train on the line between Matadi and Leopoldville to Kimbangu and Mpandi.[64] In addition to power, the messianic movements also emphasized the wealth, generosity and organizational ability of black Americans. In the new kingdom which would arise after the Apocalypse, African-Americans would teach the Africans what they knew.[65] Tomo Nyirenda promised his followers that if they agreed to be baptized and believed deeply in the millennial idea, the Americans would come and give them great wealth.[66] On another occasion, he pledged that anyone who gave the Americans a small basket of grain would get in exchange a huge cloth.[67]

The shape the African-American myth took was determined by the economic, social and political conditions of the regions in which it developed. In East, East-Central and Southern Africa, western-educated Africans, barred from meaningful participation in the white governments, white churches, and white-controlled economy, turned their backs both on the hope of living their lives side by side with Europeans and on the western rationalism required for such co-existence. While they did not abandon Christianity, they focused intensely on its apocalyptic teachings, on the promise of a liberating cataclysm and a better world to come. To bolster their status with their followers, some of them reinforced their Christian messianic teachings with traditional African messianic beliefs, while others held up the mythical image of the omnipotent African-American who would come to the rescue.

In West Africa, where there was a long-standing western-educated elite with strong ties to European culture, the African-American myth took a different shape and served different purposes.

3 African Cultural Nationalism: Contrasting Views of the African-American Myth

Unlike Africans in East-Central and Southern Africa, West Africans enjoyed several centuries of a mutually beneficial relationship with Europeans before a similar process of 'decremental deprivation' forced them to seek succor in the African-American myth. This relationship, along with the relative availability of information about America and the existence of a well-established western-educated elite, was behind the very different response of the West Africans to the decremental deprivation they too suffered at the hands of the Europeans in the late nineteenth century, as well as behind the different version they adapted of the African-American myth and the different uses they made of it.

The association between West Africa and Europe began in the late fifteenth century and was largely commercial. For about three hundred years, West Africans and Europeans were partners in trade, with minimal European interference in African political life. Unaware of the potential power of the Europeans, Africans did not develop any sense of racial inferiority and demanded and received respect.[1] From the end of the eighteenth century, socio-economic and ideological developments in Europe resulted in greater interference, on the one hand, but brought further benefits, on the other.

The Industrial Revolution created the need for raw materials and new markets, to which the slave trade was antithetical. The new economic realities, along with the concomitant strengthening of the abolitionist movement in Europe, resulted in the prohibition of the slave trade and the introduction of legitimate trade with Africa. Enforcing abolition and encouraging legitimate trade brought Europe, and especially Britain, to intervene in African commerce, social life and politics. At the same time, the cultivation of the cash crops that now made up the bulk of the intercontinental trade was left entirely in the hands of the African producers. In contrast to East-Central and Southern Africa, there were no European settlers in disease-ridden West Africa to appropriate the lucrative agricultural market.

A similar pattern of intervention sweetened by benefits occurred with the stepped-up missionary activity that developed out of the notion of the white man's burden prevalent in Europe in the late eighteenth and early nineteenth centuries. As in East-Central and Southern Africa, the intensive introduction of Christianity and western culture eroded West Africans' traditional cultures. On the other hand, in contrast to their counterparts in East Africa, West Africans who were converted to Christianity and educated in mission schools became an elite. They became the Europeans' allies in 'civilizing' Africa. A Lagos newspaper stated that the task of educated Africans was to create 'intelligent and powerful Christian Negro States'.[2] In Freetown, a leading Creole justified European activities in Africa with the claim that the abolition of slavery and the pax *Britannica* were fulfillments of biblical prophecies of world peace.[3] The Europeans, for their part, encouraged the partnership because the tropical climate and disease which earned Africa the epithet 'the white man's grave' made it convenient that Africans carry the better part of the burden of the commercial, administrative and missionary activities.

By the middle of the nineteenth century, western-educated Africans in the British domain were well established in the free professions, state administration and commerce. They were doctors, lawyers, churchmen, newspaper editors and upper-level civil servants, as well as merchants and businessmen.[4] As an educated and experienced elite, they expected to benefit from the expansion of the British sphere of influence, to be the ones who would introduce Christianity, cash crops and western administration in the British domains. In consequence, some of them even supported British imperialism. In 1894, for example, a Gold Coast newspaper urged Britain to march to Kumasi, the capital of the Ashantee Empire, and turn it into a British protectorate.[5]

This assimilated western-educated elite, identified with European culture, values and political goals, was unique to British West Africa and the Cape Colony of South Africa. It was non-existent in East-Central and most of Southern Africa, the home of messianism and millenarianism. It is this elite that shaped the West Africans' response to the crisis when it came.

THE CRISIS OF THE WESTERN-EDUCATED ELITE

The crisis in West Africa came towards the end of the nineteenth century with the deposition of the western-educated African elite. Advancing into the hinterland, the British found that they lacked the money, manpower and will to proceed with their civilizing mission and abandoned both it and their western-educated African allies. For the necessary assistance in their colonial administration, the British drew upon the traditional African rulers, who had the advantage of being familiar with their people and possessing the necessary governing experience. Integrating them into the colonial machinery minimized tension and reduced costs.

The displacement of the western-educated African elite was further accelerated by the arrival of increasing numbers of European missionaries, traders and government officials, after tropical diseases, which had been the main obstacle to a large European presence in West Africa, began to come under control.[6] For instance, in Sierra Leone, the number of Europeans increased during the last decade of the nineteenth century from 210 to 351.[7] With the threat of disease greatly reduced and ever larger numbers of Europeans in Africa, British officials decided to favor their own, reserving the responsible positions in administration, clergy and medical personnel, formerly held by western-educated Africans, for Europeans.

The reversal in British colonial policy inevitably entailed the institution of discriminatory practices. Europeans, sometimes less qualified than Africans, were installed in higher positions in the colonial civil service and salaries were set along the color line. In 1893 in Lagos colony, the native-born Henry Carr, who had been serving as chief clerk for four years with a salary of £175, was relieved of his office. The European who replaced him in his post enjoyed a starting salary of £200, which rose to £250 per annum.[8] In the same year, in Sierra Leone, western-educated Africans protested against discrimination and demanded a fair employment system which would provide salary increases on the basis of qualifications and seniority.[9] Discrimination became all-pervasive, embracing administrative, missionary and commercial circles. One western-educated African complained that the slave trade was replaced by another form of racism, no less painful: 'The wail of physical suffering has been exchanged for the groans of an intellectual, social, and ecclesiastical ostracism.'[10]

That ostracism was buttressed by the spread of social Darwinism, which seemed to provide scientific evidence that blacks were inferior. British colonial officials, quick to adopt the theory, both derided the western-educated Africans as pretenders to European status and blamed them for any political unrest that occurred in their domains. In the Gold Coast, British officials reported that the 'Cape Coast is afflicted with a number of mischievous, half-educated mulatto adventurers, whose livelihood depends on keeping alive dissention.'[11] George Thomas Carter, appointed Governor of Lagos in 1890, was openly contemptuous of western-educated Africans and declared their efforts to emulate Europeans pointless and irrational.[12] In 1909 Sir John Rodger, Governor of the Gold Coast, aptly described the

British attitude toward the educated African elite: British educational policy, he charged, involved producing 'black and brown Englishmen' and then 'cursing the finished article when the operation is complete'.[13]

The deposition of the western-educated elite in West Africa can be considered as much a crisis for them as the outrages of the white settlers were for the Africans in the east-central and southern parts of the continent. But unlike the leaders of the messianic and millenarian movements, who looked for a metaphysical force to oust the European interlopers, the West Africans were able to respond with cultural and political measures aimed at improving their lot and obtaining their fair share of power. Their long exposure to and internalization of European values obviated the appeal of messianism and inclined them to a more earth-based solution to their problems.

AFRICAN CULTURAL NATIONALISM

The response of the western-educated Africans in West Africa to their loss of status was the cultural nationalist movement. This was a loosely organized movement that emerged spontaneously in the late nineteenth century throughout the four British domains in West Africa. Led by the rejected urban, western-educated African elite, the movement attempted to grapple with the sudden problem of identity they and their followers faced as a result of their ouster by reasserting the value of Africa and Africans. It was largely an intellectual movement with political overtones, whose leaders believed that they could regain their former place and eventually attain equality with Europeans. Their hope lay in persuading the skeptical British that they were up to par and deserved to be treated as equals, to which end they published articles in African newspapers, petitioned colonial officials, and formed a variety of organizations. Both their aims and intellectual, westernized means were totally different from those of the messianic and millenarian movements in East-Central and Southern Africa, whose leaders, never members of a once favored elite and free of illusions about their ability to persuade the ruling whites to give them and their people their due, placed their hopes in a miraculous rescue by an omnipotent metaphysical power.

The cultural nationalist movement set about to refute the assertion based on social Darwinism that blacks were an inferior species of the human race with no claim to civilization or culture. They concentrated their efforts on proving that Africa had a viable past of its own, in no way inferior to Europe's, and that African culture had once been a leading one. The Liberian scholar, Edward Wilmot Blyden, thus cited ancient history, especially Egypt's, as proof of Africans' contribution to the human race. He traveled to Egypt and described how, when he looked at the pyramids, 'feelings came over me far different from those I ever felt when looking at the mighty works of European genius. I felt I had a peculiar heritage in the Great Pyramid built ... by the enterprising sons of Ham, from which I was descended.'[14] Some cultural nationalists claimed that 'Africa was the cradle of the world's systems and philosophies, and the nursing mother of its religions.'[15] Kobina Sekyi celebrated traditional African religious and cultural practices, especially those of the Fanti ethnic group, over those of the Europeans, and argued that the traditional African state was more natural than the European and could serve as a model for Europeans to emulate.[16]

Along with calling up African history and traditions to prove Africans' contribution to humanity, activists in the movement also started to question their present. They wondered if their total submission to European culture in virtually every area of their lives – dress, food, language, lifestyle, and even their names – had achieved anything. Casely Hayford, of the Gold Coast, one of the movement's leading members, answered the question with a hearty negative: European scorn for Africans, he contended, stemmed precisely from the African imitation of Europeans.[17] Others emphasized that there was no way Africans could metamorphose into Europeans. It was as ridiculous for Africans to imitate Europeans as it would be for 'Old Englanders' to borrow the customs of the Mendi ethnic group.[18] Orishatukeh Faduma observed that nature had created different races and Africans could not turn into Anglo-Saxons and vice versa.[19] Some cultural nationalists went so far as to claim that such fruitless emulation of European culture robbed Africans of their true identity. Kobina Sekyi held that when Africans learned to think like white men, they stopped feeling and thinking like Africans, and warned that Africans could completely lose their identity.[20] O. T. Nana, one of the leading activists in Sierra Leone claimed in a newspaper article that in attempting to be carbon copies of Europeans, Africans had lost their sense of direction and condemned themselves to uprooted lives.[21]

The remedy of the cultural nationalists was to reject European culture and return to their own traditional African ways. S. R. B. Solomon of the Gold Coast, for example, called upon his fellow Africans to protect their traditional institutions against erosion by European influence. 'The greatest calamity of West Africa that must be combated tooth and nail', he emphasized, 'is the imminent Loss of Ourselves. ... Rather let men rob our lands ... but let us see that they do not rob us of ourselves. They do so when we are taught to despise our own Names, Institutions, Customs and Laws.'[22] He himself changed his baptismal name to an African one, Attoh Ahuma. Other western-educated Africans followed his example. For instance, William J. Davis, of Sierra Leone, who obtained his academic education in London and served as senior master at the Wesleyan High School in Freetown, changed his name to Orishatukeh Faduma. Other Creoles did the same: A. E. Metzger became Toboku-Metzger; O. T. George became O. T. Nana; Claude George became Esu Biyi. They demonstrated their release from cultural subjection and emphasized their African heritage by reverting to African attire and African food. For instance, in 1887 leading Creoles in Freetown formed the Dress Reform Society, with James Hasting Spaine, the colonial postmaster, as president.[23]

Scholars have been inclined to regard the cultural nationalist movement as purely cultural and to disregard its nationalist element. For example, Leo Spitzer, who wrote a leading book on the Sierra Leone Creoles stated: 'From the 1880s until about 1910, Creole reactions to the increasingly racist tenor of British policies in Sierra Leone had been largely limited to the intellectual and cultural realm.'[24] Most of the measures taken by members of the movement – the return to African names, African food, and African clothing – were demonstrations of cultural, not national, independence. Nevertheless, the cultural protest was accompanied by nationalist elements. This can be seen in the activities of Mojola Agbebi of Lagos, christened David Brown Vincent. In addition to changing his name and leading a group of western-educated Africans to shed their European attire for African dress, Agbebi took the hitherto unprecedented step in Africa of leaving the white dominated church to which he had belonged and establishing a separate, independent African church. In 1888 he founded the African Baptist Church and in 1891 the United Native African Church – into both of whose services he incorporated African music, hymns, and dances. These were the first churches in West Africa run entirely by Africans. Their executive, clergy and teachers were Africans, and the church policies and decisions were made by Africans without white supervision or interference.[25]

The protest also included some political elements. These are very difficult to detect, since they were hidden under layers of avowed loyalty to Britain. Nonetheless, they did exist. Notably, Casely Hayford worked to create a political union of the four West African British domains. More generally, most cultural nationalists never reconciled themselves to their ouster from their former partnership with Britain. They saw themselves as the only possible partners in the establishment of an advanced, civilized state in Africa based on western know-how and Christian values. And they harbored the wish to regain their former role in the British colonial administration. The fact that the objective was partnership rather than independence does not diminish its political nature.

What remains true is that to the minds of the cultural nationalists, cultural development was indispensable to political progress. The cultural nationalists could not but recognize the vast gaps that separated the Africans from the Europeans, and generally concurred that closing these gaps – through what they called the regeneration of Africa – was necessary before they could take their place beside the British in governing their countries. Blyden was adamant that civilizing Africa had to be Africans' first priority, insisting that 'in this direction, and this direction only, lies the hope of Africa's future'.[26]

The question was how to achieve that regeneration, or, more precisely, through whose agency, since the racist whites who scorned and rejected the western-educated Africans that made up the movement would obviously be of little assistance. On the answer to the question, the cultural nationalists were divided. Some, who took what we term the African-American avant-garde approach, argued vigorously that external help, in the form of black Americans, was essential. Others, who took what can be termed the African avant-garde approach, argued with equal vigor that Africans could revitalize the continent on their own.[27]

THE AFRICAN-AMERICAN AVANT-GARDE APPROACH

The African-American avant-garde approach maintained that the task of regenerating Africa was beyond the capacity of Africans equipped with only their traditional values, and that the active participation and leadership of African-Americans was essential. The major spokesmen for this approach were Edward Blyden, Orishatukeh Faduma and James Johnson. All three held posts in Protestant churches and were familiar with the western world. Like the leaders of the messianic and millenarian movements in East-Central and Southern Africa, they were imbued with the African-American mythical image, believed that the descendants of Africa in the New World had already risen to the cultural and technological level of whites, and maintained that they were essential to the improvement of the Africans' lot. While the former regarded African-Americans as an omnipotent force that would miraculously liberate them from their miseries through a spectacular act of Armageddon, the African-American avant-gardists saw them as persons whose education and skills made them useful allies in Africans' efforts to rebuild and reconstruct the continent. For example, the Nigerian Bishop James Johnson held that African-American missionaries, not European ones, were needed to Christianize the continent so as to restore it to its former glory.[28] He also maintained that African-Americans were the right people to help make Africa 'industrially independent' by augmenting the natural resources and capacities of the Africans with the moral virtues, knowledge and skills they would bring from the United States.[29]

To promote their idea, the advocates of the African-American avant-garde had to explain why black Americans who lived thousands of miles away and in a very different socio-political and cultural milieu should serve as an avant-garde for Africans in Africa. To this end, Blyden, Faduma and others created yet another myth: the Providential Design theory. This myth was based on the Christian interpretation of history, whereby Providence directs the course of human events. Providence guides history, and history is given meaning through the Almighty will. Blyden, an ordained Presbyterian minister, held that Africans had been transported as slaves to the New World by divine sanction. Time and again, he put forth the idea that Africans were uprooted from their homeland and placed in slavery in a far off continent by God's will. Drawing on the Old Testament, he pointed out that God had placed the Israelites in bondage in Egypt for four hundred years before He rescued His chosen people and guided them to the Promised Land. Blyden argued that just as the history of the Israelites was directed by the hand of God, so too was the history of black Americans. There was a 'divine purpose in permitting their [Africans'] exile to and bondage in this land [the New World]'.[30] The purpose, in Blyden's interpretation, was so that they would be able to help revitalize Africa and the Africans.

Attributing the slave trade to God's will served several purposes. For one thing, it provided an answer to the question that Christian Africans could not help but ponder: how could God-fearing Christians perpetuate the horrors of slavery? The idea that slavery was part of Providential Design served to answer this question. To get around the obvious problem that the theory could also be used to justify slavery, as an expression of the will of God, Blyden argued that slave-holders distorted God's will for material gain and that slavery was a temporary phenomenon.[31] Moreover, the theory enabled Blyden to argue that the long years in bondage were not just a time of misery and hardship, but had important benefits. Africans emerged from the horrors of slavery strengthened and purified, he contended: 'Slavery would seem to be a strange school in which to preserve a people; but God has a way of salting as well as purifying by fire.'[32] In fact, he held up the entire institution of slavery, with all its hardships and agonies, as something for the benefit of the black race. Comparing the slave's lot to Christ's, who was similarly 'despised and scorned', Blyden insisted that '[A]ll the advancement made to a better future by individuals or race, has been made through paths marked by suffering. This great law is written not only in the Bible, but upon all history.'[33] More specifically, Blyden contended that slavery provided the children of Africa with precisely the advantages that would make them useful to Africans: the opportunity to absorb Christianity and to obtain a western education in the arts and sciences. Blyden held that 'The slave trade was regarded as a great means of civilizing the blacks – a kind of missionary institution', and moreover, that during their time as slaves, Africans were 'not only indoctrinated into the principles of Christianity, but they were taught the arts and sciences'.[34]

Finally, the theory gave legitimization to the African-American avant-gardists' basic idea of using American blacks for the regeneration of Africa. The theory held that black Americans' extraordinary achievements were the product of God's will, not human effort. African-Americans owed their success neither to their talent nor to the help of American whites, but to the will of the Creator of the world. In this theory, Christianity, education, and technological know-how were 'deposited' in the hands of the African-Americans to be used not for their own material gain, but for the advancement of their brethren in Africa. It is with this interpretation that the advocates of the African-American avant-garde approach felt justified in demanding that American blacks uproot en masse and come to Africa to help restore the continent. Blyden put forth this demand in dramatic terms: 'Two hundred millions of people have sent me on an errand of invitation to their blood relations here. Their cry is, "Come over and help us."'[35] James Johnson spelled out the argument quite clearly in 1915, when he addressed a group of African-Americans who came on shore at Freetown on their way to establishing a settlement in the Gold Coast: 'We greet you warmly also as Brethren because we discern in you those who are evidently intended by God, the Father of all, to be with us fellow missionaries and fellow workers for the upbuilding of our desolated Aboriginal Homeland, the repeopling of it, the regenerating of West Africa religiously, intellectually, morally, socially, and otherwise.'[36]

An article in the *Lagos Standard* summed up the African-American avant-garde concept as follows: 'America is not the destined home of the Negro. He is an alien and a stranger there. In his removal to that distant land, we can discern the hands of an All-wise Providence. His enforced exile has been for a purpose, and when that purpose is accomplished, like the ancient Israelites, he will once more be led out of Egypt to return to his original home.' Since this return was nothing less than the will of

Providence, it was bound to occur, even if there was currently little evidence of a mass migration: 'But sooner or later, by some means or another, the destined end, we fully believe, will be effected, and God's hidden purposes will be revealed in the fullness of time, of the exiles – not by tens or by scores as at present, but by hundreds and thousands – laden with the wealth of intelligence, and experience of arts and learning to be used in Africa for the elevation of their race and country.'[37]

With the Providential Design theory, Blyden and its other advocates created their own myth. Like other myths, this one had the advantage that it 'is not ... necessarily false but that its "truth" cannot be established from historical evidence'.[38] Nor could its truth be disproved by historical evidence. The advocates of the Providential Design theory had no need for historical accuracy. All they needed was to be able to turn the historical fact of slavery to their own ends. This they did, endowing slavery with transcendental meaning so as to create a sense of connectedness, shared ideals and common goals between Africans and African-Americans. In the words of the *Gold Coast Leader*: 'It is but asserting the commonplace when we say that the expatriation of some of our people to America and to the West Indies in times past, was in the order of Providence, to hasten a national consciousness; and today our brethren there are turning with longing eyes to the fatherland.'[39]

The Providential Design theory reached various parts of the continent, where it took on different forms. In the Union of South Africa, Christian Africans read the biblical verse, 'Princes shall come out of Egypt; Ethiopia shall soon stretch forth her hands unto God', as proof of the Providential Design concept. Egypt was interpreted as the United States, the place of black bondage; the princes were seen as the African-Americans who had accepted western culture and would bring Christianity to Africa.[40] James E. Kwegyir Aggrey of the Gold Coast, a firm believer in the Providential Design theory, declared that 'God sent the black man to America. Was this all a matter of chance? You who are philosophers know there is no such thing as chance; God always has a programme. He meant America to play a special part in the history of Africa.'[41] In the lower Congo, the theory underwent yet another permutation, not rooted in Christianity. This was the legend, noted in Chapter 1, that the Congolese who were taken to the New World as slaves developed, all by themselves, a rich, prosperous industrial society which made the white man accept them as equals.[42] All the variations of the Providential Design theory, though, supported the same conclusion: that Africans were able to rise to an advanced level of culture and technology only when they were removed from Africa to the New World.

The advocates of the African-American avant-garde approach both exploited and helped to propagate the larger African-American myth. With its grand idealization of American blacks, the larger myth served as the foundation for their beliefs and arguments and provided the rationale for placing the future of Africa into the hands of African-Americans. The sub-myth, the Providential Design theory, provided the justification for calling upon American blacks to uproot themselves from their familiar lives to travel to a land where they had no personal ties, of which they had no memories, and where they could only expect hardships. To this end, the advocates of the African-American avant-garde fortified their religious argument with social and racial ones. They harnessed the ugly side of African-American life to their cause. As already pointed out, Africans had ample information about the realities of black life in America. African newspapers repeatedly censured the segregation, discrimination and lynching of blacks in the southern states, the denial of their voting rights, and their poverty and lack of social and economic mobility. The African-American avant-gardists touted these abuses to intensify any feelings that African-Americans might have had of being outsiders in America and to bolster their calls for mass emigration to Africa. In visits to the United States, they argued that Africa, not America, was the true home of American blacks, and that their stay in the United States was transitory. Fearing African-Americans' successful, and hence permanent, integration into American society, they urged American blacks to maintain their distinct black identity and ties to Africa. In a speech delivered to an audience of African-Americans in the United States, Blyden proclaimed that it was 'certain that the two races will never live in a state of equal freedom under the same Government, so insurmountable are the barriers which nature, habit, and opinion have established between them'.[43] As can be discerned from this statement, the socio-political assertion that blacks were mistreated outsiders in white America was only part of a larger argument: that their racial identity was more than skin deep. Each race had its own distinctive features, Blyden repeatedly insisted.[44]

Yet even as they preached maintaining a distinct black identity, the advocates of the African-American avant-garde approach were far from rejecting white culture. On the contrary, African-Americans could serve as an avant-garde for Africans only and precisely because they had attained access to aspects of white culture that were rare in Africa: technology, higher education, and modern skills. Bishop Johnson maintained that only western-educated Africans and African-Americans, who had benefitted from extensive contact with whites, could lead the way to the regeneration of Africa.[45] Blyden struck the same note in his announcement that 'we shall resort to the same means of general culture which has enabled the Anglo-Saxon to find out for himself the way in which he ought to go'.[46] Faduma advised his brethren in the New World to bring from America those things that would benefit Africa, especially education in modern agriculture and industry.[47]

This combination of racial self-identification and exploitation of western culture and technology was seen as the means not only to the cultural regeneration of Africa but also to political attainments. The other side of the racial separatism that Blyden propounded was the notion of racial unity encompassing both Africans and African-Americans. This notion of racial unity readily lent itself to nationalistic ends. Blyden's biographer, Hollis R. Lynch, points out that Blyden's 'ultimate ideal was the creation of one or more West African States'.[48] In 1880, inspired by the recent unification of Italy and Germany along racial lines, Blyden held up the vision of a great black nation created jointly by Africans and African-Americans. Along with calling on African-Americans to take an active role in the cultural regeneration of the continent, he called on them to join their brothers-in-race in the great task of nation building.[49]

Ten years later, Blyden and other advocates of the African-American avant-garde took tentative steps to begin to make the dream a reality. The occasion was the ouster of African clergymen from the employ of the Church Missionary Society (CMS) by the society's white missionaries. The clergymen who were dismissed had worked under the direction of the respected African Bishop Samuel Ajayi Crowther, who for the previous thirty years had successfully led the CMS missionary work in West Africa. In response, Blyden and James Johnson organized two forms of protest. One was an emergency meeting in Lagos, where it was decided to establish an independent African church with Bishop Crowther as its head. The other consisted of efforts to hasten African-American immigration. Blyden and Johnson actively went out to locate suitable sites in Yorubaland for the settlement of black Americans of Yoruba descent.[50]

The African-American avant-garde concept found its way into black American circles. It is not surprising that the first American blacks to respond to the idea were clergymen. Bishop Henry McNeal Turner of the AME Church and Bishop Alexander Walters of the AME Zion Church, contemporaries of Blyden, both advocated the idea. In his 1895 speech to the Congress on Africa in Atlanta, Turner told his audience: 'I believe that the Negro was brought to this country in the providence of God to a heaven-permitted if not a divine-sanctioned manual laboring school, that he might have direct contact with the mightiest race that ever trod the face of the globe.'[51] Turner and Walters accepted not only the explanatory and apologetic elements of the myth, but also its message that American blacks should return to Africa to regenerate the continent. Turner called for African-Americans to leave the United States and move back to their ancient homeland. He was behind the AME Church program sending black American missionaries all over Africa. And his attempt to amalgamate the Ethiopian Church in the Cape with the powerful, American-based AME Church, touched on in Chapter 1, was yet another way of getting African-Americans to bring the lessons of Christianity to heathen Africans. Similarly, Bishop Walters, a champion of pan-Africanism and an AME Zion Church bishop for Africa, asked his hearers to consider the question: 'For what other purpose were the natives brought to America and caused to pass through the crucible of slavery and now to be Christianized and trained in the best schools of the nation but to aid in the redemption of Africa.'[52]

Yet another black American to take up the banner of the African-American avant-garde was Max Yergan. Yergan was appointed YMCA secretary to the Union of South Africa in 1925, after having served as the YMCA representative in Bangalore, India, and in East Africa. Yergan argued that despite the toil and suffering of slavery, 'it is possible to assert that action on such a grand scale whereby millions of Africans and their descendants have had their environment and future altogether changed has not been without real and unquestioned benefit'. He was committed to the idea that the African-Americans who had benefitted from Christianity and western civilization must return to Africa to aid their brethren in their effort to revitalize the continent. By living and working in the Union of South Africa for fifteen years, he served as a personal example.[53]

African and American advocates of the African-American avant-garde approach worked separately to realize the dream of bringing American blacks back to Africa. Blyden crossed the Atlantic several times to deliver lectures urging African-Americans to come to Africa to assist their brethren.[54] Faduma participated actively in efforts to bring them over. He was chief ideologist of the African Movement, inspired by Chief Alfred Sam of the Gold Coast, who in 1914 came to America to organize black immigrants. Faduma, who was teaching in the United States at the time, joined thirty-eight black immigrants from Oklahoma who decided to start a new life in their ancient homeland.[55]

The effort to bring African-Americans to Africa reached its peak in the 1920s with the activities of Marcus Garvey's UNIA. The highest priority of this organization, Garvey declared, was to establish a modern, independent African state extending over the entire black continent with the active participation of American blacks. This ideal, though expressed in the second and third decades of the twentieth century, was based on the nineteenth century Providential Design theory. Although Garvey never met Blyden, his writings and speeches reflect many of Blyden's thoughts. Like Blyden, Garvey regarded Africa as the cradle of ancient civilization upon which the rest of the world had drawn. He even claimed that without ancient African culture, Europe would never have attained its place in history; and he went so far as to assert that Jesus was black.[56] Garvey shared the convictions of the advocates of the African-American avant-garde approach that Africa was the only proper place for black people to live and that Africa could develop its rich natural resources and take its rightful place among the nations only with the technical help of African-Americans. Some of the UNIA members in West Africa were disciples of Blyden and probably regarded Garvey's movement as the fulfillment of Blyden's Providential Design theory.[57]

Garvey's emphasis, however, was different from that of the advocates of the African-American avant-garde who preceded him. These advocates on both sides of the Atlantic emphasized the cultural, religious and economic regeneration of Africa. Garvey stressed finding a political solution to Africa's troubles. Determined to use African-Americans to establish a new political reality in Africa, Garvey went beyond simply urging them to return to their ancestral home, as Edward Blyden, James Johnson, Bishop Turner and others had done; he took active steps on a grand scale to bring them over.

Though the colonial situation left little room for UNIA initiative in Africa, Garvey was quick to seize every possible chance to get his back-to-Africa plan in motion. Two opportunities seemed to arise at the end of World War I. One was Germany's loss of its colonies in East, Southern and West Africa. On 22 August 1922, the UNIA convention in New York decided to send a delegation to the League of Nations, which was to decide on the political fate of these colonies, to demand that they be opened up to black immigration from the New World.[58]

The other opportunity was Liberia's economic difficulties. At the end of World War I, the Liberian government asked the United States for a loan to rescue the country's economy. Since this independent republic had been established by black settlers from the New World, it was natural for the UNIA to try to make the Liberian government a partner in its back-to-Africa plan. In early 1920, Garvey launched a campaign aimed at raising $2,000,000 to develop Liberia's infrastructure.[59] This was followed head on heel by direct efforts to send African-Americans to Liberia. In the middle of the year, a UNIA delegation arrived in Monrovia for talks with the Liberian president, C. D. B. King, about the possibility of a major influx of black American settlers. The Liberian authorities seemed to welcome the idea. An agreement was drawn up, and in mid-1924 a technical team of black American mechanics, engineers and secretaries was sent to Liberia as a vanguard for the main body of settlers to arrive later that year. The advance party started building camps for the settlers and drew blueprints for future towns. Some $50,000 worth of goods, materials and machinery were purchased and most of it was sent with the advance party. Additional machinery and supplies were to be shipped on the Black Star Line along with the bulk of the settlers. Garvey made plans to transfer the UNIA headquarters to 'the city of Monrovia or any other convenient township of Liberia'.[60]

In the end, all these efforts were torpedoed by the colonial powers, mainly Britain and France. The UNIA demand that the former German colonies be opened up to black immigrants from the New World was never considered, while Britain and France exerted heavy pressure on Liberia's President C. D. B. King to renege on the agreement allowing the UNIA to operate in the black republic. The failure of Garvey's efforts brought the African-American avant-gardists' dreams of massive black immigration to Africa to an end.

THE AFRICAN AVANT-GARDE APPROACH

The advocates of the African avant-garde approach proposed a different paradigm for the regeneration of Africa. Led by Mensah Sarbah, Casely Hayford, Attoh Ahuma, Kobina Sekyi and Mojola Agbebi, they held that Africa had to be regenerated by Africans themselves. They maintained that traditional African political institutions and customs provided an adequate basis for the continent's cultural and political development and they rejected the notion of the splendid African-American who would return to his homeland and extend a helping hand to his inferior brethren. This vehement insistence on Africans going it alone had no parallel in East-Central and Southern Africa, where all the millenarian movements, even the more atavistic ones, were united in their sense of helplessness and consequent vision of rescue by an omnipotent external force.

The proponents of the African avant-garde approach attacked the very foundation of the African-American avant-garde concept: the mythical image of African-Americans. In their view, African-Americans were not at all superior to Africans but rather foreigners who had lost their African identity and were, in fact, more white than African. Casely Hayford argued that 'the African in America is in a worse plight than the Hebrew in Egypt. The one preserved his language, his manners and customs, his religion and household gods; the other has committed national suicide.'[61] Mojola Agbebi similarly claimed that American blacks had lost their cultural identity, race instincts and racial pride.[62] The *Lagos Weekly Record* argued in 1899 that African-Americans were less able than Africans. In the United States, the newspaper pointed out, blacks enjoyed the benefits of an advanced educational system, government programs and money, and politicians who promoted their interests – none of which Africans had. Considering these advantages, African-Americans' achievements were meager. If the same amount of money had been invested in African education and Africans had enjoyed similar social and cultural advantages, their attainments would be much greater. To quote the newspaper:

Indeed we are bound to say that the native African, from our limited knowledge of his achievements within the past thirteen years has shown himself to be superior to the Negro in America and has accomplished more with his five talents singlehanded and alone than the American Negro has with his ten talents and the financial aid of a great body of the dominant race in this country. The thousands of dollars spent for Negro education in the United States of America have not as yet begun to show tangible results.[63]

Nor was life in America as beneficial for blacks as the myth held it to be, the African avant-gardists insisted. At the turn of the century, the *Central African Times* lamented that 'the Afro-American has lost his original tribal morality', and went on to contend that while the African-American enjoyed civil liberty, 'his freedom is that of the wild ass in the desert and under it his character and intellect have no chance of development'.[64] Casely Hayford observed that: 'To be born an African in America, in that great commonwealth of dollars and the merciless aggrandizement of the individual, where the weak must look out for himself, and the cry of the innocent appeals not to him who rides triumphantly to fortune, is to be entangled in conditions which give no room for the assertion of the highest manhood.'[65] In 1914 the *Lagos Weekly Record* noted that living among whites had not only advantages for blacks, but disadvantages as well.[66]

The essence of the African avant-garde approach was the idea that Africa should, and could, be developed by the labor of Africans alone. Its advocates thus not only endeavored to destroy the African-American myth, they also made every effort to prove that the idea of regenerating Africa with the help of black Americans was unworkable. They pointed out that African-Americans who returned from the diaspora remained aliens in Africa; that the returnees to Liberia, Sierra Leone and Lagos established political hegemony over the indigenous Africans, felt themselves socially and culturally superior, did not assimilate into the local communities, and considered themselves 'Americo-Liberians', 'Creoles' or 'Brazilians'.[67] Mojola Agbebi declared the Americo Liberian attempt to establish a republic a failure and advised the black American settlers to disperse and assimilate with the indigenous Africans.[68] Kobina Sekyi, who contemptuously called African-Americans 'black white men', contended that were they to come to Africa, they would endanger Africans' efforts to shape their lives in keeping with their own traditions.[69] These and similar objections were probably motivated at least in part by the fear that any large-scale African immigration would inundate the small number of western-educated Africans in the British domain and vie with them for political and cultural ascendancy.

To settle the doubts of those who felt that Africans could not rebuild their continent on their own, the African avant-gardists offered the example of the Fanti Confederation, a semi-autonomous political body with its own army, judiciary, treasury and legislature, established in 1868 by traditional African rulers and western-educated Africans. Although the confederation lasted only three years, the fact that it had been formed at all was a source of great pride.[70] The confederation demonstrated that Africans had no need for an avant-garde from the New World and that an African avant-garde, inspired by genuine African political and social patterns, would be sufficient.

It is perhaps to the same end that Casely Hayford took upon himself the advocacy of one William Wade Harris, an itinerant messianic preacher and self-styled prophet who between 1913 and 1915 generated a mass movement in the Ivory Coast and Gold Coast. Traveling from village to village, he exorcised demons, destroyed fetishes, baptized the villagers, and instructed them to go to church. Hayford had little liking for black American missionaries, but threw his weight behind the Prophet Harris, as he was known. He kept a journal of Harris's activities in the Gold Coast, and was active in urging the conservative Methodist congregation there to accept him. For Harris had a double advantage. One was his African birth; he hailed from the Grebo ethnic group in Liberia. The other was that while his teachings were much the same as those of other missionaries, his success in Christianizing the Africans was many times theirs. He was thus living proof of the ability of Africans to provide their own leadership.[71]

To reinforce the idea that Africans must retain their own traditions in their progress forward, the African avant-gardists pointed out that another non-white people, the Japanese, had done precisely that, with great success. In the words of Casely Hayford:

The Japanese, adopting and assimilating Western culture, of necessity commands the respect of Western nations, because there is something distinctly Eastern about him. He commands, to begin with, the uses of his native tongue, and has a literature of his own, enriched by translations from standard authors of other lands. He respects the institutions and customs of his ancestors, and there is an intelligent past which inspires him.[72]

The self-sufficiency of the African avant-garde ideology gave its adherents a significant practical advantage over their opponents, who were constrained by their ideological dependence on the African-Americans. The African-American avant-gardists could not proceed very far without the actual arrival of the black Americans, who were slow to come. Convinced that African-Americans were essential to Africans' endeavors to revitalize the continent, they could not settle the territory they explored in Yorubaland; they could not create any viable political entity; and they could not even create a separate African church. The advocates of the African avant-garde, on the other hand, were able to form political organizations. In 1897 Attoh Ahuma, Casely Hayford and other leading advocates of the African avant-garde approach joined with traditional African rulers to establish the Aborigines Rights Protection Society (ARPS) in the Gold Coast in order to organize an African opposition to the attempt by the colony's British Governor, Sir William Brandford Griffith, to declare all unoccupied land Crown property. In their first year of operation they were able to collect funds and to mount an effective propaganda campaign against the proposed legislation, using African newspapers, public assemblies, and other forums. In 1898 the ARPS sent a delegation to London, which succeeded in persuading the British Colonial Office to order the Gold Coast authorities to rescind the bill. This success not only increased the ARPS's popularity; it also provided proof that Africans could act effectively on their own without African-American assistance.[73] After World War I, this conviction led to the establishment of a territory-wide political organization, the National Congress of British West Africa, which encompassed not only the Gold Coast, as did the ARPS, but all four British colonies in West Africa.

DIFFERENT ROADS, COMMON DILEMMAS

The advocates of the two approaches to African regeneration were at opposite ends of an ideological spectrum. Blyden, spokesman for the

African-American avant-garde approach, pleaded with black Americans to 'Come over and help us'. Casely Hayford, advocate for the African avant-garde approach, declared with equal vehemence that 'it is not so much Afro-Americans we want as Africans'.[74]

But in addition to ideology, they also differed in their geographic roots and relation to Africa itself. The proponents of the African avant-garde solution – Casely Hayford, Attoh Ahuma, Kobina Sekyi and others – all came from the Gold Coast, where there were strong ties between the traditional African leadership and the westernized African elite. According to David Kimble, the westernized African elite in the Gold Coast 'normally remained bound by family obligations (especially where the extended family had raised the funds for educating one or two chosen members) and by personal allegiance to their chiefs; even if they had moved away from their traditional communities, their enhanced status gave them a strong potential influence there'.[75] These ties led them to dig into their African past and to hold up indigenous political structures in the Gold Coast as a paradigm for the revitalization of the whole continent.

The prominent advocates of the African-American approach came from a variety of places and many of them had lived or studied in the West. They were less committed to African social and political life. Blyden was a native of the Danish West Indies and spent time in the United States before emigrating to Liberia. His studies and writings on traditional African customs and social life notwithstanding, he was part of the Americo-Liberian community, which dominated Liberia and kept aloof from the native population. Orishatukeh Faduma was seven years old when he arrived with his family in Sierra Leone from British Guiana under his birth name, William J. Davis. He was educated in Wesleyan schools in Freetown, Sierra Leone, and in England. In 1890 he moved to the United States, where he completed his religious studies at the Yale School of Divinity. He and his family were part of the Creole community in Sierra Leone, a group consisting of black immigrants and recaptured Africans who had acquired Christianity and western culture and also kept their distance from the indigenous Africans.

James Johnson considered himself a member of the Saro group – western-educated Africans originating from the Creoles of Sierra Leone who established themselves in various towns in West Africa. Johnson considered the Saro closer to black Americans than to Africans in that 'they were co-exiles, co-victims of European wickedness and greed in the age of the trans-Atlantic slave trade, and . . . co-beneficiaries of contact and association with the white man'. Johnson rejected African culture and tried to uproot some indigenous customs and institutions.[76] In short, the advocates of the African-American avant-garde approach had only the weakest of ties to the traditional African elite, to African tradition in general, and to African history in particular. They lacked the intellectual and emotional bonds that might have given them a sense of pride or security in the African past. That past for them was not a useful instrument for coping with the white man. They focused on the present by default. The African-American community provided them with the proof they needed that contemporary Africans, not Africans from the ancient past, were capable of dealing with the white man on his own terms.

Yet despite their different routes, the leaders of both groups all belonged to the modern African elite and, as such, faced the same dilemma. While they proclaimed their rejection of white culture, or at least of a great part of it, they themselves had internalized that culture and were wholly identified with it. In this they were very unlike the leaders of the messianic and millenarian movements in East-Central and Southern Africa. While most of the leaders of these religious movements were also western-educated, they had never been a part of the European commercial, cultural and administrative structures in their home territories and so could protest against the Europeans' discrimination by shedding their western veneer and returning to their atavistic roots. The leaders of the cultural nationalist movement, however, had, as they feared, largely lost their original African identities and were cut off from the African customs and traditions at which they clutched. Their protest not only took such western forms as newspaper articles and petitions, but was imbued with western values and thinking. Their major goal was to prove themselves as competent and cultured as the British colonialists.

The cultural nationalists tried to cull the benefits of western culture and Christianity from the white race. This was not really feasible. Christianity and other elements of western culture were inextricably intertwined with white people for Africans. As one study of African attitudes towards Europeans has shown, Africans found it almost impossible to separate the qualities of western culture from the white person.[77] Many members of the West African elite accused the Europeans, and especially the missionaries, of applying a double standard: their religion and culture extolled the values of equality and brotherly love, but they themselves seldom practiced those virtues. Educated Africans, however, could also be accused of not practicing what they preached: for the leaders of both camps openly acknowledged the superiority of white culture, continued to emulate it, and sought support from it.

Among the African avant-gardists, for example, Kobina Sekyi, for all his criticism of western values and promulgation of African culture, ordered his clothes from an English tailor in London, was always dressed neatly in European attire, and carried a silver-handled walking stick; he indulged in European luxuries like expensive wines and Egyptian cigarettes, which he ordered from Malta; and he admired English literature, philosophy and music.[78] Casely Hayford had no choice but to resort to the English language in his advocacy of African values. This led to some ridiculous situations. For example, he addressed a crowded audience in the Wesley Chapel in Accra wearing traditional African clothing, but his lecture had to be translated into the Fanti language by an English missionary, the Reverend E. Bruce.[79]

More substantially, the leaders of the African avant-garde pinned the realization of their most basic aspirations in Africa on British cooperation and know-how. Politically, their aim was not to abolish colonial rule but to reclaim their once substantial role in the colonial administration, and the fulfillment of this aim necessarily depended on British participation. This was so from the earliest days of the movement. The mentor of the African avant-gardists was the Sierra Leonean physician James Africanus B. Horton, who had been instrumental in the establishment of the Fanti Confederation in the nineteenth century and was a great admirer of the British. According to Horton, 'Africans are not incapable of improvement but ... by the assistance of good and able men they are destined to figure in the course of time, and to take a prominent part in the history of the civilized world.'[80] The 'good and able men' he referred to were the British, whom he described as the 'best civilizing element' on the African coast.[81] The constitution of the Fanti Confederation, which he inspired, integrated traditional African and modern British methods of government.

Half a century later, Casely Hayford called upon educated Africans to cooperate with whites in establishing the African political entity that he envisioned in British West Africa. His dream was to modernize the region along western cultural lines, to open up the hinterland to commerce and civilization, and to connect the territories by railways, roads, telephone and telegraph. To realize that dream, whites and white know-how were essential. Thus, Hayford argued that the key to African development and even survival was cooperation not only among Africans themselves but between blacks and whites.[82]

Ironically, even the cooperation among black Africans did not and could not include traditional Africans, but was, inevitably, restricted to a very narrow group of western-educated, Christian Africans and depended on their shared European culture. This could be clearly seen in the National Congress of British West Africa established in 1920, which united western-educated Africans from the four British dominions in West Africa and brought Hayford's dream to fruition. The western-educated Africans in the various British colonies were culturally and socially closer to each other than to their respective countrymen. Despite their geographical distance, the western-educated Africans of Freetown had more in common with their peers in Cape Coast and Lagos than with their African neighbors who lacked western education. Moreover, politically, the congress had not the remotest wish to create an independent African political entity based on traditional African models. Adapting Hayford's view that 'West Africa's salvation entirely depends upon a clear conception of her place within the British Empire', the leaders of the congress asked to share power in the British colonial government, not to replace it.[83]

In the other camp, the leaders did not conceal their admiration for European culture. Blyden, though he believed that European rule was temporary, urged Europe and the United States to take control over Africa – control which, to his mind, was essential for the intellectual, social, economic and political advance of the Africans.[84] His belief in the superiority of western culture kept him from protesting about the atrocities that were being perpetrated in the Congo Free State, in the conviction that they were necessary to King Leopold's mission of civilizing the peoples there.[85]

Western-educated Africans were in a bind. They could not live with European culture, nor could they live without it. Advocates of the African model were unable to come up with a working program to implement their ideas. Neither Attoh Ahuma, Kobina Sekyi, nor Casely Hayford could define the precise proportions of western culture and African culture that would be needed to revitalize Africa. Advocates of the African-American avant-garde solution, for their part, circumvented the dilemma. They sought salvation for Africa not in the marriage of western and African cultures but rather in Africa's adoption of western culture. For all that they saw themselves as cultural nationalists, they took for granted the superiority of western culture and regarded it as the only remedy for Africa's ills. At the same time, though, they neatly dispensed with the assistance of whites, pinning their hopes instead on the assistance of African-Americans, who had acquired the best of white culture but were black.

Thus, the advocates of the African-American avant-garde approach emphasized what they regarded as the numerous advantages of the African-American over the African. O. T. Nana, who published his opinion in the *Sierra Leone Weekly News*, pointed out that black Americans, as a minority, were fully exposed to western civilization, while Africans in the continent where they were the majority were excluded from direct contact with European culture.[86] The very fact that black Americans had long lost their African identity was seen as beneficial. An article in the *Lagos Weekly Record* attributed the achievements of black Americans to the extinction of their tribal identity. In the view of the newspaper, the African-American's emergence from the ordeal of slavery as a 'tribal nondescript' was an 'advantage rather than disadvantage to him', and it would be good if the same thing occurred in Africa.[87]

The advocates of the African-American avant-garde theory hoped that with the help of the African-American, Africans could have their cake and eat it too. Africa would get western culture, but that culture would be painted black. The Providential Design myth provided the legitimization for using the black diaspora; for, in it, the regeneration of Africa did not depend on the good will of Europeans, but was destined by divine order and would be brought about by descendants of Africa who were no less educated, cultured, or Christian than Europeans.

In fact, the appeal of the mythical image of the African-American was so strong that even the proponents of an all-African avant-garde had to admit that the black community in the United States had some redeeming qualities. Casely Hayford, for all his censure of black life in America, in fact, came very close to Blyden's views when he stated, 'In the order of Providence, some of our brethren were suffered to be enslaved in America for a wise purpose. That event in the history of the race has made it possible for the speedier dissemination and adoption of Western culture; and today Africa's sons in the East and in the West can do peculiar service unto one another in the common cause of uplifting Ethiopia and placing her upon her feet among the nations.'[88] Kobina Sekyi, though he regarded African-Americans as representatives of an alien culture and ruled out the possibility that they might contribute to revitalizing Africa, nonetheless held that Africans could benefit from commercial and economic ties with them.[89]

In the end, the claims and programs of the African-American avant-gardists hardly went beyond academic discussion. All attempts to translate their theoretical conceptions into reality were doomed to failure. Few African-Americans had any inclination to leave their homes and migrate en masse to Africa. Blyden himself gradually came to realize that his fervent preaching brought few followers and ultimately abandoned the African-American avant-garde concept to which he had so dedicated himself. The advocates of the African avant-garde could claim some concrete, though limited, achievements. They established some independent African churches and the ARPS, which remained active until it was replaced after World War I by the National Congress of British West Africa. Nonetheless, they never effected the return to African cultural traditions that they promulgated, never regenerated the continent, and never reclaimed their place as partners in governing their own countries.

The main achievement of the cultural nationalists was largely inadvertent: their efforts and debate enabled the western-educated Africans who made up the movement to cope on an intellectual level with the colonial situation. The very existence of these two schools of thought is evidence that West Africans were attempting to deal with the challenge of western domination and were seeking a solution to the complex problem of African identity in the modern world. Their efforts bolstered their self-confidence and self-efficacy, gave them organizational experience, and laid the intellectual foundation for their more active efforts to deal with the changing political situation in Africa after World War I.

4 African-American Models in African Politics

World War I brought important changes in the status of Africans *vis-à-vis* the colonial powers and eroded their erstwhile acceptance of colonial rule. During the war, Africa was a battleground for competing European interests, and Africans contributed significantly to the war effort both as soldiers and laborers. The dependence of the colonial powers on their contribution opened up unprecedented opportunities for Africans to demand economic, social and political reforms and, moreover, convinced them that they had earned the right to do so.

The seeds of this change were first sown in French West Africa, where Africans were a vital source of recruits as well as providing food and raw materials for war-time France. France's heavy demands on the African population led to disorders in various parts of the French African empire. In 1917 the Governor General of French West Africa, Joost Van Vollenhoven, warned his superiors that further mobilization of African recruits would lead to yet more disturbances, as well as to a decline in the food production so crucial to the army. To deal with the emergency, the French Minister of Colonies took an unprecedented step. In January 1918, he asked Blaise Diagne, the first Senegalese native to have been elected to the French Parliament, to assume the responsibility for drafting Africans. Diagne agreed, on condition that France implement its declared assimilation policy in its colonies and grant the African inhabitants of the Four Communes, which he represented, full French citizenship.

The French authorities gave their word and Diagne became the first African Commissary General of Colonial Troops, a rank equal to that of the Governor General of French West Africa. In his new position, Diagne traveled extensively throughout the French territories and was received in one territory after another with all the pomp and circumstance previously accorded only to the white Governor General. His position accorded him authority and acceptance hitherto withheld from Africans. In particular, it provided a model to which the western-educated Africans in British West Africa, who were blatantly discriminated against and barred from senior positions in the colonial administration, could aspire. The impact can be seen in the *Sierra Leone Weekly News* coverage of Diagne's 1918 visit to Conakry, the capital of what was then French Guinea. The African reporter who was sent to cover the visit described the state welcome – the band, the dancing girls, Diagne's clothes, and the official reception in his honor, to which 200 people were invited – with great relish. He also took the opportunity to point an accusing finger at Britain by reporting the rumor that when Diagne had traveled through British-controlled Nigeria, he had not been permitted to use a sleeping car reserved for whites.[1]

The appointment also provided an opportunity for British liberals to speak up against their country's colonial policies. For example, the London-based newspaper *West Africa* picked up the story and quoted the critical comments of the former British colonial official Sir Harry Johnston: ' "I consider the French nation since 1871 has dealt more wisely, considerately and successfully with the negro problem. . . . If the Negro has to visit a European country he is certainly happier in France than he is with us." ' The newspaper concluded that Britain should not lag behind any other power in its relations with the peoples of Africa.[2]

With the end of the war, it suddenly seemed possible for Africans to realize their developing aspirations. The German defeat raised the question of the proprietorship of the former German colonies. Having made a significant contribution to that defeat, Africans felt that they were entitled to a say in how these territories would be governed. They also felt entitled to be consulted on the broader issue of self-determination for colonized peoples, which, along with the future of the former German colonies, was to be discussed at the Versailles Peace Conference held at the end of the war.

The postwar era saw a rush of political, intellectual and creative activity on the part of both Francophone and Anglophone Africans who were determined to have a say in the new world order. Roughly, their activities were divided along two conceptual lines: the global and the regional. The global approach held that the best way for Africans to attain their aspirations was with the help and support of the black community in the New World. The regional approach maintained that the best way for Africans to make progress was by relying on their own efforts within their colonial frameworks. The African-American myth was manifest in both approaches, with the division in the political realm similar to that in the cultural realm discussed in Chapter 3: the globalists sought the participation of African-Americans; the regionalists rejected their involvement as detrimental to eventual African self-government.

TWO GLOBAL MODELS: GARVEY AND DU BOIS

The global approach was based on two distinct political models, both of which originated in the United States: Marcus Garvey's back-to-Africa movement and W. E. B. Du Bois's pan-Africanism. Both ideologies linked the improvement of black life in America with the liberation of Africans from colonial rule as part of the same struggle for racial equality. Both emphasized the unity of black peoples. But here they parted ways. Garvey's was a militant ideology that stressed the affinity between black Americans and indigenous Africans and that began and ended with Africa. As Garvey saw it, the only way for New World blacks to solve their problems was to emigrate en masse to Africa and to join with the Africans in ousting the colonial powers and creating an independent black republic encompassing the entire continent. Du Bois's was both a more moderate and more inclusive ideology, which eschewed violence, extended Garvey's sense of racial affinity to all people of color, and made room for whites. As Du Bois saw it, American blacks would have to solve their problems at home, and African self-rule and cultural progress would be best attained through international diplomatic channels.

In the eyes of his African followers, Garvey was the 'Moses' and 'modern Joshua' who would bring freedom to the children of Africa, the 'Paramount Chief of the Negro Race' who would govern them in place of the white colonialists, and the great leader whose eagerly awaited ships promised to bring wealth and prosperity, freedom and independence. The hopes Garvey inspired in Africa made his UNIA the only secular African-American organization with actual branches on the continent. In Liberia, Sierra Leone and Nigeria, Africans established active branches; in other parts of West Africa, supporters held informal UNIA gatherings.[3] In the Union of South Africa, which boasted more UNIA branches than any other territory, African activists founded five official chapters in the Cape Town area, one in Pretoria, and another in East London.[4] Throughout Africa, the *Negro World* and other UNIA publications were widely disseminated and read by Africans who were not members of UNIA branches.

The UNIA branches avidly spread the word of Garvey. As noted in Chapter 1, the Lagos branch ordered 200 copies a week of the *Negro World* and hundreds of copies of the UNIA constitution for distribution in the British colonies of West Africa. They were also active in promoting the Black Star Line, which would bring African-American immigrants to the continent. The Freetown branch put a model of the first Black Star Line ship on public display. The Lagos branch announced the sale of 100,000 shares in the shipping company at $5 or 30 shillings each.[5]

The branches boosted their attractiveness with a range of social, cultural and educational activities that had broad, popular appeal. The Sierra Leone branch introduced music and dancing at its meetings, and the Lagos branch set up a brass band and undertook educational activities with the aim of assisting 'in civilizing the backward tribes of Nigeria'.[6] The Freetown branch launched a fund-raising campaign to build a vocational school for girls on the American model.[7]

The UNIA influence spread beyond the branches and beyond the readers of the *Negro World* to African commercial circles. The scarcity of ships during and after World War I led the British to discriminate against African traders in favor of European trading companies and Lebanese and Syrian merchants in the allocation of the scarce trading vessels that were available. This intensified the economic hardship of African traders, who, like traders around the world, were suffering from the steep postwar decline in international commerce. The UNIA branches took up their cause, and under their influence, African traders came to see Garvey's Black Star Line shipping company as a potential solution to their problems. The enthusiasm is conveyed in a rhapsodic article published in the *Times of Nigeria*:

> The idea of establishing a line of steamers owned and controlled by Africans [blacks, that is] is a great and even sublime conception for which every body of African origin will bless the name of Marcus Garvey. The humiliating discriminations to which blacks have been and are being subjected in connection with white-owned vessels have long created a yearning, and pointed to the urgent necessity, for the inception of a Black Star Line of steamers, and the promoters of the scheme may well count upon the heart-whole support of every sane-minded African.[8]

Notable in this glowing praise is the view that African-Americans can help their African brethren out of their troubles and the readiness to follow the African-Americans' lead.

Du Bois, Garvey's senior and rival in the United States, was a very different type of leader with a very different message. Born in New England in 1868 of free American blacks, he was a highly educated, unabashed elitist, who neither sought nor attained the mass appeal that Garvey attracted. Du Bois's long life was rich in both scholarly and political activity. On 10 July 1905, he took a lead in founding the Niagara Movement, a small organization of black intellectuals that campaigned for civil rights. At its demise in 1909, he joined with like-minded white and black intellectuals to found the interracial National Association for the Advancement of Colored People (NAACP) to fight racial discrimination and to secure social, economic and political equality for African-Americans.[9] Although, like Garvey, Du Bois strove for full and immediate civil rights for blacks, his outlook was more encompassing. While Garvey shunned whites and abhorred mulattos, Du Bois was willing to work with whites and insisted that American blacks were bound by their race to colored peoples every-where. Avoiding the trap of racial determinism, he wrote in *Dusk of Dawn: An Essay Towards an Autobiography of a Race Concept*, first published in 1940, that 'the social heritage of slavery; the discrimination and insult; . . . binds together not simply the children of Africa, but extends through yellow Asia and into the South Seas'.[10]

This identification with people of color throughout the world led him to adopt a global, pan-African approach to counter the mistreatment of colored peoples wherever it occurred. In 1900 he played a leading role in the Pan-African Conference held in London, where he asserted that 'The problem of the twentieth century is the problem of the color-line'[11] – that is, the divide not simply between whites and blacks, but between whites and all non-whites. After World War I, to make the black voice heard, he brought together American blacks and Africans in a series of pan-African congresses.

On 9 September 1918, Du Bois proposed to the NAACP that issues relating to Africa's future be brought before the Versailles Peace Confer-ence. The NAACP sent him to Paris on a dual mission which linked the interests of American and African blacks: to investigate complaints by black American soldiers of maltreatment and discrimination in the United States expeditionary forces and to look after Africans' interests at the Versailles Conference.[12] On the way, Du Bois joined up with Robert Russa Moton (Booker T. Washington's successor as President of Tuskegee), whom President Wilson sent to France to visit the black troops there.[13] Du Bois tells that it was on the ship that he decided that the best way to make the black voice heard at the conference would be to organize a pan-African congress with the aim of 'bringing to bear all pressure possible, on the Delegates at the Peace Table in the interest of the coloured peoples of the United States and of the world, and to press the question of the interna-tionalization of the former German Colonies'.[14]

Both Francophone and Anglophone Africans participated in the various pan-African congresses that he organized. In West Africa, Du Bois's ideas were hailed by those who felt that a unified response was required to effectively introduce the problems of blacks to participants at the Versailles Conference. When the First Pan-African Congress convened in February 1919, the *Gold Coast Leader* stressed that it 'presented a united front upon race questions' and 'raised certain specific issues which the Peace Confer-ence cannot possibly ignore'.[15] When the congress came to an end, the *Sierra Leone Weekly News* stated in triumph: 'The Pan-African Congress is an established fact.'[16] The editor of the *Gold Coast Leader* held the con-gress up as a forum that represented black interests across colonial borders and geographical distances, advising his readers to 'brush up on their French for British and French interests in West Africa stand or fall together now and in the future'.[17]

About two years later, similar praises were sung of the Second Pan-African Congress. *West Africa* declared, 'It is all to the good that Africans of the British, French, Belgian, American and other countries should meet and make known to the rest of the world . . . what programmes they have in view.'[18] In another issue, the newspaper asserted, 'men of color must unite if they are not to be submerged during this troublesome period of readjustment'.[19]

To be sure, the praises of the congresses never reached the rhapsodic heights of the celebrations of Garvey in Africa. Unlike Garvey, Du Bois did not help to spread the African-American myth; nor was he himself mythologized. However, one may wonder whether without the myth the congresses would ever have got off the ground. For it was the myth that made it possible for the African-Americans to take the lead in organizing the congresses and to bring together the Francophone and Anglophone blacks. African globalists, feeling unable to cope on their own with the enormous tasks of coordinating the various groups and of advocating black aims on the world scene, were happy to leave the leadership of the congresses to the larger than life African-Americans. Both Francophone and Anglophone Africans acknowledged the superiority of the African-American community in at least two matters: financial resources and administrative talents.

Isaac Beton, a young schoolmaster and publisher from Martinique who served as General Secretary of the Pan-African Association, asked the African-Americans for financial help when the association met with a cash flow crisis.[20] His assumption that American blacks could provide such help was probably based on the fact that the black American community had taken upon itself the burden of financing the London session of the Second Pan-African Congress.[21] Beton was also of the opinion that African-Americans had better organizational ability than Africans.[22] Other Africans apparently shared that view. The *Gold Coast Leader* called African-Americans 'our intelligent brethren on the other side of the Atlantic'.[23] The correspondent who covered the meetings of the Second Pan-African Congress for the London-based *African World* wrote that the congress could achieve great things, but 'It is evident that for a time the lead must be taken by the American Negro. Upon him . . . rests a large part of the responsibility. If he, working with other groups, meets this responsibility then the Congress can and will be made a great and powerful international weapon for the bringing of justice, long denied, to the 400 million coloured people of the world.'[24]

The notion of African-Americans' financial and organizational superiority was supported not only by concrete facts, but also by the entire mythical aura that surrounded their image in Africa. Advocates of the global approach waxed poetic in their descriptions of African-Americans. John Alcindor, M. D., a pan-African activist from Trinidad who participated in the 1900 Pan-African Conference and from 1921 was President of the London-based African Progress Union, described American blacks as 'patches of blue in the cloudy African sky'.[25] Faith in the African-American myth ran so deep that pan-African activists believed that the black American community could carry almost any financial burden. A discussion at one of the meetings of the Second Pan-African Congress is illustrative. The item on the agenda was the financial crisis in the Republic of Liberia, the only independent black state in West Africa. After the war, Liberian President C. D. B. King negotiated a $5,000,000 loan from the United States, but the conditions for receiving it were stiff and undermined Liberia's sovereignty. Discussing ways of helping Liberia, the Reverend E. G. Granville Sutton, a native of Sierra Leone, suggested that 'If the President [King] had gone to them [African-American leaders] and not to the American Government he would have received instead of five million dollars, fifteen million dollars'.[26]

Against the background of the African-American myth, Garvey and Du Bois, each in his own way, provided Africans with political direction in the years after World War I. In the late nineteenth century, the African-American myth had led some cultural nationalists of West Africa to look to black Americans as an avant-garde for the cultural and technological development of Africa. At the end of World War I, their spiritual descendants again placed African-Americans in a position of leadership for all blacks. The driving myth remained the same; only now the leadership expected was not cultural and technological, but political.

THE NATIONAL CONGRESS OF BRITISH WEST AFRICA:
THE REGIONAL APPROACH

The advocates of the regional approach rejected both Garvey's and Du Bois's models. They emphasized the Africans' own role in improving their social, cultural, economic and political situation; denounced the participation of African-Americans in African politics; and, ironically, sought the assistance of the British colonial power in preparing them to take their place among the modern nations. The regional approach was consistent with the postwar outburst of nationalist sentiment among diverse groups in

Europe and the Middle East. Like the global approach, it also had adherents among both Anglophone and Francophone blacks.

In British West Africa, the regional approach was given political expression by the National Congress of British West Africa (NCBWA). This was a territory-wide organization encompassing Africans from all four British colonies in the sub-region. It was the brainchild of Casely Hayford of the Gold Coast and Dr Akiwande Savage of Nigeria, who was living in the Gold Coast at the time. Hayford and Savage began to recruit support for their idea in the Gold Coast in 1914 and 1915. In 1919 they formed two territory-wide committees, one in the Gold Coast and one in Sierra Leone. The Gold Coast Africans took upon themselves the tasks of encouraging the establishment of more such committees and of coordinating them into a single body, which, it was thought, would have more clout than disparate local committees.[27]

Their labor bore fruit on 11 March 1920, when forty-five delegates from the four British territories in West Africa met in Accra to attend what was termed the Conference of Africans of British West Africa. For nineteen days, in the course of which the name of the body was changed to the National Congress of British West Africa, the delegates hammered out a corpus of resolutions that, among other things, demanded the participation of West Africans in the governing of the territory. To be sure, the resolutions did not seek to oust the colonial government. The delegates agreed to retain the colonial structure, represented by the British-appointed and -dominated Executive Council (consisting of the colonial governor and colonial officials) and the British-appointed Legislative Council in each of the four colonies. Along with this, however, they demanded that half the Legislative Council be elected by the people of the territories and they called for the establishment of a new body, the House of Assembly, to consist of the elected members of the Legislative Council and of 'financial representatives' elected by the Africans. They also passed resolutions calling for the abolition of racial discrimination in government administration and for the establishment of municipal boards in every town, with four-fifths of the representatives elected by the town's taxpayers.[28]

The call for the inclusion of Africans in the territory's political life was accompanied by resolutions demanding social, educational, economic and legal reforms which would place Africans in a better position to govern themselves in the near future. These included resolutions demanding the introduction of compulsory education in British West Africa, raising primary and secondary school levels, and establishing a West African university; the protection of African traders and businessmen from the powerful European commercial firms; the allocation of resources to the development of banking, shipping and commerce in the territories; a fairer judiciary, with the establishment of a West African Court of Appeals; the elimination of the residential segregation of races; and the end of the colonial trustee-ship of African land. In a session devoted to 'The Right of the People to Self-Determination', a resolution was passed condemning the partition of the former German colonies by the Allies without regard for the wishes of the inhabitants.[29]

The Accra meeting was an expression of the regionalists' determination to take the life of the territory in hand by themselves. They had a clear idea of what they wanted and created a region-wide political structure to confront the colonial authorities. Moreover, resolved to make the British hear their claims, they deliberately violated the regulation stipulating that Africans could present petitions only to the colonial authorities in the colonies them-selves and sent a delegation to London to present their demands directly to the British Colonial Office.[30]

By and large, the National Congress at Accra spurned the African-American myth. Its resolutions were directed to London and made no reference to any role for African-Americans. Moreover, in the important area of education, which was then on the minds of western-educated Africans throughout the continent, the congress pointedly snubbed them. Shortly before the congress convened, the Phelps-Stokes Education Com-mission, to be led by prominent figures in black American education, was getting ready to visit West Africa. The National Congress rejected the com-mission entirely, claiming that the experience of running black schools in the United States was irrelevant to Africa.[31] Given that at the time of the Accra session, the African-American was something of a cultural hero in Africa and the Phelps-Stokes Commission was eagerly awaited by African intellectuals, this was a forceful rebuff.

Following Accra, the National Congress met again in Freetown in January–February 1923 and in Bathurst in December 1925–January 1926. During these sessions and throughout the decade of its existence, the National Congress continued to rebuff all American influence.

During part of this time, Hayford was in contact with Du Bois about West African representation in the pan-African congresses. In March 1919, shortly after the First Pan-African Congress, he wrote to Du Bois express-ing interest in it and his regret that the colonial government did not permit any West Africans to attend. In response Du Bois invited Hayford to par-ticipate in the Second Pan-African Congress. In December 1920, Hayford sent a friendly reply, promising Du Bois that he would exert his influence to obtain West African representation in the congress and inviting the pan-African leader to come 'to address our Congress'.[32] But nothing came of the gesture. Nor did anything ever come of the efforts of Robert Broadhurst, secretary of the African Progress Union, to get the National Congress executive to authorize setting up a joint body to raise funds for the pan-African movement and to send delegates to London to open a West African branch of the pan-African movement there.[33]

The members of the National Congress were a tightly knit, homogeneous group with little interest in cooperating with others. Though they were spread out over four separate colonies, the local NCBWA committees in each territory were made up of people of similar socio-economic and, in many cases, similar religious backgrounds.[34] Most of them were urban, western-educated Africans who belonged to an elite group consisting of the descendants of the Sierra Leone Krio expansion in the nineteenth century. Most of them were businessmen and professionals – lawyers, doctors, journalists and teachers – who represented the small and exclusive middle and upper-middle classes of the four territories.

As a cohesive group, they disparaged the heterogeneous pan-African congresses. They felt that the homogeneity of their own leadership made them more effective than the pan-African congresses, and they were uncomfortable with the cosmopolitanism inherent in pan-Africanism. Moreover, the NCBWA members felt that their socio-economic status entitled them, and them alone, to share power with Great Britain in governing the West African colonies. President of the Accra session, Thomas Hutton-Mills of the Gold Coast, stated in his keynote address, 'Apart from the fact of the delegates to the conference being the natural leaders of the people of their several communities, they have in themselves the right to appeal to His Majesty's Government for such constitutional reforms as in their judgment are necessary.'[35] Seeing themselves as the natural and rightful leaders of their territories, they rejected the contending claims of both the pan-Africanists and Garveyites to speak for African blacks.

In fact, the regionalists were opposed to any and all involvement by African-Americans in Africa's political life. Like their nineteenth-century predecessors, they distinguished sharply between African-Americans and 'genuine' Africans. After centuries of slavery, they contended, American blacks had lost their African heritage and no longer qualified as Africans, while they themselves were 'genuine' Africans despite their European ways. In the words of a National Congress delegate to London: 'Although we have frequently been described as Black Englishmen, yet we have no intention of losing our race individuality.'[36]

The regionalists based their claim for leadership in West Africa on the conviction that, as Africans, they knew better than anyone else what had to be done to improve their lot. Non-Africans, even if they were black, simply did not know enough about Africa and could only do harm. Writing in the *Gold Coast Leader*, a regionalist warned that African interests could be 'compromised' by the pan-African congress that was being held at the time and urged the National Congress to anticipate and act against the danger.[37] Analogously, Casely Hayford pointed an accusing finger at UNIA, which, in his view, had done more than any other organization to bring 'to the notice of world opinion the disabilities of the African race'.[38]

At best, the regionalists viewed American blacks as foreigners who would have to internalize African values before they could be of any use. As the *Gold Coast Leader* argued, 'before the American Negro can hope to be of any other than temporary assistance to the Negro race in general . . . they must acquire the African point of view'.[39] Given this attitude, it is not surprising that Garvey's plans for mass immigration evoked a great deal of opposition. An article in the *African World* warned vigorously of the potential damage: 'Suppose for a moment 15,000 American negroes really descended upon Africa . . . what would be the result but acute tribal antagonism between the reforming newcomers and the more or less contented indigene?'[40] Kobina Sekyi, writing in the *Gold Coast Leader*, expressed the same view:

> In fact our brethren from beyond the seas, with their American ideas and ideals, would confuse us a good deal more, because then we should have here not only a medley of English and Akan-Fanti ideas and ideals, but a worse potpourri of American and English and Akan-Fanti modes of life and thought. This would surely be confusion worse confounded; and this would probably mean jumping from the frying pan into the fire.[41]

Some African newspapers went so far as to advise Liberia not to admit African-American settlers.[42]

Politically, the convictions of the National Congress regionalists were diametrically opposed to the essentials of both Du Bois's pan-Africanism and Garvey's radical nationalism. The National Congress did not believe in a comprehensive struggle of or on behalf of all blacks. It sought equality and political and social rights for Africans alone, and – more narrowly still – only for those who lived in a specific part of the continent. They even rejected the idea of power sharing with traditional Africans who lacked the benefit of western education.[43] Moreover, despite the word 'national' in its title, the National Congress was not a nationalist organization in the accepted sense of the term. It had no aspirations for political independence. The term 'national' in the congress's title referred to the unity of the

Africans in the region and their right to hold meetings and to suggest ways of improving their situation.[44]

Most of the NCBWA activists were what might be termed conservative nationalists. They aspired to equality and greater political and civil rights, but all in the framework of the British empire and all by constitutional means. Like the advocates of the African avant-garde in the late nineteenth century, they regarded the ruling colonial power, Britain, as the only party with whom to negotiate, and believed that their aspirations would be realized only through full cooperation with the colonial power. In the words of the *Sierra Leone Weekly News*: 'Our cry has never been to be delivered from the rule of England and be independent of them as a race; it has rather been a cry of loyal and grateful people to remind their rulers of their faithful and sincere connection with them.'[45] As products of British culture, the National Congress leaders believed that they still needed Britain to direct and instruct them in the art of governing a modern state.

This entailed the attainment of self-rule through strictly legal means. As the *Nigerian Pioneer* stated, 'We should all wish to go forward in the march of progress, but it must be on constitutional lines.'[46] The paper rejected UNIA's militaristic schemes to establish an independent black republic in Africa as 'a pipe dream' on the grounds Africans were not ready for self-rule. Instead, it advocated measured, incremental steps towards self-government, certain that Britain would show the way and open the door: 'Great Britain has given practical proofs, time and again', the paper declared, 'that as soon as a Colony is ready for a small form of self-government, even if only a quarter or a half-way measure, she will lend a ready ear to any sound appeal, emanating from a fully representative body of the people.'[47] The 'representative body' that the writer had in mind was probably the National Congress. It is this affinity for Britain, this sense of themselves as loyal British subjects whose interests would be best served under Britain's tutelage and protection, that led the National Congress at the end of the Accra session to send its delegation to the Colonial Office in London rather than to any of the pan-African congresses or any of the UNIA conventions.

The regionalists' continued perception of themselves as part and parcel of the British empire made both the international apparatus of the pan-African congresses and the UNIA irrelevant. Moreover, it made many of the specific features of Garveyism positively anathema. The opposition of the National Congress to Garvey's militarism has already been pointed out. Garvey's plans for an independent black republic in Africa were similarly out of line with their views. His call for an armed struggle against the colonial powers was seen as grandiose and preposterous. The *Sierra Leone*

Weekly News vigorously rejected what it presented as his pretensions to empire while it maintained allegiance to Britain: 'We therefore deprecate any attempt by any empire of ours to incite us to change our national allegiance to those under whose fostering care we have hitherto been defended and governed.'[48] *West Africa* pointed out the absurdity and lack of realism in his scheme: 'On the surface there is nothing more alluring than the force and solidarity of one nationality running from one end to another in Africa as a basis of political union. But is such a scheme possible in Africa of today? Was it ever possible in Africa?'[49] The *Nigerian Pioneer* termed Garvey's call for 400 million blacks to take Africa by force 'big words' and asked 'What is the truth about Garvey's rodomontade? without a single soldier, a single warship, or a single Negro state organized for his special object.'[50]

Garvey's racism also evoked strong opposition as totally inconsistent with the National Congress's aspirations for cooperation with whites. The *Nigerian Pioneer* emphasized the incompatibility of his racism with the National Congress's cooperative efforts: 'Marcus Garvey is trying to light the fire of racial hatred, whilst the sane men on both sides are endeavoring to work together for the good of Nigeria.'[51] The *Sierra Leone Weekly News* affirmed: '[O]ur aspirations are towards obtaining equal rights for ourselves and our children with our fellow subjects without discrimination of race.'[52]

The opposition to African-American participation in African affairs was strongest in the Gold Coast, the birthplace of the National Congress and home of its hardliners. In the late nineteenth century western-educated Africans from the Gold Coast were the standard bearers of the all-African solution to the continent's problems. This exclusivity persisted in the twentieth century, when their descendants led the opposition to American influence, to Du Bois's pan-Africanism no less than to Garvey's radical nationalism. Gold Coast Africans had the advantage of an independent political tradition going back to the second half of the nineteenth century. The Fanti Confederation, established in the Gold Coast in 1868, and the Aborigines Rights Protection Society, founded there in 1897, were political organizations which operated within colonial law but were organized and run mainly by Africans to put forward Africans' political demands. These organizations provided the western-educated Africans of the Gold Coast with the political heritage and concrete political experience that gave them the confidence that they could promote the political interests of Africans without the assistance of American blacks.

The regionalists in the National Congress regarded the Garveyites as a more serious challenge to their leadership than Du Bois. Du Bois's moderation, gradualism, and readiness for dialogue with whites was considerably closer to NCBWA thinking than Garvey's revolutionary ideology. Moreover, the pan-African movement never endangered the National Congress's hegemony in British West Africa. The pan-African congresses were held entirely in Europe and the United States, and most of the Africans who attended them were residents of Europe. This distance left the National Congress free to ply its own ideology.

The UNIA, in contrast, distributed literature, founded branches and hosted meetings throughout West Africa, and the back-to-Africa propaganda and revolutionary message of the *Negro World* reached thousands of African readers. Moreover, the West African UNIA branches seemed to have real power. Under the impact of their propaganda, which elicited widespread public rapture with the Black Star Line, the National Congress was compelled to support economic cooperation with the UNIA. Resolution Number 5 of the Accra session stated: 'That in view of difficulties hitherto experienced in the matter of space in British Bottoms by legitimate African traders and shippers this conference welcome [*sic*] competition in the shipping line with particular reference to the Black Star Line.'[53] The necessity of cooperating with the UNIA, when it otherwise rejected everything associated with African-Americans, can only have intensified the National Congress's fear and dislike of the organization.

The above analysis differs somewhat from Langley's conclusions to the effect that 'the majority of the . . . nationalist leaders of the N.C.B.W.A., on the whole, tended to be more sympathetic to Garvey's Pan-Negro nationalism and its economic goals, than to the more majestic, more intellectual but ineffective movement of W. E. B. Du Bois'.[54] Langley's view was based on Kobina Sekyi's writings defending Garvey's activities in the United States and Liberia.[55] But it can be argued that, as a cultural nationalist, Sekyi was committed first and foremost to the struggle against European racism and that his defense of Garvey stemmed not from agreement with the latter's philosophy but from his conviction that the fierce attack against him by 'Englishmen or anglicised Africans' was motivated by racism.

The apprehensions of the National Congress proved to be unfounded. In its struggle with the Garveyite movement, the National Congress had the upper hand. It garnered supporters from all four British territories of West Africa, while the UNIA branches never spread beyond Freetown and Lagos. Moreover, the Gold Coast, where the UNIA did not have a single branch, provided the NCBWA with a power base deeper-rooted and more solid than anything that the UNIA could ever hope to attain in any part of British West Africa.

Politically, the UNIA branches never got off the ground. Most of their activities remained in the cultural and commercial spheres. They provided no alternative whatsoever to the National Congress's conservative nationalism. The UNIA branches in West Africa were as moderate and constitutionally oriented as the NCBWA. The Lagos UNIA branch went out of its way to affirm that it was operating 'in compliance with our loyalty to the Crown under the protection of the laws of the country'.[56] In general, the UNIA branches in West Africa embraced whatever the African-American community could offer in the commercial realm, but firmly rejected Garvey's revolutionary approach. Thus, the *Lagos Weekly Record* took care to qualify its support for Garvey's economic program with a condemnation of his militarism: 'While we would hesitate to endorse the political programme of Marcus Garvey with its aggressive and militaristic tendencies, we entertain no doubts whatever in the soundness of his doctrine of world-wide cooperation among Negroes for their economic and industrial uplift.'[57]

The UNIA in West Africa never developed a political program of its own distinct from its rival's naive, gentlemanly approach. At the same time, it suffered from the stigma of association with its radical American parent and was widely seen as an organization which jeopardized the Africans' struggle for equality and political rights. Kobina Sekyi, who had split with Casely Hayford when the latter left the Aboriginist Rights Protection Society to found the National Congress, went out of his way to declare, 'If any of us desire to assist West Africa in this its hour of need, he or she would do better by supporting the Congress movement than in directly giving help to Marcus Garvey.'[58]

The UNIA branches had only a short life-span in Africa. After Garvey's 1925 imprisonment for postal fraud in the United States, the movement waned and the branches disappeared. They petered out because they lacked an independent program and reason for existence. Their support and *raison d'être* in Africa derived from the grand hopes that Africans placed in Garvey's commercial enterprises. When the American organization collapsed, along with the Black Star Line, so did its African offshoots.

At first glance, the rapid demise of the UNIA branches might seem to justify the regionalists' contention that black Americans had little to offer Africans. The National Congress, however, soon came to its own end, outwitted by the British. In 1923 the British colonial authorities permitted a limited number of Africans to be elected to the Legislative Council in Nigeria and soon extended the policy to the Gold Coast and Sierra Leone. This totally undermined the National Congress's regional framework, as Africans in the individual territories established local parties which concentrated on purely local issues.[59] In 1930 the National Congress ceased to function, without having achieved any substantial gains. The British move was no more than a ploy. Only two or three African representatives ever sat in any of the legislative councils – a far cry from the equal partnership to which the National Congress had aspired.

BLACK FRENCHMEN, AFRICAN-AMERICANS AND THE PAN-AFRICAN MOVEMENT

The Pan-African Congress of 1919 was the first international gathering to bring together African-Americans and both Anglophone and Francophone Africans. Its predecessors, the Pan-African Conference of 1900, the Universal Races Congress of 1911, and the International Conference on the Negro held in 1912, had also attempted to serve as international forums from which people of African descent could broadcast their problems, and their participants referred to themselves as representatives of all black people. But Francophone blacks did not take part, largely on account of French colonial policy.

This policy was to simultaneously assimilate the western-educated Africans in the French territories into the colonial administration while strictly forbidding them any independent political activity. The two-pronged approach effectively turned the western-educated Africans in the French colonies into agents of French colonial interests and prevented them from joining the black political movements that emerged at the beginning of the century. Moreover, the lack of a common language, the exclusion of non-French missionaries from French-controlled territories, and the fact that there were almost no French African newspapers all added to the isolation of Francophone blacks and effectively prevented their direct contact with Anglophone blacks in Africa and the New World.

World War I changed all this, making the first cracks in the wall that separated the Francophone blacks of Africa and the New World from their Anglophone brethren. Their meeting took place neither in Africa nor in the New World, but in Paris, home to the Versailles Peace Conference and the postwar nexus of international politics, where the restrictions on political activity imposed by the French colonial administration did not apply.

Serving in Paris at the time were a small group of black French officials – administrators, army personnel, lawyers and other black African professionals in the employ of the French government – who were thoroughly assimilated in the political and social life of France. The four most prominent were the African deputies to the French Parliament: Blaise Diagne of Senegal, Gratien Candace of Guadeloupe, and Rene Boisneuf and M.

Lagrosilliere from the French Antilles. When Du Bois and Moton arrived
in Paris, they were strongly affected by the Africans serving in high public
office, especially by Diagne, and for a brief time saw in them the embodiment of racial equality and the fulfillment of every black man's dream.[60]
This idealization, along with the utility of Diagne's prestige and close
personal ties with the French President George Clemenceau, led Du Bois
to ask Diagne to join him in organizing the First Pan-African Congress,
which took place in Paris between 19 and 21 February 1919.[61]

Diagne accepted the offer, seeing in Moton and Du Bois embodiments
of the African-American myth. He was impressed by their accomplishments as leading black intellectuals and by their unflagging commitment
to the black cause, and he believed that their moderation and gradualism
were consistent with his own determination, as an assimilated Frenchman,
to work within, not against, the colonial structure. Despite his well-known
ambition and egocentricity, he agreed to share with Du Bois the leadership
of the major committees of the congress.[62]

The relationship, however, soon entered rocky seas, and ceased altogether with the end of the Second Pan-African Congress in September
1921. Behind the rift were fundamental differences in point of view, as
well as self-interest. In the course of the rift, the myth of the all-powerful
African-American was turned on its head, and the power that had initially
been seen as a power for good came to be seen as a power for harm.

Ideologically, a major element of the partnership between Diagne and
Du Bois was their shared antipathy to Garvey's UNIA and their rejection
of black nationalism. Du Bois, though sharing Garvey's aspirations for an
end to colonial rule, contemptuously dismissed his militant approach as
bombastic and unrealistic. Their mutual dislike was a matter of public record
and often issued in nasty mudslinging.[63] Diagne, for his part, was intent on
social and political equality with the French colonial rulers, not Garvey's
'Africa for the Africans'. In a letter to Garvey, he expressed solidarity with
African-Americans, denounced racial discrimination in the United States,
and offered the good services of the French people, black and white alike,
in bringing international public opinion to bear on behalf of black Americans
– but made his support contingent on the UNIA's abandoning its 'revolutionary propaganda' in Africa.[64] Together, Du Bois and Diagne prevented
UNIA representatives from participating in the First Pan-African Congress.
As Diagne wrote: 'our American friends and brothers under the leadership
of Burghardt Du Bois presented their opposition to the theories of Marcus
Garvey'.[65] They totally ignored Garvey's telegram of protest, which claimed
that Du Bois had no right to represent African-Americans on his own.[66]

Nonetheless, the congress soon revealed fundamental differences in the perspectives of the American and French partners. The black French officials regarded the congress somewhat as a social gathering where blacks from different parts of the world could come together to discuss issues of common concern – only neither the issues nor the discussions were to be political. The emphasis was to be on cooperation with the French colonialists. As Diagne subsequently put it: 'Our first congress gave us, with the French, the occasion to proclaim our desire for a moral union with all our brothers, in the framework of our respective nationalities.'[67] The black French officials who Diagne represented were products of French culture and assimilated into French society and the French political system. They regarded themselves as Frenchmen, were patriotic to France, and extolled the French colonial system as the only basis for black advancement. Du Bois, in contrast, rejected assimilation and emphasized the uniqueness of the colored races. Like Diagne, he aspired to equality for blacks and colored minorities, but, unlike Diagne, he also promoted self-rule for Africans and saw the congress as a body that would exert pressure on the international community to rectify the injustices against blacks throughout the world.

The resolutions of the First Pan-African Congress represented a compromise between these opposing points of view. The congress gingerly skirted the sensitive subject of self-government for Africans. Paragraph C outlines the principles by which Africans were to 'be governed', not by which they were to govern themselves. Section V of paragraph C demands not the right of self-rule but the right of Africans to 'participate in the Government as fast as their development permits', postponing that participation to some time in the indefinite future.[68] Immanuel Geiss points out that this resolution was not at all revolutionary at the time, but a retreat from the principle of self-rule which had already been accepted nineteen years earlier at the Pan-African Conference of 1900.[69] Moreover, the black French officials did whatever they could to turn the congress into a podium for the praise of French colonial policy. Diagne out and out lauded French colonial rule, and the black Francophone delegates carefully avoided even the mildest criticism of the notorious atrocities in the Portuguese and Belgian territories.[70]

The congress satisfied neither of the parties. Diagne dismissed it as irrelevant. 'Let us state clearly that the problems [discussed at the First Pan-African Congress] did not particularly concern the natives of our African colonies', he asserted in retrospect. 'Everyone at the Congress agreed with us that these people have no complaint of any importance and they declare themselves to be satisfied with their lot under the humane and gracious authority of France.'[71] Du Bois, for all his admiration for the French colonial system in general and for Diagne in particular, could not but have been disappointed with the lukewarm and regressive resolution on self-government.

By the time of the Second Pan-African Congress in the summer of 1921, both sides had put a certain distance between them. Unlike the first congress, which was held in Paris, the second one consisted of three consecutive sessions: in London, Brussels and Paris. As chief organizer, it was probably Du Bois who pushed for the London venue, in the knowledge that the black French officials would be reluctant to attend meetings in an English-speaking and culturally alien city, which would enable the American delegation to pass more progressive resolutions. The black Frenchmen, for their part, duly absented themselves, though Du Bois had consulted with Diagne on preparations for the congress and they probably received formal invitations.

The resolutions passed in the London session under Du Bois's leadership were clearly political and much more demanding than those passed at the First Pan-African Congress. 'The Manifesto to the World' published by the London meeting contained six points. Five of the six demanded education, freedom of religion, cooperation with the rest of the world, black ownership of land in Africa, and elimination of racial discrimination. One point, the second, called for 'local self-government for backward groups, deliberately rising as experience and knowledge grow to complete self-government under the limitations of a self-governing world'.[72] The London motions were a sharp departure from what Diagne saw as the proper aims of the congress, which, in his view, was to be no more political than the first: 'We, the representatives of the black elite', he told an interviewer, 'would have been mad if at this congress we would have wanted anything other than scientific verification that there are no inferior races and that it has become urgent to actively educate our race.'[73]

The explicit call for 'local self-government' with the ultimate aim of attaining 'complete self-government', albeit very gradually and hedged by many conditions, was particularly unacceptable. Diagne and the black French officials he represented opposed any manifestation of independent black identity separate from the French colonial scheme. Diagne repeatedly reiterated his conviction that nations are defined by common culture and not by race, so that people of different races could be members of the same nation.[74] He and most other French officials ardently believed that the only way for the blacks under French rule to advance was to adopt French culture and integrate into the French nation. Their identification with France was expressed even in the way they referred to themselves. While Anglophone delegates called themselves 'we Negroes', the black French officials participating in the congress termed themselves 'we Frenchmen'.[75]

'We Frenchmen', Diagne wrote in a letter dated July 1921, 'want to stay French. France has given us all the liberty and, without any thought, admits us like its own European children.'[76]

At the Brussels session, where Diagne was once again at the helm, he prevented the London motions from being voted on.[77] At the Paris session, he succeeded in incorporating into the congress's final resolutions a commendation of France, 'who had done [more] in granting equality than any other country'. But, to his chagrin, the African-Americans and the black and white socialist delegates from Belgium and France pushed through a resolution calling for African self-government.[78] With this affront, the black French officials split for good from African-Americans and all cooperation between them ceased.

The severing of ties was accompanied by a mudslinging campaign on the part of Diagne and his colonialist backers, which turned the African-American myth, which had underpinned the cooperation between the black Frenchmen and the African-Americans, on its head. The campaign had begun when it became clear that the African-Americans supported African self-rule. Launched by French and Belgian colonialists, the crusade associated all reservations, however moderate, about colonial rule with the twin bogies of communism and bolshevism and linked these threats with both Garveyism and Americans in general.

American blacks, European liberals and British socialists all came under fire as Garveyite, communist or bolshevik. The response in colonialist circles to the Phelps-Stokes Education Commission's 1921 visit to the Belgian Congo provides a striking example. As noted earlier, the visit was part of a tour of West, Central and Southern Africa commissioned by the various colonial administrations to obtain recommendations on African education. With the single exception of James Kwegyir Aggrey, the commission was made up entirely of white Americans. Nonetheless, the Belgian journalist Pierre Daye called the commission an agent of the Garveyite movement, linked its visit to the discovery of copies of the *Negro World* in various parts of the Belgian Congo, and roundly castigated the Belgian colonial authorities for allowing it entrance. To bolster his allegations, he accused one of the Second Pan-African Congress activists, Paul Panda Farnana, a native of the Belgian Congo and Secretaire de l'Union Congolaise de Bruxelles, of being a Garveyite and of having persuaded two Belgians, Senator La Fontaine and Professor Paul Otlet, to assist the black nationalist cause.[79]

The campaign against America and Americans was particularly virulent. The *Revue Indigene*, an organ of the black French officials, emphasized the supposed danger of American 'agitators' to Belgium's 'simple and . . .

impressionable' black subjects.[80] In another article it accused the United States of colonialist designs on the Congo and of cynically exploiting the fervor generated by Garvey's back-to-Africa ideology to free the country of its black citizens by sending them to Africa.[81]

Du Bois too came under attack. In a typically confused way, Pierre Daye reported in the Belgian magazine *Flambeau* that Du Bois was 'one of the most trusted disciples of the well known prophet, Marcus Garvey'.[82] A leading Brussels paper, *Neptune*, reflecting the ideas of Belgium's capitalist circles, whose wealth had sources in Africa, claimed that Du Bois's and Moton's mission to Europe was financed by bolsheviks and charged the NAACP with being a bolshevik organization which 'organized its propaganda in the lower Congo' and could cause 'grave difficulties' there.[83]

Diagne picked up the banner. The day after the Paris session ended, a French colonial paper quoted him as saying that 'the black bolshevism of Mr. Garvey can only lead to ruin and devastation'.[84] His account of the congress echoes the language and ideas of the anti-American crusade. The opposition of the colonialist press to the congress stemmed, according to Diagne, from the Garveyite propaganda that presented the congress's aims as the fulfillment of the revolutionary 'Africa for Africans' slogan. Diagne claimed that Du Bois and the African-American delegation had tried to force the Brussels and Paris sessions to 'adopt without discussion the American decisions [taken in London] which followed theories approaching those of Garvey'.[85] In an article published in the government magazine *Depeche Coloniale* fifteen months later, he argued that Du Bois's 'political inter-nationalism was a step closer to the great march of Bolshevism' and told that at the congress 'we had to fight against our American comrades led by Du Bois, who became more our enemy than Garvey'.[86]

Diagne's condemnation is not inconsistent with his well-known aversion to communists. As a devoted French nationalist – a 'patriot' as he preferred to call himself – Diagne came into constant conflict with the French Communist Party in the National Assembly. Aware of Du Bois's socialist leanings, he could well have placed Du Bois in this enemy camp. But it is equally unlikely that he actually believed the propaganda he mouthed, especially given Du Bois's role in excluding Garvey from the First Pan-African Congress. He was also probably fully aware that the modest demand of the London resolutions for 'local self-government', which would become 'complete self-government' only very gradually and on condition, was far removed from Garvey's call for the immediate establishment of black rule all over Africa and his threat to resort to armed force to attain it.

Diagne's motive seems rather to have been his fear of being tarred by the same brush as the Americans. As the first African ever elected to the

French National Assembly, Diagne was voted in with the support of the natives and against the will of the French establishment in Senegal. However, once in office, he soon learned that to survive politically he would need the support of the French Colonial Ministry and the French commercial companies operating in Senegal. Gradually, he reneged on his promises to his African constituency and increasingly came down on the side of the colonial authorities and commercial circles. For example, in 1923 Diagne would sign a 'Pacte de Bordeaux', backed by the Minister of Colonies and by the Governor-General of French West Africa, procuring for himself the political support of the French trading companies in exchange for his promise to see to it that they would be represented in the District Council and in his party.[87] It is more than likely that the fierce colonialist crusade against the Americans showed Diagne what was in store for him should he be, or seem to be, associated with them.

The passage of the African self-government resolution, coming as it did on the heels of the colonialist propaganda linking even the most moderate expressions of black independence to the bogies of Garveyism, bolshevism and communism, and depicting all Americans as dangerous enemies of the colonial order, could not be glossed over. It presented a real danger, threatening to undermine Diagne's standing in the French colonial system and to divest him of the support of the French colonialists. In order to stay alive politically, Diagne had to totally disassociate himself from the black Americans. He did so in action, by refusing to let the London resolutions come up for a vote and by withdrawing from the pan-African movement when the resolutions were passed, and in word, by joining in the mudslinging.

The split between the black French officials and the African-Americans was a political act with political motives. At the same time, the manner in which it occurred suggests that the African-American myth figured in the break just as it had in the initial partnership.

The black French officials' cooperation with Du Bois in the First Pan-African Congress was predicated on the myth, and their experience there seemed to support it. The Americans organized and financed the congress as well as all the committees that were set up to implement its resolutions and carry on its work. Without Du Bois's initiative and formidable organizational skills, the congress would probably never have got off the ground.[88]

The black American delegates served as the essential bridge between the black French officials and the Anglophone Africans. The black French officials could not help but be cognizant of the vital American role, which, by its nature, reinforced the mythical image of the powerful

African-American, who not only had the wealth and competencies to do what Africans alone could not, but could somehow make things happen, bring peoples together, and take command in the international arena. The conflict during the Second Pan-African Congress did not lead to a disavowal of the myth, but turned it on its head. Diagne did not break with his erstwhile allies because he came to see them as weak or to feel that they could not deliver on their promises. On the contrary, he and the other French colonialists who railed against African-Americans attributed to them the same extraordinary power, ability, wealth and influence as the myth did. Only now these qualities were not a source of inspiration, but the features that made African-Americans seem so dangerous. Larger than life, African-Americans could now stir up civil unrest in Africa and bring down the colonial order. The fact that the American delegates were able to get their motions passed in London in the absence of the black Frenchmen could only have confirmed the black American's superabundant power to do harm. Interestingly, this view of African-Americans as a power for harm was inspired by whites and adopted by the Africans who, more than any others, longed to be like white Europeans and accepted by them.

Diagne's withdrawal from the pan-African movement marked a definitive break with Du Bois. Du Bois made a supreme effort to keep the pan-African movement alive and succeeded in organizing two more congresses, but never again in Francophone capitals and never again with the participation of the black French officials, or any other Francophone blacks. Nonetheless, the myth on which he rode persisted among Francophone blacks. One known example is Tiemoho Garan-Kouyate of the French Sudan, today Mali. A Paris-educated communist activist, Kouyate met American blacks at the international trade union conferences he attended. He was impressed by their touted financial and organizational abilities and was aware of the part Du Bois and other black Americans had played in the pan-African congresses. In 1929 he asked Du Bois to help him organize and finance the League Against Imperialism, of which he was a presiding member.[89] Though nothing came of the request, it does show the persistence of the myth.

In some respects, the views of the black French officials and of the NCBWA activists were similar. Both advocated a gradual approach based on constitutional action to resolve the political problems of Africans. Both regarded the active support of the colonial powers as essential to the future of their people and sought solutions within their respective colonial structures. Both ultimately rejected the participation of African-Americans in African politics.

But ultimately the perspectives of the two groups were very different. The black French officials advocated assimilation. Their goal was to replace African culture, which they considered inferior, with European (i.e. French) culture. The NCBWA leadership also admired western culture, but they saw themselves as Africans; they wished simply to enhance European culture, not to supplant African culture. The black Frenchmen rejected the idea that race might be a determining part of a people's identity. As far as they were concerned, it was not race that distinguished Africans from Europeans, but culture. They believed that the barriers between Africans and Europeans would melt away as soon as the cultural gap was closed. Their major objective in the pan-African congresses was not colonial reform but proving that color was not indicative of ability. The National Congress supporters also rejected racial discrimination, but they believed that each race had its own cultural characteristics, and, like their nineteenth-century predecessors, they were interested in developing them.

The two groups also differed in their attitudes toward African-Americans and the African-American myth. The National Congress hardliners rejected both totally. They discounted the African origin of New World blacks and considered them foreigners, no closer to Africans than whites. They repudiated the view inherent in the myth that African-Americans were superior to Africans and the accompanying notion that they could make a contribution, whether monetary, organizational, or ideological, to Africa's development. The black French officials accepted the myth and rejected American blacks not for themselves but for their political views. Garvey's revolutionary politics and Du Bois's pan-Africanism both proved too radical for them. The potency the myth attributed to African-Americans lurked behind both the black Frenchmen's initial alliance with the Americans and their subsequent repudiation of them as dangerous subversives.

PAN-AFRICAN NATIONALISTS AND AFRICAN-AMERICANS

The First and Second Pan-African Congresses were dominated by black French officials who used them to promote their own social and political agendas. Their views, however, did not represent those of the entire black Francophone community living in France. At the end of World War I, Paris was the center for black Francophone political activities, where western-educated Africans and liberal and socialist groups gathered and put forward their social and political programs. Without the severe restrictions on political expression that French colonial law imposed on its African subjects, Francophone blacks in Paris were able to express their political views freely, through associations and newspapers and other printed literature.

After World War I, nationalist and proto-nationalist groups from all over the French empire made Paris the center of their activities.[90] One of the major groups was headed by Marc Kojo Touvalou-Houenou, a scion of the royal family of Behanzin, the last King of Dahomey. Touvalou-Houenou became involved in politics under the influence of the political changes wrought by World War I and of the pan-African congresses.[91]

Like many other Francophone Africans, Touvalou-Houenou did not belong to the world of black French officialdom and did not share their political ideology. Along with other Francophone Africans of his persuasion, whom we term 'pan-African nationalists', he advocated far-ranging changes in the French colonial structure. The views of the pan-African nationalists made them undesirable partners to the black French officials in the First and Second Pan-African Congresses. Du Bois skipped over them, along with all other Francophone Africans, in the Third Pan-African Congress that he organized in London and Lisbon and in the Fourth Pan-African Congress in New York. The pan-African nationalists, for their part, had little use for Du Bois. They rejected his moderate evolutionary approach in favor of Garvey's revolutionary thinking and assumed that the African-Americans he led were agents of the American government. They probably reasoned that since Diagne was part of the French political system, Du Bois was similarly part of the white American establishment. Du Bois's visit to Liberia in 1924 as US President Calvin Coolidge's official representative must have confirmed their suspicions. In 1934 a group of black Francophone activists went so far as to organize a congress of their own and to work out 'a common program of action around which world unity among the blacks can be achieved'.[92]

In 1924 Touvalou-Houenou and a group of followers established their own organization, the Ligue Universelle pour le Defence de la Race Noir (LUDRN), with its own newspaper, *Les Continents*. These names reveal the direction in which Touvalou-Houenou and his followers were heading: black racial unity, the protection of blacks all over the world, and the development of the African continent.[93] Lamine Senghor, another pan-African nationalist, adopted much the same course. A war veteran from Senegal, Senghor started his political life as a member of the Ligue, but in 1927 split with Touvalou-Houenou and established the Comité de Defense de la Race Negre (CDRN) and its newspaper, *La Voix des Negres*, whose name was later changed to *La Race Negre*.[94] The aims of the Ligue and the Comité were formulated in general terms and were probably influenced by other pan-African gatherings. However, unlike their predecessors, the Ligue and the Comité both took Marcus Garvey as their political mentor and the UNIA as a source of inspiration. Touvalou-Houenou became acquainted with Garvey's ideology through the *Negro World* and was so impressed that he smuggled issues of the paper to his native country, Dahomey.[95] *Les Continents* and *La Race Negre* printed Garvey's speeches and accounts of UNIA conventions in America and gave wide coverage to African-American affairs. *La Race Negre* reprinted Garvey's poem 'Africa for the Africans' and maintained its pro-UNIA stand even after Garvey's imprisonment and deportation in 1925.[96]

These and other black newspapers published in Europe played a major role in spreading Garvey's ideas among Francophone Africans, mainly in Paris but also in Africa. Of all the Francophone Africans, Touvalou-Houenou was probably the most strongly influenced by Garvey's thinking. Even the name of his organization, Ligue Universelle pour le Defence de la Race Noir, was, as Immanuel Geiss points out, a near translation of Garvey's UNIA: Universal Negro Improvement Association.[97] The ties between the Ligue and the UNIA were strengthened when Touvalou-Houenou visited the United States in 1924. On 18 August he attended the UNIA Annual Convention in Harlem and delivered a speech to an audience 5,000 strong denouncing social discrimination in the United States and praising Garvey and his movement. He in turn was highly praised and elected to the highest office of the UNIA.[98] Before returning to Paris, he was taken to Philadelphia, Chicago, and other cities where UNIA membership was large. The visit gave him direct contact with the African-American community and enabled him to assess for himself the strength of the Garveyite movement.

Four years after Touvalou-Houenou's visit to the United States, Garvey visited Paris as part of his European tour. By 1928, Garvey had lost his strong base in America and was trying to gather new support abroad. Denied a visa to the various countries of Africa, he had to confine his efforts to Europe. Garvey arrived in Paris from London in August, not as the triumphant head of a dynamic black organization, but as a hobbled leader trying to shore up his waning powers. He made an all-out effort to attract many Francophone black followers in Paris as compensation for the meager support he had received in his London tour.[99] In Paris, he hoped to find a more sympathetic audience in the pan-African nationalists who were already familiar with his ideology.[100] Garvey addressed an audience at the Club du Faubourg and opened a UNIA Paris branch. Despite his efforts, the European tour was actually a failure and he was forced to give up his plan of establishing permanent headquarters in Europe.[101]

The foreign visits made by Touvalou-Houenou and Garvey had a dramatic impact on both, leading them to change their views on how to promote black development. Ironically, though, the conclusions they reached after getting to know one another were diametrically opposed. Early on in his career, Touvalou-Houenou had campaigned for equality for Africans within the French colonial system. His position was consistent with the high regard in which black Frenchmen in general held French culture and with the views of the black French officials at the pan-African congresses. He differed from his Francophone rivals only in that he publicly accused the French colonial authorities of obstructing the immediate assimilation of all Africans. If Diagne and the other black French officials shared this perception, they dared not say so out loud. Up until his visit to the United States, Touvalou-Houenou never waved the banner of African self-rule. Even when he spoke as a guest at UNIA meetings, he remembered to praise France's assimilationist ideology. But once back in Paris, he changed his tune. It may be conjectured that in his face-to-face meetings with the masses of UNIA supporters in the American cities he visited, he came to appreciate their commitment to Garvey's radical stand and to feel the strength of the movement.

In 1924 the pan-African congresses were disintegrating while, as far as one could see, the UNIA seemed to be going strong. Du Bois's international pan-Africanism must have struck him as a defunct idea. Garvey's national pan-Africanism, with its masses of followers and apparent backing by the political and economic power of the black race, must have seemed the more dynamic and viable approach. Soon after his return, he abandoned his assimilationist ideology and adopted Garvey's black nationalist approach. He began to call for the liberation of his native country, Dahomey, from French rule.[102] In an interview with an African-American reporter, he demanded 'home rule or autonomy' for all African races. The reporter noted that in Paris, Touvalou-Houenou was regarded as 'the Marcus Garvey of Europe'.[103] His new political attitude provoked a strong reaction from French colonial authorities. When he returned to Dahomey in 1926, he was arrested, subject to the Indigenat Code, which outlawed political activity by Africans. That arrest put an end to his political activities in the Ligue which had been driven underground as a result of the schemes of the French administration. Touvalou-Houenou died in Dakar in 1936.[104]

Garvey's reaction to the Francophone blacks he met in Paris was similar to Du Bois's a few years earlier. Like his more conservative predecessor, Garvey developed a certain regard for the French colonial system. When he first arrived in Paris, Garvey presented his all-encompassing nationalist position and attempted to recruit black Frenchmen under the banner of 'Africa for Africans'. He even claimed success in rallying French blacks to his cause. 'We have already cemented a working plan with the French Negro by which we hope to carry out the great ideas of the UNIA', he proclaimed in the 11 August 1928 issue of the *Negro World*.[105] However, there were indications that this arch anti-colonialist, who had declared the colonial powers enemies of the black race, had begun to soften. The 27 October issue of the *Negro World* relays that in a speech at the Club de Fauburg, Garvey declared that 'France is the only country which offers to the Negroes legal equality and the humane rights of citizenship.'[106]

In the course of his stay in Paris, he became so enamored of the French assimilationist policy that he even proposed that 'the French republic must continue to aid the Negro in his ambition to establish his own country and his own government in Africa'.[107]

The about-face of Touvalou-Houenou and Marcus Garvey did not bring them any closer to the realization of their ideas. Touvalou-Houenou's black nationalist approach was effectively thwarted by the French colonial administration. Marcus Garvey left Paris without winning the support of the French colonial administration for the establishment of an independent black nation in Africa. For reasons of self-interest, both the black French officials and the pan-African nationalists in Paris became involved with American blacks. Though the major concerns for both groups were the problems of Francophone blacks, each group linked up with a different African-American political movement. The black French officials joined forces with Du Bois's moderate pan-African movement while the nationalist pan-Africans identified with Garvey's radical black nationalist movement.

In both cases, the Francophones' brief readiness to entertain an American ideology rested on their faith in the African-American myth. The myth led them to attribute tremendous intellectual, administrative and financial prowess to the African-American community and lent force and viability to the ideologies that sprang from it. For a brief time, the myth led black Frenchmen, who traditionally regarded themselves more as part of the French nation than of the black race, to join forces with African-Americans. The political impact of the myth was short-lived, though, lasting only through the 1920s, before the Francophone blacks and African-Americans once again went their own political ways. Somewhat longer-lasting were the myth's cultural repercussions.

NEGRITUDE AND THE HARLEM RENAISSANCE

Francophone Africans were inspired not only by the political ideologies of the black American community, but also by its cultural activity – namely by the Harlem Renaissance. The Harlem Renaissance, also known as the New Negro Movement (after an anthology of black American literature published by the black American writer Alain Locke), was created by black writers, artists and musicians who congregated in Harlem in the 1920s and the 1930s. Like Garveyism, it grew out of the burgeoning civil rights movement that followed World War I and gave expression to the developing consciousness among American blacks.[108]

A cultural movement, it was inextricably linked with the social issue of African-American identity. It drew black artists in all fields who felt alienated from white American culture and unwilling to express themselves in its terms. In their search for their true selves, the artists of the movement strove to find meaning in their being part of the black race. They defined themselves both by the experiences they shared with other blacks and in terms of intrinsic racial features reflected in a 'black personality' different from that of whites. Their conviction was that in rediscovering themselves, they would be able to consciously assert their valuable role in American civilization both for themselves and to others.[109]

The emphasis on racial solidarity and black personality went hand in hand with a focus on Africa. These black American writers, artists and musicians considered their work a link in the long chain of black civilization and culture which had started in Africa. Most of them had only limited knowledge of the black continent and its inhabitants, but that did not deter them from looking to Africa for inspiration for their artistic creativity. They were connected by a sense of kinship and drawn by the alternatives to white western culture that African art offered.[110]

In the 1930s, Francophone Africans drew inspiration from the Harlem Renaissance for a renaissance of their own, focused on the concept of negritude. Like the idea of a unique black personality, the concept of negritude entailed the assumption of a distinct black way of being that all blacks, whether in Africa or the diaspora, shared. The idea was developed by a group of Francophone blacks in Paris. The members of this group were, like Diagne and his coterie of black French officials, products of the French assimilation policy. But unlike them, they were dissatisfied with their status and openly recognized the fundamental injustice of French colonial policy: that while a small black elite were integrated into French society, the vast majority of the population in the French colonies were not and were discriminated against in every area of life. This fact made these black Frenchmen highly insecure about their position in French society, a feeling which intensified as they personally encountered prejudice in Paris. At the same time, they felt overwhelmed by French culture and, like their American predecessors, felt that they had lost their genuine personality. According to Leopold Senghor, one of the founders of negritude, many Africans who had integrated into French society and appeared to have attained their goals came to have uneasy second thoughts about their future as black Frenchmen: 'we had become aware within ourselves that assimilation was a failure; we could assimilate mathematics or the French language, but we could never strip off our black skins or root out black souls'.[111]

The concept of negritude developed from these second thoughts. Like the Harlem Renaissance, the Negritude Movement entailed a radical change in the way Francophone blacks defined themselves and perceived traditional African society. For the first time, there were western-educated Francophone blacks who defined themselves as Africans rather than as black Frenchman.[112]

And, like their American models, the members of the Negritude Movement also embarked on the rediscovery of Africa and turned all things African into a potent source of identification, inspiration and symbolization. The Negritude Movement was driven by many of the same forces as was the Harlem Renaissance. According to Codjo Achode, 'the identification of Africans with the New Negro Movement was less the result of Negro American commitment to the cause of Africa than it was the result of the perception of the movement by Africans as a projection of similar conditions. That identification was perfect as both the Negro Americans and Negro Africans were members of the same race.'[113]

Like their American counterparts who formed the Harlem Renaissance, the Francophone blacks who developed the idea of negritude were perpetual outsiders. Though educated in French schools and residents of French towns and cities, Francophone blacks were no more fully integrated into French society than American blacks were integrated into American society. In both cases, integration was largely a formal matter. In America it was sanctioned by the ideas of equality in the Bill of Rights and anchored in the Fourteenth Amendment to the Constitution. In the French colonial system, it was rooted in the ideals of the French Revolution. But in neither context was it fully supported by the surrounding white society. Both black Americans and black Francophones felt the tension between the formal ideology and the social reality.

At the same time, both western-educated Francophone Africans and black Americans were uprooted from their African traditions. They regarded themselves as French or American. But since neither French nor American society truly accepted blacks as equals, those who were most assimilated were, in some ways, also most vulnerable. Africans who had maintained their traditions were able to fall back on their traditional community and way of life in their encounter with the modern world. Assimilated blacks were alone, with neither social support nor an inner standard to bolster them. In addition, they had reason to be insecure in their host countries.

In particular, black Frenchmen feared losing their privileged position. Disillusioned and uncertain, both groups came to feel that whatever integration they might have attained only deprived them of their authentic African selves. It was out of this feeling that they embarked on a search for their African roots. The concept of negritude and the Harlem Renaissance movement held Africa and Africans as symbols for the inner integrity and authenticity of the black race and provided an anchor for black identity.

The founders of the Negritude Movement saw in the writings of the Harlem Renaissance authors their shared African roots. In a 1966 speech at Howard University, Leopold Senghor rendered 'well-deserved homage to the poets whom we translated and recited and in whose steps we tried to follow: Claude McKay, Jean Toomer, Countee Cullen, James Weldon Johnson, Langston Hughes, Sterling Brown'.[114] Francophone African intellectuals sought in the writers of the Harlem Renaissance the same cultural leadership that those writers sought in Africa. The works of the Harlem Renaissance writers provided an antidote to the assumption, shared by western-educated Africans, of the superiority of European culture and inspired the writers of the Negritude Movement to produce art and literature that 'had its own integrity, independent of white European roots'.[115] In the 1930s this sense of shared roots and shared purposes led to joint cultural endeavors when Harlem Renaissance artists came to Paris and mingled with French blacks. One of their main meeting places was the salon of Mademoiselle Paulette Nardal, a Francophone black from Martinique, where people came together to listen to jazz, Negro spirituals, and each other's literary productions.[116] Francophone and American blacks who attended these meetings later joined forces to publish the bi-lingual literary magazines, *La Revue du Monde Noir* and *Presence Africaine*.[117]

The Harlem Renaissance and the Negritude Movement of the 1920s and 1930s show some striking parallels to the cultural nationalist movement that developed in West Africa in the last quarter of the nineteenth-century. The nineteenth-century movement had also been created by western-educated Africans whose efforts to integrate into European culture were rebuffed and who were trying to redefine their lost identities in traditional African terms. Moreover, all three movements grew out of the special pressures that modern life exerted on blacks. The cultural nationalists tried to find a place for traditional African values as Africa was increasingly affected by European culture and technology. Both the Harlem Renaissance and Negritude Movement can be seen as reactions to the breakneck industrialization of Europe and the United States after World War I.[118] During the half century or so of modernization that spanned the three movements, the cultivation of African art, values and culture provided blacks in Africa, France and the United States with a means by which to identify themselves in a rapidly changing world.

The Harlem Renaissance had its own appeal for Africans, but it is very likely that its attraction was founded on the conceptions that Francophone blacks already had about the intellectual, organizational and financial talents of African-Americans. This is suggested by Senghor's account of how he came to the Harlem Renaissance writers: 'Studying at the Sorbonne I began to reflect upon the problem of a cultural renaissance in Black Africa and I was searching – all of us were searching – for a "sponsorship" which could guarantee the success of the enterprise. At the end of my quest it was inevitable that I would find Alain Locke and Jean Price-Mars.'[119]

The Harlem Renaissance was apolitical, though its artists dealt with political issues in their works. Negritude was similarly a socio-cultural movement, but it soon became the crucible in which many black Frenchmen were transformed into African leaders. The best known example is Leopold Senghor, the first President of the independent Republic of Senegal. Ultimately, the cultural movements, the Harlem Renaissance and Negritude, were stronger and more enduring than the political movements that were inspired by black Americans. Pan-Africanism was accepted enthusiastically by the black French officials in post-World War I Paris but rejected within two or three years, and it had almost no support at all in the French colonies in Africa. Garveyism found favor among the pan-African nationalists in Paris, and the UNIA succeeded in disseminating its ideas through copies of the *Negro World* smuggled into Senegal and Dahomey. But Touvalou-Houenou's nationalist activities were swiftly blocked by the French colonial rulers. The Harlem Renaissance, on the other hand, had concrete political results through its impact on the black French intellectuals who gathered around the concept of negritude.

Prior to World War I, the African-American myth inspired Africans to seek the aid of African-Americans largely in the cultural regeneration of their continent. The political potential of the myth, expressed in Blyden's vision of a black nation created jointly by Africans and American blacks, was still embryonic. With the upheavals of the war, the cultural ramifications of the myth receded, while its political potential rose to the fore. In the 1920s the myth gave power to two American-based political models, which provided Africans with more active and focused ways of trying to deal with the colonial situation. The myth was part and parcel of the political discourse of both Anglophones and Francophones.

Like the nineteenth-century cultural nationalists, both groups had their yea sayers and their nay sayers. The yea sayers (the globalists) felt that they could not have a say in the postwar world order without the help of African-Americans. The nay sayers (the regionalists) felt that they could. The Anglophone yea sayers were divided between Europe and Africa. Most of those in Europe supported Du Bois's pan-Africanism, while those in Africa tended to rally behind Garvey's UNIA. This is because the Africans in Europe, in the thick of international events, came to adopt a cosmopolitan viewpoint, while the Africans in Africa tended to focus solely on Africa, much as the UNIA did. The nay sayers were concentrated largely in Africa itself, where they established the NCBWA, which sought to advance African political interests with the help of the British rather than the African-Americans. The dichotomy notwithstanding, the NCBWA had more than it realized in common with the UNIA branches that it so adamantly opposed. For the UNIA yea sayers adapted mainly Garvey's commercial message and rejected his racism and radical nationalism as firmly as did the NCBWA, while the NCBWA gave its blessing, albeit reluctantly, to the Black Star shipping line. For all the emotions and rhetoric, the overlap was possible, and even to be expected, because the western-educated Africans on both sides shared the same status in the colonial machinery and the same naive belief that Britain would further the political development of the territory.

Among the Francophones, both the yea sayers and the nay sayers were located primarily in Europe, where they had the freedom of speech and association that they were forbidden in the French colonies in Africa. The black French officials in Paris initially accepted but ultimately rejected Du Bois's pan-Africanism, while the pan-African nationalists embraced Garveyism. The black French officials were drawn to pan-Africanism as long as they thought they could keep it a cultural movement that would advance their assimilation in the French colonial system, but were quick to abandon it when they could not contain its political demands. The pan-African nationalists, who did not share the officials' faith in French promises of total assimilation, were drawn to Garvey's separatism and political message. There was little if any overlap between the views of the two sides. In contrast to the Anglophones, the Francophone nay sayers and yea sayers had very different political status in the French colonial system. The black French officials were part of the colonial machinery and were bound to reject any political model that threatened their privileged position. The pan-African nationalists did not enjoy the same political privileges, and they sought in the Garvey model the political solution that was closed to them, and that they knew was closed to them, under the French colonial system.

In neither Anglophone nor Francophone Africa, however, did either of the African-American political models leave an enduring mark. By the end of the 1930s, no trace was left of either Du Bois's pan-Africanism or Garvey's UNIA. More successful was the African-American cultural message, which became the basis for the Negritude Movement. Paradoxically, the Francophones of the 1930s discovered their African heritage by way of the Harlem Renaissance – whose cultural message of racial identity was then expressed in political action.

5 Africans and African-American Educational Models

Just as World War I catapulted Africans into a fervor of political activity bolstered by the African-American myth, so too it ushered in massive changes in African education influenced by the myth. Up through the early part of the twentieth century, education in Africa was largely the province of the missionaries, who used it as a powerful means of attracting converts. By the end of the nineteenth century, Africa had an extensive network of missionary-operated elementary schools, seminaries, technical schools, teacher-training colleges and some secondary schools, which provided western education for hundreds of thousands of Africans.[1]

Western education was a commodity that Africans were eager to obtain and ready to convert for. As the basic requirement for employment in the European commercial firms and colonial administrations, it was the key to social and economic mobility.[2] At the same time, increasing numbers of Africans came to consider western education the *sine qua non* for regenerating the black continent. Reverend Peter Kawa, a superintendent of schools of the Church of England in the Cape Colony, asserted in 1902 that 'the South African Native must be educated, if he be expected to take his place among the nations of this land'.[3] The *Gold Coast Chronicle* had reached the same conclusion a year earlier: progress by blacks, it asserted, would be achieved 'not by fighting, but by . . . educating ourselves'. For modern western education was the tool 'as would fit us to hold our own in the race of life'.[4] The *Gold Coast Times* reiterated that point in 1924: western education, it wrote, would enable Africans 'to take their rightful place in the council of nations'.[5] In his book *L'Aventure Ambigue Recit*, the Senegalese novelist Cheikh Hamidou Kane has a traditional African woman urge her young relative to attain western education on the grounds that it will enable Africans to regain command of their lives: 'One hundred years ago, our grandfather . . . threw himself upon the newcomers. His heart was without fear and he valued liberty more than life. Our grandfather and his elite were defeated. Why? How? Only the newcomers know. One has to ask them to explain. One has to go and learn from them the art of winning without being right.'[6]

The work of the missions notwithstanding, beginning at the turn of the

112

century repeated complaints could be heard throughout almost all of Africa about the inadequacy of the educational facilities and the low standard of education for Africans. The schools established by the colonial governments, missionaries, and Africans themselves could not meet the growing demand for western education. There were not enough secondary schools and only a few colleges in all of Africa. Only two institutions of higher education in Africa were recognized internationally: Fourah Bay College in Sierra Leone and the School of Pharmacy in Dakar.[7] A description in the *Nigerian Pioneer* of the educational situation in Nigeria concluded: 'In all those schools the standard is that of elementary grade except in a few schools at Lagos which are denominated secondary schools but the result of whose work does not show ability to pass an examination of the Matriculation Standard.'[8] The South African Native Affairs Commission, looking into the low level of education in the Union, concluded decisively that 'the supply of Native teachers is far from equal to the demand and that many of those whose services are available are of inferior attainments'.[9] Similarly, the British Colonial Office was aware of the poor quality of African education and was looking for a comprehensive educational policy to apply to their colonies.[10] Africans, foreign missionaries, and the colonial regimes were all united in their dissatisfaction with the state of African education.

THE DEBATE OVER CURRICULA: VOCATIONAL VERSUS ACADEMIC

Africans differed, though, as to the type of education they believed was needed. Some favored a vocational curriculum, others an academic one. The advocates of a vocational curriculum attributed the current superiority of whites mainly to their technological skills. In her comprehensive study of the image of Europeans in Africa in written and oral sources, Veronika Gorog-Karady shows that, more than any other quality, Africans were impressed by Europeans' technical ability, which they linked directly to the European's formidable superiority.[11] The natural conclusion was that to attain such power for themselves, Africans too must acquire technological and agricultural skills. Thus, as early as 1899, the *Lagos Weekly Record* hammered home the point that Africa 'needs colleges, seminaries, schools of technology, mineralogy, civil engineers, electricians, telegraphers and railroads; these are the greatest civilizing agencies in the world'. The correspondent went so far as to assert that: 'The planting of a school for the industrial training of young Africans in the principal cities and towns where civilization has obtained a foothold in Africa is of more vital importance that [*sic*] the establishment of missions.'[12] Such views gained momentum in the early decades of the twentieth century. In a 1920 article entitled 'Industrial Education: A Pressing Need', the *Colonial and Provincial Reporter* argued strongly for vocational education as the way to make Africans 'a really producing community' as a step toward reaching 'the goal of material prosperity'; this type of education, the newspaper claimed, would 'lead us to much needed manliness and independence of character by giving us the much coveted power to employ ourselves'.[13] In 1927 M. Mokete Manoedi, from Lesotho, argued that to create a modern society Africans would first have to acquire the Europeans' technological skills:

> But the problem of building modern railways, and supplying rolling-stock, improving the waterways and harbors, constructing ocean and river crafts, providing medical and sanitary services, is far beyond the intellectual and financial resources of the Negro. . . . [T]he Negro has not as yet reached the point of achievement which the white man has reached; and until he does reach that point, he must make use of the knowledge and skill of the white man with a view to preparing himself to reach that point.[14]

In his book *Le Pauvre Christ de Bomba*, the Cameroonian author Mongo Beti has his hero say that the motive for conversion to Christianity was to learn the secrets, not of the Gospel, but of western technology: 'The first of us who ran to religion, to your religion, came as if to a revelation; that's it, a revelation, a school where they would acquire the revelation of your secret, the secret of your strength, the power of your airplanes, your railroads, and whatnot.'[15]

The paradigm of vocational education with which Africans were familiar was the Tuskegee model developed in the United States by Booker T. Washington. Booker T. Washington provided the philosophical foundation for the vocational education that the AME Church, the AME Zion Church, and other African-American missions gave their pupils along with their education in Christianity and the three R's.[16] As recalled, Booker T. Washington's philosophy emphasized black self-help through vocational training. His own extraordinary rise from slavery made him a symbol of the 'regeneration of his race' for many blacks.[17] The clear success of Tuskegee Institute, which he founded in 1880, seemed to prove the soundness of his approach. Tuskegee Institute was an industrial school for blacks which taught not only skills, but also a way of life and a set of values. Above all, it propounded and served as a model of black self-sufficiency.

The students and staff were all blacks and they produced their own food and other necessities. The students labored on the school's land and in its workshops, and they received salaries and invested their savings in the school bank. When it opened, Tuskegee had thirty students and one teacher and was located in a rented church in three small buildings on 100 acres of land. Within three decades, it developed into a famous black institution known throughout the world. In 1915, when Booker T. Washington died, Tuskegee had a staff of 230 serving 2,415 pupils, in 111 buildings.[18]

Between the end of the Civil War and Booker T. Washington's death fifty years later, American blacks had progressed from a nearly 100 per cent illiteracy rate to a 75 per cent literacy rate.[19] Although much of the work was done by the black elementary and high schools and academically oriented black colleges which sprung up within a few decades of emancipation, many Africans associated the enormous educational advances of African-Americans with Tuskegee. In both Africa and the United States, Tuskegee was an enormous source of pride – a symbol of black self-sufficiency, ability and achievement. The combination of work and study exemplified by Tuskegee was emulated all over the American South. More industrial and agricultural colleges were established, and the Tuskegee approach was adopted by the already existent Hampton Institute in Virginia. From the American South, the influence of the Tuskegee model was carried to Africa.

Black American missionaries in Africa and Africans educated in the American South adopted and transferred Booker T. Washington's Tuskegee philosophy to Africa. Judging by its name alone, Chilembwe's Providence Industrial Mission owed much to the Tuskegee concept. Charles Domingo, the Nyasalander head of the American-based Seventh Day Baptist Church, established a central boarding school modelled on Tuskegee in Chipata, Nyasaland.[20] John Dube, on his return to Natal from Oberlin, established the Ohlange Institute modelled on Tuskegee. The black missionary William Sheppard of the Southern Presbyterian Church in Virginia, who in 1890 was sent to establish a mission among the Bakuba ethnic group in what was then the Congo Free State, trained the students at his mission school in Iuebo as brickmasons and carpenters and employed them to fortify the walls of the mission and to make furniture for it.[21] The black American missionary, Samuel B. Coles, who himself graduated from Talladega College in Alabama, based the instruction in the schools he established in Angola, where he served from 1923 to 1953, on the Tuskegee philosophy. Students worked on the school farm most of the day before starting classes. Coles was in charge of instruction in agriculture not only in the schools but also for the villagers in the surrounding area.[22]

Colonial authorities were also evangelists of the Booker T. Washington philosophy, inviting Tuskegee graduates and faculty members to provide agricultural training for African farmers in their colonies. In 1900 the German government formally asked Tuskegee to send a team of experts to what was then German Togo. Three Tuskegee graduates led by one of their teachers, J. N. Calloway, arrived in Togo to teach Africans to grow cotton. Two years later, three more graduates were sent to the same German colony and worked on the project for six more years.[23] In 1903 British colonial authorities appointed John Wesley Hoffman, head of Tuskegee's Department of Agricultural Botany and Chemistry between 1894 and 1897, to serve as Director of Agriculture in Nigeria.[24] In 1906 another team was sent from Tuskegee to what was then the Anglo-Egyptian Sudan to teach the local people to develop the cotton crop there.[25] The head of the British South African Company, Lord Grey, invited Booker T. Washington himself to introduce his educational philosophy into the areas in Southern Africa under the company's jurisdiction.[26]

Though Washington never visited Africa, the work of the Tuskegee people in various parts of the continent had a cumulative effect. The very fact that they were invited by the colonial regimes to teach, direct, and give advice demonstrated to Africans the potential of Tuskegee-type education and greatly enhanced its value in their eyes. Many Africans associated the vocational curriculum developed in Tuskegee and Hampton with the self-improvement and success that they so much wanted. African leaders expected the Tuskegee system to perform the same miracles in Africa as they believed it had wrought in the United States. In 1902 the Lozi king, Lebusi Lewanika, asked the AME Church missionary A. A. Rideout to establish an independent school emphasizing industrial education in his chiefdom in Northern Rhodesia.[27] Harry Thuku of Kenya was so taken by Tuskegee that he regarded it as 'our asylum where the hunted downtrodden and oppressed Negro may hasten to seek help or advice', though it was thousands of miles away. In 1921 the East African Association which Thuku headed asked Booker T. Washington's successor at Tuskegee, Robert R. Moton, to send graduates to start a trade school in Nairobi.[28] The advocates of the vocational curriculum could point to the Tuskegee example to support their position.

The demand for an academic curriculum can be traced back to the 1860s. James Africanus Beale Horton, a Sierra Leonean who was trained as a physician in England and was appointed to high ranking medical and administrative positions in British West Africa, suggested in his book *Western Africa, Vindication of the Negro Race*, published in 1868, that the Fourah Bay Institute in Sierra Leone be turned into a university to serve as an instrument in the regeneration of the continent. In the early 1870s, James Johnson and Edward Blyden again raised the idea of turning the Fourah Bay Institute into a West African university. As cultural nationalists, they emphasized the African aspect of the anticipated university, which would be designed for African students and staffed by black faculty from all over the world. Blyden preferred a secular academic institute while James Johnson, as a Church Missionary Society (CMS) official, wanted the church to take an active part in handling the university.[29] In the 1920s, the National Congress of British West Africa (NCBWA) carried on the idea of a West African university. In articulating its educational goals, it deliberately shunned the vocational curriculum, which was identified with the African-American model. In the Accra session, 11–29 March 1920, the congress advocated the establishment of a British West African university as well as comprehensive reform of the entire educational system on the model of the Japanese.[30]

The idea of a West African university was supported by Sir Harry Johnston. Relying on his experience as a colonial official in East-Central Africa and his commercial activities in West Africa, he argued that Africans 'require a University education of the best'.[31] Johnston, unlike many whites in his position, believed that Africans possessed the ability to undertake and benefit from academic studies. He felt that traditional European liberal arts education would not only uplift Africans culturally, it would also make it possible for them to contribute usefully to the colonial administration and the commercial activities in the British colonies.[32] Interest in an academic curriculum was not confined to West Africa. Africans in the Cape Colony led by John Tengo Jabavu tried to establish an institution of higher education for Africans modelled on the British system.[33]

The advocates of an academic curriculum, no less articulate than their opponents, held that higher education in academic institutions would do more for the development of Africa and Africans than vocational education. Some advocates of the academic curriculum were probably motivated at least partly by their rejection of the African-American myth and the politics of the UNIA in which the myth was embodied. But mostly they believed that a narrowly vocational curriculum did not adequately meet Africa's needs. Indeed, there were staunch supporters of the academic curriculum who generally accepted the African-American myth. Their objections to the Tuskegee model paralleled those that were raised by certain black Americans against the dominance of vocational training for blacks there.

In the United States, the academic versus vocational education controversy had been fought out at the beginning of the twentieth century. The apostle of academic education for black Americans was W. E. B. Du Bois. New England born, with a B.A. from the black Fisk University, a Ph.D. from Harvard, and postgraduate studies at the University of Berlin, Du Bois was a teacher and scholar in his own right, with numerous books and articles to his name. In 1905, when he was in his mid-thirties, he wrote *The Souls of Black Folk*, where he took up verbal arms against Booker T. Washington's philosophy of accommodation to white supremacy and his 'programme of industrial education' related to it.[34] Some of Du Bois's objections to vocational education were practical. He argued that academic education was required to provide the black community with the more highly qualified people – the 'talented tenth' he called them – that it needed to advance: teachers for black elementary and industrial schools; professionals, such as lawyers and physicians; and leaders with the broadness of vision and soundness of judgment to steer their people towards equality without 'mob rule'.[35]

But the main thrust of his argument was ideological. Industrial education was too narrow and materialistic in his view. He objected to the 'economic cast' of the vocational approach 'becoming a gospel of Work and Money to such an extent as apparently almost completely to overshadow the higher aims of life'.[36] The real aim of education, Du Bois maintained, should be to bring civilization and culture to its possessors. Industrial education, Du Bois argued, answered the immediate needs for economic betterment of black Americans, but to address 'the broader question of the permanent uplifting and civilization of black men in America, we have a right to inquire, as this enthusiasm for material advancement mounts to its height, if after all the industrial school is the final and sufficient answer to the training of the Negro race; and to ask gently, but in all sincerity, the ever recurring query of the ages, Is not life more than meat and the body more than raiment?'.[37] Education, he insisted, 'that encourages aspiration, that sets the loftiest of ideals and seeks as an end culture and character, rather than bread-winning' must not be a privilege reserved for whites. Blacks have the same yearning to 'read the riddle of the world' and need, perhaps even more than whites, universities 'to furnish the black world with adequate standards of human culture and lofty ideals of life'.[38]

In Africa it was Orishatukeh Faduma of Sierra Leone, one of the major advocates of the African-American avant-garde, who took up the banner of academic education. Faduma had spent five years studying divinity and the philosophy of religion at Yale and seventeen years preaching and teaching in the American South. He was undoubtedly familiar with the debate there and with Du Bois's stand. But, more than influence, there seems to have been an affinity of predilections and values. Like Du Bois, Faduma was exceptionally well educated, with a B.A. from the University of London and Doctor of Divinity from Harvard, and his background and disposition seem to have fostered a similar respect for learning in the broader sense of the word. In an April 1918 article in the *Sierra Leone Weekly News*, written to propose the establishment of a 'co-operative Missionary Training School' in West Africa, Faduma expressed admiration for scholarship and traditional classical learning, and wrote with great respect of African 'self-taught experts in both technical and academic fields' and of Africans 'of giant intellects in general, and biblical literature'.[39] The 'training school' he proposed was to be a cross-denominational institution consisting of four separate schools – of religion, theology, bible, and 'Christian Sociology and Practical Ethics' – and was to teach such subjects as 'Anthropology and Race Psychology' and comparative religion. Despite its misleading name, Faduma envisioned much more than a vocational school to churn out church functionaries. The scope of the school, he wrote, was to be 'broader than that we have hitherto had', and its aim was to be nothing short of teaching the underlying truths of all religions, including paganism, 'to know what religion is in one-self and what it is in the other man'. In other words, what Faduma advanced here was solid academic education to broaden the mind and widen the horizons.[40]

About three-and-a-half years later, in the fall of 1921, Faduma dealt more directly with the vocational versus academic controversy in two articles written for the *Sierra Leone Weekly News*. Both articles focused on African-Americans, though it is safe to say that their ideas applied to Africans as well. The subject of the articles was what Faduma called 'phases' of African-American development: religious, mental and social. To all of them, education is the key, Faduma maintained. Significantly, vocational development is not treated as a separate phase. In the first article, of 24 September, Faduma pointed out that the religious development of the black American was promoted by missionaries who 'with the Bible in one hand and their Spelling Book in the other . . . made religion to the freedmen rational and ethical and enlarged the boundaries of his mind'.[41] He further argued that the African-American's mental development, to which academic education is crucial, is of primary importance.

Considering the neglect of centuries due to his separation from the world's highest centers of culture followed by physical slavery, the need for his intellectual training is reasonable. There is no emancipation from slavery where the mind's power to reason is not trained and where men cannot acquire the art of reading and writing, among the best means of acquiring and disseminating knowledge.[42]

Only in the second article, of 1 October, did Faduma turn to vocational education. Like Du Bois, he argued that vocational education must be underpinned with academic learning:

Industry of a high grade to which Negroes everywhere should aspire requires Intelligence of a high order. To be a skilled farmer requires a thorough knowledge of insect, plant and cattle life, as well as a practical if not scientific acquaintance with the nature of soils. To be a first rate builder requires more than an elementary knowledge of mathematics, but also a knowledge of the science of architecture.[43]

Also like Du Bois he insisted that vocational training alone is too narrow and, to be meaningful, must be backed up by academic studies: 'Industrial education is a power for good only when it is realized by the aid of spiritual forces which are moral and intellectual.'[44] Aware of the educational debate, Faduma lamented that 'There has been a cry against Higher Education for the Negro.' The outcry, he argued vigorously 'is not justified by the case either in Africa or in the United States of America', where quality institutions of higher learning for blacks were scarce, and strongly urged that blacks 'if necessary, traverse oceans and seas for their highest intellectual equipment'.[45]

Faduma's frame of reference and terminology are different from those of Du Bois. Du Bois upholds education as a vehicle for culture and civilization. Faduma speaks of education as a means of broadening the mind, developing its powers of reason, and disseminating knowledge. But both, while recognizing its role in the economic advancement of black people, ultimately see education as a means of raising the spirit. They are fellow travelers on a road leading in much the same direction. The myth and model of the United States seem to have provided the background for the advocates of the academic curriculum no less than for the advocates of the vocational curriculum.

THE PHELPS-STOKES COMMISSIONS: THE TUSKEGEE MODEL

The first thorough study of education in Africa was carried out by the Phelps-Stokes Education Commission. The idea for a study of African education can be traced back to the inter-denominational World Missionary Conference held in Edinburgh in 1910. This conference, like other similar but less known and influential ones, was organized by European missions, which bore the brunt of educating Africans and were so strapped by financial problems that some of their schools were on the verge of collapse. The

Edinburgh conference addressed not only the problem of funds but all the inadequacies of African education, including the curricula. The committee that was authorized to find solutions to these problems in the British domain recommended to the British Colonial Office that a professional commission of enquiry be established to conduct a thorough investigation of the educational facilities and needs of the British West African colonies.[46] In 1914 the Colonial Office rejected the recommendation on the grounds of insufficient funds.[47]

The matter did not end here, however. The secretary of the Continuation Committee was J. H. Oldham, an Anglican missionary who was already well-known in missionary and government circles. In 1912 Oldham had visited the United States and became convinced that the Tuskegee model was exactly what was needed in the British colonies in Africa. Oldham was determined that the British Colonial Office's refusal to investigate African education would not thwart his endeavor to bring the Tuskegee model to Africa and decided to initiate an inquiry on his own. To do so he turned to America. He joined forces with the American Baptist Missionary Society, and together they held talks with the American Phelps-Stokes Fund, which was dedicated to improving black education in America and provided support for schools there that employed the Tuskegee approach. On 19 November 1919 an agreement was reached to establish a commission to survey educational conditions in Africa and to recommend a suitable educational program. Interested missionary societies would contribute, but the major financial burden was to be borne by the Phelps-Stokes Fund.[48]

The Phelps-Stokes Education Commission started its work on 4 September 1920 in the British colony of Sierra Leone. From there, it went on to the Gold Coast, today Ghana; Nigeria; the Republic of Liberia; the Belgian Congo, today Zaire; Angola and the Union of South Africa. Four years later a second commission was sent, this time to East and East-Central Africa. The second commission started its work in January 1924 in Ethiopia, from where it proceeded to the British and Portuguese colonies in East and East-Central Africa and then revisited the Union of South Africa. Basically, the aims of the two tours were the same: to study the state of African education in the various territories, to investigate the Africans' educational needs, and to recommend an educational program in keeping with the religious, economic, social and health conditions in each area.[49]

Most of the commission members were American. Its head, Dr Thomas Jesse Jones, was a Presbyterian minister and sociologist by training who had made a name for himself as an expert on African-American education. An ardent supporter of vocational education for American blacks, Jones had worked at Hampton Institute from 1902 to 1909 before becoming Education

Director of the Phelps-Stokes Fund. In that capacity, he authored a survey on black American education, whose dominant theme was the importance of industrial and vocational education for blacks in the American South. He deprecated the black academic institutions of which Du Bois was so proud and went so far as to suggest that their liberal arts courses be subordinated to courses in the manual arts and home economics. As Jones saw it, the future welfare of American blacks was dependent on their commitment to industrial education and they should 'grasp every opportunity' to attain it. To his credit, it can be said that he was genuinely concerned with improving the quality of life for black Americans in the predominantly rural areas in which they lived. The problem was that he hardly saw beyond that to the possibility that they might some day leave the rural region for the metropolis; moreover, to the extent that he did, he envisioned their role there as semi-skilled laborers rather than as the movers and shakers of a modern, industrial society.[50]

Jones's tours of the various territories and countries in Africa reinforced the convictions he came with. The regions he visited in East, East-Central and Southern Africa were largely agricultural and some of them had white settler communities. In Jones's mind, they were thus comparable to regions in the American rural South where blacks outnumbered whites. It was only natural for him to transfer to Africa the same educational system that had been developed for the American blacks. As was to be expected, the commissions came down firmly on the side of vocational training. The commissions' recommendations were published in two books written by Jones, *Education in Africa* and *Education in East Africa*. As far as the African-American model was concerned, these recommendations had three major components: 1) to send Africans to study at Tuskegee- and Hampton-type schools in the United States so that they could come back to administer and teach in such schools in Africa; 2) to send African-Americans to Africa to set up and teach in vocational schools there; and 3) to introduce, especially in East Africa, the Jeanes Fund system of itinerant teachers. This system, in effect in the American South since 1907, had been established by the principals of Hampton and Tuskegee to provide supervision for out-of-the-way rural schools.[51] The Jeanes teacher went from school to school and developed courses closely related to the rural life of the community. The system had the additional aim of keeping school graduates from leaving their rural communities for the cities by developing employment opportunities in the countryside. Africans, according to Jones, had much the same needs.[52]

The proposed curriculum was significantly different from that of the missionary schools to date. In the mission schools, vocational education was a tool for spreading Christianity. Children were taught some vocational skills along with religious and academic subjects, but the trades remained secondary. In the schools Jones proposed, vocational training would take center stage and academic subjects would be pushed well to the sidelines. The commissions' recommendations for education in Africa were more reductive than anything Booker T. Washington ever conceived of for black people. Tuskegee, Hampton and the other vocational colleges that sprung up in the American South had as their students adolescents and young adults who had already received some grounding in academic subjects in elementary and high school. Their vocational training came at the end of an education which, in principle if not in quality, was similar to what American white children received and which had developed their minds. It also conveyed the academic background necessary to properly master and advance in the vocations that were taught.

The Phelps-Stokes Commissions made vocational training the be-all and end-all of all levels of schooling for Africans, beginning in the elementary grades. Their recommendations removed or drastically reduced the teaching of academic subjects, which, ideally, set the ground for analytic thinking, prepared children to become free-thinking citizens of a democratic country, and underpinned a mastery of a vocation, as both Faduma and Du Bois argued. The curriculum was also different from what many African supporters of vocational education sought. With its emphasis on agricultural education and simple crafts, it did not come anywhere near providing the sophisticated technical education that would enable Africans to become the equals of whites or the masters of their environment. There was no progression from the simple agricultural and industrial skills they would learn to the engineering skills required for their building railroads, designing roads, and developing the continent's resources on their own.

The Phelps-Stokes educational program for Africans in America was similarly restrictive. It channeled the African students it supported to study in all-black agricultural or vocational schools of the Tuskegee type, where, along with a trade, they would be taught the Booker T. Washington values of patience, hard work and racial harmony, even at the cost of acquiescence to discrimination. The program discouraged academic education and education in predominately white institutions. It attempted to persuade African students enrolled in white academic institutions to transfer to Tuskegee or Hampton. And the program intentionally selected African applicants for study in the States whom it expected to be compliant and tractable.[53]

The limited nature of the program in both its African and American phases can be attributed to two major factors. One was that Jones was not an egalitarian. In the tradition of the American South where he had spent the

better part of his adult life, he saw whites and blacks as having different needs and different potentials, and hence requiring different education.
Like others of his time, including Aggrey and many of the Africans who
placed such hopes in the Phelps-Stokes Commissions, Jones believed that
Africans, as well as black Americans, needed white guidance to raise them
to a higher plane of civilization. 'The Native people depend upon European and American groups for the machinery and achievements of civilization', Jones stated.[54] He differed from Aggrey and other Africans in that
he believed that Africans were permanently on a lower plane and would
need guidance perpetually.[55] His underlying assumption was that African
societies would remain rural indefinitely, while providing the European-
dominated sectors with the raw materials and labor necessary to support
industrialization.[56]

The other motive was to allay the apprehensions of the colonial regimes
regarding American education for Africans. By and large, the colonial
authorities saw education as a means of providing the colonial administrations and commercial interests with the steady stream of labor needed to
feed their expanding and profitable enterprises, but feared that the recipients of such education could pose a challenge to their authority. Their
apprehension is evident in the fact that although Jones's recommendations
were geared to all the territories the commissions visited, they were implemented only by the British and the South Africans, and even they were
wary. The Advisory Committee on Native Education in Tropical Africa,
appointed by the British Colonial Office to oversee the implementation of
the recommendations of the first Phelps-Stokes Education Commission,
stipulated that: 'Education should be adapted to the mentality, aptitudes,
occupations, and traditions of the various peoples . . . Its aims should be
. . . to promote the advancement of the community as a whole through the
improvement of agriculture, the development of native industries, and the
improvement of health . . . and the inculcation of the true ideals of citizenship and service.'[57]

The British colonial authorities also had strong reservations about sending Africans to study in the United States. The 1915 rebellion led by the
American-educated Chilembwe in Nyasaland was not far from their minds.[58]
The inquiry commission set up by the Colonial Office had reached the conclusion that Chilembwe's uprising was related to his studies in the United
States and to his ongoing ties with American blacks. It also pointed out
that Chilembwe had transferred African-American political notions to dis-
contented educated Africans who assisted him in his uprising.[59] In the
early 1920s, their fears may have been exacerbated by the political activities stemming from the United States: Du Bois's pan-African congresses

and, even more, Garvey's well-publicized plan to send African-Americans to settle in Liberia.

British authorities were especially concerned lest radical American ideas brought in by returning African students unsettle the growing circle of western-educated Africans who were not able to find jobs in the colonial administration or in commercial firms and filled the ranks of the un- and under-employed.[60] To ward off the danger, the British put obstacles in the way of African students returning from America to the colonies. This policy was first instituted in 1920 by Sir Edward Northey, Governor of Kenya, in response to racial tensions in the country. It was later adopted by the Colonial Office and lasted until World War II.[61] The casualties of this policy were mainly those who were educated in academic institutions. Graduates of Tuskegee- and Hampton-type schools were treated more leniently. Among the victims were Daniel Sharpe Malekebu, who had studied medicine, and his wife. In March 1921, when they completed their stay in the United States, the colonial authorities turned down their application to return to Nyasaland. They had to wait five years before finally receiving permission to enter. The reason for the refusal, Malekebu writes: 'It was told us by those in the know that I would be another John Chilembwe.'[62]

Once they did return, American-educated Africans were regarded with distrust. Nnamdi Azikiwe, who would become the first President of Nigeria, noted: 'throughout Africa, the native who was educated in America was regarded with suspicion, and such persons were generally assumed to be disloyal and anti-British'.[63] In 1927 an article in the *Gold Coast Leader* remarked that 'local governments have adopted every device to make contact [between Africans and African-Americans] difficult, if not impossible'.[64]

They also made it difficult for American-educated Africans to find suitable employment. The growth in the number of western-educated Africans after World War I, mainly in the British dominions in West Africa and to a lesser extent in the Francophone territories, put pressure on the limited quantity of posts available in the modern sector. Graduates of Tuskegee- and Hampton-type schools had less trouble than others finding work because they were accepted by the colonial regimes and the missionaries.[65] Those who graduated from mainly white and/or academic institutions had to overcome intentionally erected obstacles before they could find jobs comparable with their training. Hastings Banda and Alfred Xuma, who graduated from American medical schools, had to take additional courses in British universities before being given their professional licenses in the British territories. Others had to search long and hard in the already highly competitive job market. The suspicions of the colonial officials made their situation even harder. As K. A. B. Jones-Quartey of the Gold Coast described it:

> The results of this prejudice were disastrous to any African foolish or headstrong enough to have defied it and gone to the States for higher education. I used to know – many others used to know – a few Africans with perfectly good American degrees who literally went knocking from door to door seeking decent employment in vain – men who could teach, write, speak as well as any of their European-trained contemporaries, and better than many.[66]

Jones was sensitive to British concerns and seems to have tailored his program with them in mind. In a somewhat self-congratulatory memorandum dated 1934, he patted himself on the back for having allayed their fears: 'It is very significant that this very favorable recognition of American education by the British has developed during the postwar period when nationalism in Asia and other parts of the world and even in some parts of Africa tended to limit the influence of American schools.'[67] The type of education recommended by the Phelps-Stokes Education Commissions was meant to ensure the continuing dominance of whites by promoting Africans only horizontally, making them better farmers and craftsmen but not providing them with the conceptual skills to enter the free professions and academics, or, needless to say, to become political leaders of their people.

Jones saw the transfer of the Booker T. Washington philosophy to Africa as a means of producing docile and compliant African laborers.[68] He believed that black Americans and Africans who were inculcated with Booker T. Washington's philosophy would be immune to the bolshevism, pan-Africanism and nationalism that the colonial regimes so feared, and he presented the vocational and agricultural schools of the Tuskegee- and Hampton-type as antidotes to these dangers.[69] His aims were entirely consistent with those of the colonial authorities and other whites, who wanted an educational system which would help them incorporate the Africans into the colonial structure and, thereby, to control them.

THE FAILURE OF THE TUSKEGEE MODEL IN AFRICA

Jones's program initially seemed to be full of promise. Even before the recommendations were published, the Phelps-Stokes Commission was welcomed with enthusiasm by supporters of the vocational curriculum. In Sierra Leone, the estranged wife of Casely Hayford urged the Phelps-Stokes

Commission to 'stretch out a helping hand' in support of education 'in matters appertaining to what is technically known as the "applied sciences" or in pursuit of practical and mechanical industry'.[70] Henry Carr, a prominent Nigerian educator who had served as sub-inspector of schools for the Church Missionary Society and inspector of schools for the entire Lagos Colony, looked to the commission for a solution to Africa's educational problems. Though he himself had received his M.A. and B.C.L. from the University of Durham, England, he addressed the commission in the following words: 'We therefore look to our friends from America, and to their constant support and co-operation in the efforts that we put forth to resolve the difficulties with which we are confronted.'[71]

We saw in Chapter 4 that the NCBWA pointedly snubbed the Phelps-Stokes Commission. But UNIA supporters in Africa were happy to bask in the commissions' reflected light, as can be seen in a 1920 article in the *Lagos Weekly Record* which tried to link the success of African-American vocational education with the activities of the Garveyite National Negro •Business League: 'there can be no question', the writer contended, 'that the Booker Washington idea has scored the greater measure of success with American Negroes; for through industrial co-operation and freedom and under the auspices of the National Negro Business League they have been able to amass wealth, win fame and position and exert considerable political momentum within the American commonwealth'.[72]

Once the recommendations were published, Jones proved adept at winning over the hesitant British colonial authorities to his program. To gain their support, Jones included in the commission, as its only black member, his friend James Aggrey, the American-educated African who rose in the ranks and earned the respect of white folks. With a degree from Livingstone College, South Carolina, Aggrey served as living proof of the miracles that could be wrought by American education. Though his own education was academic, he functioned as a zealous and articulate spokesman for the Tuskegee model, winning over both the white colonialists and the colonized blacks. Aggrey was the ideal African for Jones's purposes. Ignoring racial slights, preaching hard work, moderation, and cooperation with whites to his fellow Africans, Aggrey did not threaten Africa's white rulers and, as shown in previous chapters, was regarded as a positive asset. This view is clearly expressed by Charles Templeman Loram, a white educator who joined the Phelps-Stokes Education Commission in South Africa. Aggrey, he declared, is 'a living example of the black man who lives the Christian life . . . who has trod the steep path to civilization and has not tried to get there by shortcuts, who knows the weaknesses of the black man and can interpret them to us. We want him as an example of what can be done by work and prayer.'[73] Aggrey also served as an example and inspiration for Africans, many of whom associated him with the Tuskegee model. For example, during his 1924 visit to their country, a group of young Kenyans asked Aggrey to help found a 'Tuskegee' in their native land: 'We have learned . . . of your remarkable career both in Education and moral senses, in United States of America. We are [*sic*] the Natives of Kenya mostly young Kikuyu Generation and the Bantu of Eastern Africa, beg to request your kind recommendation to our local Government, that this colony have the college established.'[74] Peter Mbiyu Koinange, a native of Kenya who graduated from Hampton, explicitly credits Aggrey: 'When I heard that man [Aggrey] speak, I quit my job in Nairobi and walked twenty-five miles to my home in one day and told my father, I must go to America where that wonderful African was educated.'[75]

In 1923 the British Colonial Office accepted the recommendations of the first Phelps-Stokes Education Commission and set up the Advisory Committee on Native Education in Tropical Africa to implement them. In 1924 it appointed Aggrey assistant vice-principal at Achimota College, modelled after Tuskegee, in the Gold Coast, and commissioned a second tour by the Phelps-Stokes people. These steps were all triumphs for the Africans who advocated the American vocational model. For almost two decades after 1920, the Phelps-Stokes Fund, along with several other American philanthropic foundations, worked assiduously to introduce the Booker T. Washington educational system to Africa.

Throughout much of this period, Jones also succeeded in promoting the program with the missionaries, colonial bureaucrats, educators, and other people who would have to implement it. Jones was aware that it was not enough that the commissions' recommendations were accepted. They could still die a quiet death on a dusty shelf. To drum up enthusiasm and facilitate their implementation, he launched an intensive marketing campaign which consisted of organizing visits for missionaries and colonial officials to Tuskegee and Hampton and other sites in the American South. In 1922 the Phelps-Stokes Fund set up a visitor program, which he vigorously promoted. For instance, on 20 December 1926 Jones wrote to the Rev. Hooper, secretary of the Church Missionary Society, inviting him and his wife to 'have a personal acquaintance with American experience in education related to rural and racial conditions'. The Phelps-Stokes Fund allotted $500 for the Hoopers to take a four to six week tour of the American South.[76] Between 1922 and 1932, a total of 224 directors of colonial education and supervisors and teachers in mission schools from British, French and Portuguese territories visited the American South at a cost of nearly $40,000.[77]

Most of the visitors returned to Africa convinced of the value of the Tuskegee educational model. Margaret F. Grant, a Scottish missionary in Northern Rhodesia, came back from her study tour in 1923 to set in motion the Jeanes School system in the Mwenzo District.[78] H. S. Keigwin, an experienced colonial official in Northern Rhodesia, today Zimbabwe, who served as Commissioner, Magistrate, and Director of Native Development, similarly returned from his tour with his preconceived ideas of black capacities completely overturned and ready to put the program into action. 'Now, more than ever, I stand, and can only stand, for the fullest opportunity of development for the coloured man and woman', he wrote to Jones.[79] He became involved in implementing the Tuskegee concept in Northern Rhodesia and volunteered to direct the Dombashawa Native School there. Gordon Guggisberg, the Governor of what was then the Gold Coast, came back from Hampton and Tuskegee with his faith in the capacity of Africans reaffirmed and a new-found respect for Tuskegee-type education: 'The first and most satisfactory thing that I have learned from my American experiences is that my belief in the potentiality of the African is *completely* confirmed', Guggisberg said, and added that it is the 'type of education which the American Negro has received, and which he has wholeheartedly received, that has made him the valuable asset he is in the United States'.[80] Robert MacPherson of the Scots Mission, Kenya, who visited the American South in early 1935, returned with a new-found faith in the ability of blacks: 'as a direct result of this tour we return to Africa fully convinced that learning and the arts, culture and progress are not impossible to the African just because of his colour'.[81] One of the few discordant notes was sounded by W. H. Seaton, Inspector, Native Development Department, Northern Rhodesia. In a pamphlet entitled, 'Linking School and Community in Southern Rhodesia', published in October 1930, he criticized both the African-American vocational curriculum and its implementation in Africa. In a letter to Jones dated 25 October 1930, he stated quite forcefully that 'Much of the work at Hampton did not appeal to me, because . . . there is no help there for our problem of connecting the school with the community.'[82] But such reservations were far and few between. Most of the visitors who toured under the auspices of the Phelps-Stokes Fund were duly impressed.

Moreover, there seemed to be indications on the ground that the program was working. The Jeanes system that Margaret Grant introduced in Northern Rhodesia apparently worked well enough for her to ask the Phelps-Stokes Fund for £100 to enlarge it.[83] In 1926 Phelps-Stokes Fund officials received a copy of a letter that African teachers had sent to the principal of the Jeanes School in Kenya, stating: 'We are very glad that we were invited to attend the Jeanes School to be taught the best ways of teaching and the best things to teach. We are thankful that the Jeanes School is here in our country for it will bring progress to our people. . . . We do not want you to think when you read this letter that it is written simply to please. These thanks are in our hearts.'[84] The program's promoters on both sides of the Atlantic were so satisfied with that letter that Oldham, the advocate of Jones's program on the British side, quoted part of it in a memorandum entitled 'Recent Tendencies in African Education'.[85]

Nonetheless, the program turned out to be a failure. For its sponsors, the first blow was Aggrey's sudden death in 1927. L. A. Roy, office secretary of the Phelps-Stokes Fund, wrote to Jones of his concern: 'Now that Aggrey is gone we have got to do our best to keep our name alive until a new man can be raised up.'[86] About two weeks later, Jones wrote to the President of the Fund, Dr Anson Phelps-Stokes, expressing similar apprehension: 'Though I firmly believe in the victorious life of dear Aggrey, I cannot avoid feelings of depression at times when I think of all the possibilities that seem to be temporarily retarded by his passing.'[87] Finding a replacement for Aggrey was not easy. The first replacement Jones suggested was Ross Lohr of Sierra Leone, who was studying at the time at Ottenbein College in Ohio. Jones described Lohr as a man 'who seems to me to have great possibilities as one of Aggrey's successors'.[88] To realize that potential, however, it was necessary to steer Lohr to Hampton and provide him with some training at Tuskegee Teachers College, Department of Rural Education. Even so, things did not work out. Lohr was slated to become Assistant to the Director of Education in Sierra Leone on his return from the United States but, because of lack of budget and an unexpected change in the directorship of the Education Department, he was never appointed to the post.[89]

Plans for two other replacements also went awry. One was Eyo Ita of Nigeria. Educated at the Hope Waddell Training Institute in his own land, he attended the Teachers College Department of Rural Education in 1930, and the next summer was sent by the Fund to Hampton and Tuskegee.[90] On his return to Nigeria in 1933, he joined the staff of Baptist College, in the remote section of Ogbomosho, Calibar, from where he tried to implement the principles he had learned. But, instead of filling Aggrey's shoes, he underwent a change of heart. 'The gospel of better industry and more production seems . . . futile', he wrote to Jones in 1934, 'for already the people have more than enough to eat and the surplus finds no market anywhere.'[91] Eyo Ita's realization that the Tuskegee philosophy was not suited to local conditions led him to establish his own school, the West African People's Institute, which was independent of both the government and missionary authorities and inspired by a philosophy quite different from the acquiescence taught at Tuskegee. Education, Ita proclaimed, must 'make our youth hyper-sensitive to the sacredness of equal social justice . . . It must fill our youth with sublime moral passion, must teach them to respect themselves, their land and its cause.'[92]

The third candidate was Ernest Kalibala of Uganda, who had studied at Tuskegee in 1924 under the joint auspices of the Phelps-Stokes Fund and the CMS. Of the three projected replacements for Aggrey, Kalibala was the only one who had been a student at Tuskegee prior to Aggrey's death. And even he, after a year at Tuskegee, decided to transfer to the academically oriented Lincoln Academy in North Carolina, despite Jones's strong protest, from where he proceeded to advanced studies at New York University and Columbia University.[93] Nonetheless, the Phelps-Stokes Fund paid the then enormous sum of $400 to cover the costs of his return to Uganda to serve as Assistant Educational Secretary to the CMS. Once back home, he soon came to the realization that the Jeanes School model for village schools was inappropriate to the rapidly changing conditions in the rural areas of his native land. Wary that working under the CMS would not permit him the independence he would need to develop the rural schools in Uganda along more suitable lines, he broke with the mission and, like Ita, established his own independent, academically oriented school, the Aggrey Memorial Institute in Kampala.[94]

These difficulties of finding a replacement suggest that more fundamental problems than Aggrey's death were behind the disintegration of Jones's program. Essentially, the Tuskegee model was unsuited to African realities. Ita and Kalibala were not the only persons who found the program unworkable in the social and economic conditions of the black continent. P. H. Moyo, a British instructor at Tjolotjo industrial school in Southern Rhodesia, pointed out that the forty-mile distance which separated the African reserve from the nearest train station made it almost impossible for the Africans to trade or sell their products.[95] The black American missionary Samuel B. Coles, a graduate of Talladega College in Alabama, is another case in point. Coles was not directly associated with Jones's program, but he was imbued with the Tuskegee philosophy and tried to put it into practice in the agricultural school he and his fellow American missionaries ran in Angola. Using the Jeanes system, the school made an all-out effort to keep African farmers and artisans in their rural villages and to discourage them from moving to the cities where they could be exposed to dangerous philosophies. In Coles's words: 'That was a milestone in our effort to teach the people around Galangue, who love the bush and are rural at heart, that they are better off on their own fields than crowding into the cities where they fall prey to communism and other influences that are bad for them and for Africa's future.' He soon discovered, however, that Africans trained as carpenters and masons in the industrial schools could not make a living in the rural areas so would have to be retrained as farmers.[96] In short, there was little demand in rural Africa for the trades that the students were taught; and where there may have been demand, there was no adequate infrastructure to bring the goods to market.

Very few, if any, of the advocates of the Tuskegee model in Africa considered the need to adapt the vocational studies to African socio-economic realities, to say nothing of changing those realities. Jones brushed off Eyo Ita's complaint that the farmers he taught could not market their surplus with the retort that the matter was beyond both Ita's ken and concern, and attributed the defection of his various protégés to the dangerous ideas they acquired by being too long in the United States.[97] In the United States, a Tuskegee or Hampton graduate could earn a living, boost his or her self-esteem, and hope to become a productive member of society by providing needed skills. A graduate of a Tuskegee-type school in Africa could not necessarily do any of these things. The colonial regimes, white governments, and missionaries regarded the Tuskegee approach as a magic wand to mold Africans into docile, productive subjects. They were ready to establish vocational schools to do so, but not to set new priorities or to build the infrastructure to enable African enterprise. In fact, they erected barriers. In areas settled by whites, the best land was reserved for the settlers and Africans were not permitted to raise crops that would compete with theirs. In other areas, European commercial companies were given virtual monopolies in trade, again making African entry virtually impossible.

The American arm of the program did not go well either. At first glance, the educational activities sponsored by the Phelps-Stokes Fund in the United States should have opened new avenues for African students who wanted to study abroad. In many respects, Jones's plan was similar to much of what the African-American churches had already done. As noted in Chapter 1, these churches encouraged Africans to train in their educational facilities in the United States so that they might return to work as missionaries and school principals in Africa.[98] Jones's plan, however, had the advantage of being broader in scope and more systematically organized than the churches' activities and was backed up by the considerable resources of a number of well-endowed American funds. The churches financed both their church activities and educational work mainly through scattered and irregular contributions from African-Americans. The lack of steady income limited the extent of the educational activities and the number of African students the black churches were able to support. To illustrate the contrast: while Bishop Small of the AME Zion Church kept several African students in his own home, providing for their needs ('out of his own purse he aided Frank Arthur and other African students'), the Phelps-Stokes Fund spent $21,000 over thirty-six years on the African students it supported in the United States.[99]

The problem was that the education that Jones and the Phelps-Stokes Fund were offering was not quite what many Africans wanted. To be sure, there were Africans who were eager to go to the United States for technical studies. One African from the Johannesburg area who had attended Tuskegee said that he went there because 'I wanted to get an education that would make my people do what white people do.'[100] But many African students had other ideas. Once they were brought to the United States by the Phelps-Stokes Fund, more than a few of them switched from vocational to academic colleges. Peter Koinange, who had been so impressed by Aggrey, fulfilled his dream in 1927 when he traveled to America. Upon the advice of his headmaster at Alliance High School, G. A. Grieve who had recently visited the American South as the guest of the Phelps-Stokes Fund, Koinange enrolled at Hampton.[101] Though he began his studies at Hampton, Koinange went on to the academically oriented Ohio Wesleyan University and did postgraduate work at Columbia University in New York, and Cambridge University in Great Britain. On his return to Kenya in 1938, he turned down the post of principal of a government school that was offered him and, instead, went on to establish a school of his own, Kenya Teachers College, in which he integrated the traditional age-group system for the division of labor and roles prevalent among several ethnic groups in Kenya.[102]

Similarly, two African teachers from the Union of South Africa, Miss Makanya and Miss Njongwana, came to the United States to study at Tuskegee at the expense of the Phelps-Stokes Fund, under the recommendation of Charles Loram while he was a member of the Native Affairs Commission of the South African government. To the chagrin of Phelps-Stokes officials, after some time at the vocational school, both women transferred to an academic institution.[103] Another South African student, Mark S. Radebe, who declared his intention to study at Lincoln University, was refused financial aid.[104] However, the reality overcame the declared policy and for the most part the Fund often did support the defectors. The Phelps-Stokes financial report covering the fiscal year 1933–4 revealed that out of ten African students who received financial aid in the United States, at the sum of $1,532.01, only four were attending Hampton. The other six were attending academic institutions throughout the United States.[105]

The Fund officials nonetheless persisted in their efforts to channel the African students in the United States into a single vocational track, with little recognition of the diversity or legitimacy of their interests. L. A. Roy, for example, complaining that two African students supported by the Fund had asked to be transferred from Tuskegee to Teachers College, Columbia University, admitted that the 'Tuskegee teachers did not have a proper concept of the conditions for which these boys were preparing to meet and, therefore, could not help them much'. Nevertheless, his attitude towards the students' desire to choose what they would learn was patronizing and censorious: '[T]hey wanted to know what education is so that they can go back to the Gold Coast and tell their people what education is and themselves determine what is the right type for their people', he dismissed them, adding, 'In this respect they have the minds of children.'[106]

Moreover, though Jones had expected that Aggrey would win African students over to his program in the United States, many who were thus inspired to study there opted for an academic education. Hastings Kamuzu Banda, who would become the first President of independent Malawi, tells that he determined to become as learned and articulate as Dr James Aggrey after hearing him speak in 1921. But he enrolled at the Wilberforce Institute, affiliated with the AME Church, and then continued his studies at Indiana University, the University of Chicago, and in 1932, at Meharry Medical College.[107] Nnamdi Azikiwe was so fired up by Aggrey's talk and personality when he first heard him speak in Lagos at the age of sixteen that he too decided to follow in his footsteps and continue his own education in the United States.[108] As Azikiwe describes it, 'I became a new man and my ideas of life changed so much that I lived in daydreams, hoping against hope for the time when it would be possible for me to be like Aggrey.' But, making use of a reference book to black American institutions of higher learning that Aggrey gave him, he enrolled first in Storer College in West Virginia, and later in Lincoln University, Pennsylvania, both academically based.[109] Kwame Nkrumah similarly decided to follow in Aggrey's footsteps and study in America after listening to him hammer home his ideas for uplifting the African people, but he too avoided the vocational track and enrolled in Lincoln University.[110] In Kenya, several young Africans responded to Aggrey's address supporting vocational education by handing him a note telling him of their need for identical education to that given to white children and for access to university level institutions in Africa and abroad.[111]

By the middle of the 1930s, Jones's program on both sides of the Atlantic had proved a failure. The Tuskegee curriculum was shown up as totally unsuitable for Africa. Many students who the Phelps-Stokes Fund brought to and supported in America opted for academic education, and the African students who came back from the United States were unwilling to implement the program in Africa. The Phelps-Stokes recommendations did not answer to the aspirations of even those Africans who supported the vocational curriculum. The training in agriculture and simple crafts which the commissions recommended was very far from the advanced technical education they had envisioned and offered little if anything that would enable them to take their place in the community of modern nations.

ACADEMIC EDUCATION AND THE SECOND GENERATION OF AFRICAN STUDENTS IN AMERICA

The failure of the Tuskegee model to take root in Africa did not put an end to Africans' faith in American education. On the contrary, Africans continued to look to the United States for educational models, and African students continued to study in American colleges and universities. Only what they sought and what they studied differed from the technical education that the Jones program offered. It also differed from the largely religious education that the black American churches provided. As discussed in Chapter 1, African students had been studying in black American church schools since the end of the nineteenth century. These students belong to what can be called the first generation of African students in America.[112] Most of them were converts or children of converts motivated by deep religious feeling who received financial assistance and moral support from various African-American churches. Most of them became professional churchmen and bore the title of Reverend.[113] On their return to Africa, most of them continued their church work and pursued the same aims as the black American missionaries who had sent them, that is to spread Christianity and western culture among the Africans, further convinced by their experiences in the States that these were the keys to Africa's future. Some of them went so far as to repudiate not only African paganism but all of African culture. John Chilembwe, for instance, insisted that the members of his congregation dress in neat and clean western clothes and adopt the white man's manners.[114] Some of the first generation (as shown in Chapter 3) were staunch supporters of the African-American model for the advancement of Africa and labored to turn the African-American myth into a reality. Most ascribed to the Providential Design theory and supported calls for the return of American blacks to their African homeland.

The Africans who went to study in the United States after World War I can be called the second generation of African students in America. Like their predecessors of the first generation, they were also graduates of mission schools, but they were less committed to missionary work and more accepting of African culture. In the United States, many did not attend mission schools. They studied subjects ranging from agriculture and education through medicine, literature, and political science. Back in Africa, they engaged in a variety of professions. There were entrepreneurs and journalists, agricultural consultants, educators and politicians.

This second generation was also inspired by a different aspect of the myth than the first generation. More sober and less romantic in their assessment of the African-American community, they abandoned the Providential Design theory and, with it, the notion that the salvation of Africa would come on the shoulders of American blacks. There were no more calls for an African-American avant-garde or for mass immigration of black Americans to Africa. On the contrary, the second generation of students were committed to the principle that Africans had to help themselves, much as the African avant-garde advocates of earlier generations had been. But unlike them, these students were keen to take from America what America had to offer.

More than all else, African students of the second generation were fired with the political features of the African-American myth: the strong conception of America as a free and open society. We saw in the first chapter that for fifty years, Africans all over the continent regarded America as an upholder and model of liberty. African pupils adopted the American culture heroes. Jones-Quartey tells that when he was at school in the Gold Coast, he and his friends ordered biographies and collections of speeches by George Washington, Patrick Henry and Abraham Lincoln.[115] Azikiwe, who had sung 'John Brown's Body' along with the other pupils at the CMS Central School at Onitsha, Nigeria, which he attended, was so moved by the legend of the American 'who died that others might live and enjoy the good things of the earth', that the first thing he wanted to see when he came to study at Storer College was John Brown's fort. Passing the Statue of Liberty as his ship sailed into New York harbor, he contemplated the motto, 'Liberty, lightening the world', inscribed on the pedestal and recalled the successive waves of Europeans who had sought religious and political freedom in America. 'I could appreciate the meaning of this living symbol of Americanism', he wrote in his autobiography.[116]

The distinguishing mark of the second generation of African students who sought higher education in the United States is their quest for liberty – or, to put it differently, their politicization. This set them apart not only from the first generation, but also from those Africans who received their education in British government or missionary schools and made up what

Martin Kilson calls the 'upper echelon' of the African elite. These were the lawyers, doctors, journalists, administrators and teachers selected by the colonial administrations to represent Africans in government.[117] Relative to other Africans, they had fairly comfortable lifestyles and financial security. Over time, their dependence on the colonial governments brought them to respect and identify with the colonial regimes. The second generation of American-educated Africans repudiated this model.

The difference is well illustrated in the development of Nnamdi Azikiwe's attitudes to Garvey, whose American-based UNIA held out, for a brief time, the promise of political liberation for Africans. The young Azikiwe learned about Garvey from a classmate at the Hope Waddell Training Institute, who told him about a great black man who would bring a great army to liberate Africa. Initially, Azikiwe says,

I was not aware of the fact that Africa needed liberation. My father was a First Class Clerk in the civil service. We seemed to be people who lived well. He gave me facilities which were not everyone's lot; and he gave me my pocket money of four shillings a month regularly. So naturally I never thought of any problems, excepting those of compound interest, which my West Indian teacher had assigned to my arithmetic class as home work. Therefore I spoofed the idea of a Negro coming from America to redeem Africa, and I told my friend that we were being educated to take the place of our fathers.[118]

These were much the ideas of the African elite educated in the British system, to which Oved Azikiwe, Nnamdi's father, belonged. But the young high school student soon had a change of heart. When he went home for a school break and told his father, who had a position in the colonial administration, about Garvey, the latter warned him not to be found with anything written by 'that man' and refused to say anything more on the issue. Not satisfied with his father's uninformative warning, young Azikiwe continued to read the *Negro World*, and went so far as to copy Garvey's motto, 'One God, One Aim, One Destiny', into his notebook.[119]

When the time came for him to go to college, he chose not Britain, but the United States. In the 1930s and 40s, the pressing need, as western-educated Africans saw it, was not for vocational and agricultural development but for political liberty. They took as their model not Booker T. Washington but Marcus Garvey, who in the 1920s had brought to Africa the ideal of political self-help. They respected Aggrey, who had made a strong impression on many of them in the 1920s. But they were affected more by his personal example, as an African whose American education enabled him to travel as an apparent equal with whites, to serve on a prestigious commission, and to speak before packed audiences of both races, than by his declared message. Even those, like Azikiwe and Nkrumah, who explicitly acknowledged their debt to Aggrey, paid short shrift both to his political conservatism and to the politically sterile vocational program he touted, and when it came time for them to go to the United States, opted for an academic education, as he himself had.

The racial discrimination in the United States did not deter Africans who wanted to continue their education there. As pointed out in Chapter 1, Africans were well aware of America's mistreatment of its black citizens. The British, smug in the understatement of their own culture, tended to exaggerate the impact of this knowledge. For example, the white principal of Achimota College, A. G. Fraser, observed in a 1926 newsletter: 'Here they fear American suggestions, although they may be very, very good. But the tendency is to think that any American suggestion must be meant to keep the African down. And they think of America as a place where the African has to travel in Jim Crow cars. . . . And often they think of America as the place which has given the African lynch law.' In comparison, Fraser pointed out, England treats blacks much better: 'I do not suppose one man in ten thousand in England knows anything about the statistics of lynching, for instance. I did not. In England, I should not have been able to tell that eighteen Africans were lynched last year and no white men, or that over four thousand had been lynched during the last forty years.'[120]

Black Africans apparently saw things differently. They evidently found the covert eddies of British racism more offensive than the overt and violent abuses of America. 'My fellow passengers in the compartment were behaving as though they had not seen me', a Gambian student complained of his experience on a train in England.[121] Nnamdi Azikiwe similarly complained of the racism he encountered traveling on a British ship from Liverpool to Accra, where he and a Liberian friend were seated in a remote corner of the dining room, set apart from the white passengers. 'I was peeved because here was the ogre of the colour bar rearing its horrid head to mar my homeward voyage', he wrote in his autobiography.[122] He also had plenty of evidence of British racism in the Gold Coast, where it was reflected in the behavior of his own people and rankled even more. When his ship reached Accra, the African boat boys who carried passengers from the surface boats to the shore on special chairs refused to take him before they transferred all the white passengers, the 'masters'.[123] Back in Africa he found that the British authorities at Achimota College did not hire qualified Africans to teach there and that the staff was 'an exclusive preserve for white Britons'. Even Aggrey was appointed only to the low-level post of assistant vice-principal, Azikiwe felt, 'to make it possible for lilliputians to deride his academic qualifications, in spite of his valued experience in handling human situations'.[124]

For many Africans of the second generation, British racial discrimination was more painful than American, because it was intertwined with colonialism and imperialism. This distinction is implicit in the description of Jones-Quartey, who had studied in the United States from 1937 to 1946:

> though the color situation was even worse than I had preconceived it, there were two significant facts about it. First, not only was it wrong and unlawful in the eyes of the Constitution of the United States, but the federal government itself, and most of official America, was actively and permanently committed to combating this evil ... And second, in spite of its unavoidable evidence and influence everywhere, race discrimination in America did not and could not prevent the development of a fine community like Negro Atlanta, or of fine Negro personalities.[125]

As western-educated Africans saw it, in the United States racial discrimination was illegal at the federal level and various US presidents tried to combat it, while in Africa it was approved by the colonial governments. In America, discriminatory practices did not impede the development of blacks, even in the heart of the racist South, but in Africa they did. In America, racism was a social problem, which could be eliminated by providing blacks with proper education; but in Africa, it was a political problem to be overcome, according to Azikiwe, Nkrumah and others of the second generation, only by an end to colonial rule.

A good portion of the second generation set their sights on an informal political education in the United States, which would give them the tools with which to strike out against colonialism. It was widely believed that American education fostered the leadership skills that Africans would need to develop their countries and to attain political freedom. Already at the end of the nineteenth century, Reverend Makone of the Ethiopian Church in the Cape Colony clearly set out the view that the AME Church educational network should cultivate leadership in its African students: 'We want a man of some qualification', he insisted, 'one who will stand for the prejudice, one who will fight for the equal rights for the race on the face of the globe. ... We want the men who passed their degrees who can face an opposer with great power.'[126] A quarter of a century later, Harry Thuku of Kenya struck much the same note in a letter to the secretary of the Tuskegee Institute, 'We suffer beyond imagination from the want of such men and leaders of our own race to guide us in every walk of life, and the result is that our progress in the sphere of Trade, Industry, Agriculture and the last but not the least important, Politics, is seriously hampered.'[127] Education at Tuskegee, the complaint implied, would give Africans the skills, in politics no less than in more concrete spheres, to combat their oppression. After World War II, Prince Ikejiani of Nigeria, who studied in America, articulated the same idea in somewhat bombastic but even more emphatically political terms: 'The first skirmishes in the struggle for political freedom of the 21 million people of Nigeria are being fought today – in the colleges of the United States.'[128]

African students were drawn to America by its promise of an education in liberty and by the fact that the United States was not a colonial power. Azikiwe tells that Hogan Edem Ani-Okokon, a Nigerian student, decided to study in the United States because he believed that Africans could learn about freedom and democracy there.[129] As for himself, Azikiwe reported that his motives were initially more commercial: to acquire moneymaking skills that would enable him to earn a living independent of the colonial structure. But once in America, he made a New Year resolution, in which he vowed: 'First, that, henceforth, I shall dedicate my life to the emancipation of the continent of Africa from the shackles of imperialism and to the redemption of my country from the manacles of foreign rule.'[130] Young Nkrumah chose Lincoln University in Pennsylvania in order to prepare for the fight against colonialism. It was while studying there that he wrote his first book, *Toward Colonial Freedom*, in which he stated, 'We believe in the rights of all peoples to govern themselves.'[131]

The political education that the second generation sought could obviously be better obtained in an academic institution than in the narrow, politically sterile technical frameworks to which the Jones program tried to restrict its students. Azikiwe and Nkrumah thus both accepted financial assistance from the Phelps-Stokes Fund, but pointedly opted for an academic track.[132] The movement towards academic education, as we saw, was already under way when the Phelps-Stokes Commissions made their tours of Africa in the early 1920s. In the 1930s, when it was apparent that Tuskegee-style vocational education had failed, the movement became more pronounced.[133] On the whole, American education seemed to have fulfilled its political promise, and more. Africans who studied in the United States came back to Africa equipped with not only professional training, but also with a slew of distinctly American values and skills, which drew yet other African students and served those who were so inclined towards advancing their people.

One such value was the pragmatism of American education and culture. After almost a quarter century in the American South, Orishatukeh Faduma returned to Sierra Leone to commend 'the practicalness and many sidedness' of American education as something he would like to see in African education.[134] A student from the Gold Coast at Lincoln University in Pennsylvania similarly lauded the utilitarian quality of American education: 'The education we are getting from the States brings American pragmatism into balance with European intellectualism, and the results cannot but be good for Africa.'[135]

A related virtue discovered in America, and not to be acquired by a British education, was an anti-aristocratic respect for hard work. Nnamdi Azikiwe is a case in point. His first exposure to this value was when he was still a high school student in Nigeria, when he received as a school prize the book *From Log Cabin to White House* that told the biography of US President James Garfield. According to Jones-Quartey, the story of this poor, fatherless boy reared in the wild west, who became the twentieth President of the United States, made a deep impression on the young Azikiwe, convincing him that he, too, could achieve his goals with persistence and hard work.[136] But, as Azikiwe himself makes clear in his autobiography, it took actually being in the United States to drive the lesson home. When he reached Storer College in West Virginia, Azikiwe writes, he went to the home of the President of the college, Dr MacDonald, who, dressed in shabby attire, was working in his garden. But never having seen MacDonald before, Azikiwe did not identify him and innocently asked 'the gardener' for directions. 'The gardener' asked him some questions. Azikiwe, angry at his presumption, replied that he was a student from Africa who was born and bred as an English gentlemen, 'and it was not the business of a gardener to find out the nature of discussion between gentlemen'. When Azikiwe, with his British-style public school education, finally learned who 'the gardener' was, he was astonished that a college president was doing manual work for all to scc. 'I was pcrplcxcd', hc wrote, 'because in Africa I and my colleagues thought it *infra dignitatem* even to wash the plates used for eating. It was the job of stewards!'[137] Many years later, when he was well known as a leader in the struggle against British colonialism in West Africa and the young Nkrumah asked him for advice on studying in the United States, Azikiwe, having internalized this lesson in labor, asked the young student at the start of his career whether he was able-bodied and 'would be willing to do any type of odd job and soil his hands so as to work his way through a university?'.[138]

Some of the Africans who studied in America returned to their countries with the skills and motivation to become leaders. Some became leaders in education for their people. As noted above, Eyo Ita, Ernest Kalibala and Peter Koinange, who had been sent to America by the Phelps-Stokes Fund, came back to establish independent, academically oriented schools, which ranged far afield of the original Phelps-Stokes conception. Others assumed the responsibility of political leadership. James Coleman showed that most of the West African students who studied in the United States during World War II became actively involved in Nigerian politics upon repatriation.[139] Three African leaders who led their countries to freedom, Kwame Nkrumah of Ghana, Nnamdi Azikiwe of Nigeria, and Kamuzu Banda of Malawi, all received their political education while attending black American schools.

The American educational system, black and white alike, apparently encouraged a degree of independent and critical thinking that other systems did not. Sir Eric Ashby, master of Clare College, Cambridge University, spelled out the differential impact of American and British education on their African graduates: 'There [in American universities] they saw that European academic tradition had undergone massive adaptations . . . which seemed appropriate for Africa. . . . A period of study in Britain frequently consolidates in an African a respect for the British educational system. A period of study in America frequently nurtures a dissatisfaction with the British system.'[140] Horace Mann Bond, President of Lincoln University from 1945 to 1947, emphasized that black American schools were unique in promoting leadership skills: 'These were principles of leadership and techniques for exercising leadership for colonial peoples, not available for the student at any University in the British Commonwealth of Nations, nor in Western Europe, nor in any Soviet Republic, nor in Asia, nor elsewhere in the world.'[141]

The Africans who studied in America came back with a deep appreciation of what America had to offer and encouraged other Africans to follow in their footsteps. After his rise to political power in Nigeria, Azikiwe offered scholarships to young Africans to study in the United States and encouraged parents who had the wherewithal to send their sons to black American educational institutions.[142] Between 1935 and 1938, he persuaded fourteen Africans to study in the United States and helped them to gain entrance to the academically oriented Lincoln University.[143] Nkrumah, for his part, returned to Africa full of gratitude for the education in freedom he had received in America. Passing the Statue of Liberty on his departure from the United States, he declared: 'You have opened my eyes to the true meaning of liberty. I shall never rest until I have carried your message to Africa.'[144] After the African states gained their independence, Nkrumah in Ghana, Azikiwe in Nigeria, and Tom Mboya in Kenya all appealed to America for help to build universities in their countries.[145]

The story of the two African-American educational models, the vocational and the academic, in Africa is laced with irony. In bringing to Africa the African-American model of vocational education, grounded in the philosophy, experience and knowledge of black Americans, Jones and the Phelps-Stokes Fund in a way realized the ambitions of the late nineteenth-century advocates of the African-American avant-garde. The initial enthusiasm with which Jones's program was greeted, the positive expectations it evoked, and the credit Africans gave it for many years rested not only on the idea of technical education but also on the African-American myth promulgated by Blyden, Faduma, James Johnson, Aggrey and others, and disseminated by the black American missionaries. But none of the early African-American avant-gardists ever dreamed that their avant-garde would be used not to elevate the Africans but to keep them in their place. Jones turned their intentions inside out, but only to see his narrow and restrictive approach superseded by the academic model, sought by Africans who aspired to the broadest possible liberty and liberation.

The career of Aggrey exemplifies some of the strange twists and turns. Aggrey whole-heartedly supported the application of the Tuskegee approach to Africa and the philosophy of accommodation to white rule that went with it. During his 1921 visit to the Union of South Africa with the Phelps-Stokes Education Commission, for example, he told a large mixed African and white audience: 'When education is offered to you to learn how to work at trades, to till the soil and to become first-class citizens, just jump into it.'[146] On his way to accept the appointment at Achimota College, he wrote to Jones enthusing about the promise that the African-American vocational model held for Africa: 'Today many are every year going to America to study her [black vocational] schools in order to benefit Africa. Thinking of it all, I am grateful to exclaim, "What hath God wrought".'[147] Yet his own education was emphatically academic. Many of the students who were fired by his speeches and personal example eschewed the vocational model and sought an academic education for themselves. And he himself left his post at Achimota after only a year and a half to return to the United States to complete his doctorate on 'British Rule in West Africa' at Columbia University.[148]

The Phelps-Stokes effort to educationally engineer a 'good African' was thwarted by the realities of Africa itself. Jones's reductive version of Booker T. Washington's Tuskegee approach proved utterly impossible to implement on African soil by everyone who tried. Moreover, the winds of change that blew over the continent after World War I soon made Jones's program an anachronism. Jones and the British colonial regime exploited the African-American myth to promote an educational program that they considered beneficial to whites. Aggrey, embodiment of the myth, was their bait. Africans, increasingly antagonistic to colonialism, read the myth differently, taking from Aggrey's example not the compliance and compromising spirit, but the promise of the eagle's flight.

After World War I, the African-American myth supported two types of activities in Africa: one political, the other educational. The political activities soon came to naught. The educational activities survived and bore fruit, but only those educational activities that the Africans themselves chose and which reflected the themes in the myth that they themselves decided had value and meaning. These themes were liberty, egalitarianism, democracy and utilitarianism. Even if they did not formally study politics, the Africans who went to study in the United States after World War I sought and received there a political education, which, after World War II, they would use to make political changes in the map of Africa.

6 The South African Liberal Movement and the Model of the American South

In South Africa the African-American myth was adapted by both blacks and whites in the country's tiny liberal movement. Like believers in other parts of the continent, South African liberals looked to America for solutions to the problems created by white rule. The liberal movement was concentrated in the larger towns, especially Johannesburg and Cape Town, where whites and Africans intermingled in large numbers. It consisted of people of both races held together by a general liberal ethos. South African liberals rejected the prevailing social-Darwinist view that consigned Africans to a fixed place on the lower rungs of the social and biological hierarchy and strove to establish a society that would permit Africans social and economic mobility. At the same time, they were essentially a highly moderate movement. They borrowed the slogan of Cecil Rhodes, the Cape Prime Minister who promised in 1897 'equal rights for all civilized men'.[1] The liberals focused on securing the rights not of all Africans, but of only the relatively limited number of Africans who were civilized, in the sense that they possessed western education and property.

They were divided among themselves along both racial and geographic lines as well as the pattern of race relations that they envisioned. Roughly speaking, there were three schools of thought on this matter: full integration, propounded primarily by pre-Union Cape liberals; bi-racialism, with separate but equal coexistence; and white paternalism within a system of benign segregation under which natives would be permitted to develop economically but not to achieve equal status with whites. All of them, though, waged their struggle against apartheid peacefully and constitutionally. They worked within the prevailing system of segregation, with and through white politicians. They strove to eliminate its abuses in gradual, careful stages, using as their weapon not the gun but western education. They dedicated themselves to the formidable task of trying to persuade the bulk of South African whites of the need for the races to live together in harmony.[2]

Liberal pressures first arose in the British colonies of Natal and especially

145

the Cape in the late nineteenth century, in response to successful efforts on the part of the Afrikaner Bond Party in the Cape and the ruling white minority in Natal to rescind social and political rights which educated Africans had till then enjoyed. The pressures were extended to the rest of South Africa and a clearer, more organized liberal movement emerged with far-reaching political changes following the unification of the British-ruled Cape Colony and Natal with the Boer republics of the Orange Free State and Transvaal in the Union of South Africa in 1910. The unification created a state, unique in sub-Saharan Africa, in which a small minority of white settlers governed the entire country and all its black inhabitants totally free of control by any imperial power. With the exit of the relatively more tolerant British colonial authorities, the country's new, largely Afrikaner government promptly extended the harsh discriminatory regulations in force in the Boer republics to the entire country, systematically depriving Africans of any right to participate in South Africa's social, economic and political life. The Union government progressively chipped away at the limited franchise that the British had extended to educated and propertied Africans in the Cape and, to a lesser extent, in Natal. It systematically ejected Africans from their arable lands and concentrated them on largely unfertile reserves. In addition, it sharply curtailed Africans' freedom of movement, including their rights to live in the white dominated cities, by stringent pass regulations.

The liberal movement worked to counter the progressively more draconian restrictions through a range of organizations, with overlapping aims but with somewhat different emphases and memberships. One set of organizations, consisting of Joint Councils of Europeans and Bantu, the Cape Native Welfare Society, the Bantu Men's Social Center, the Helping Hand Club for Native Girls and others, focused primarily on building racial understanding through social and educational activities which brought together well-educated whites and Africans.[3] The other consisted of a single organization, the South African Native Congress, after 1923 renamed the African National Congress (ANC), formed in 1912 by Pixley Ka I. Seme. This was a largely native organization (though it included some colored activists) aimed at drawing together Africans of all cultural levels and social backgrounds for the purpose of exerting political pressure on the Union governments. These differences notwithstanding, the leadership of the two overlapped considerably in the period under discussion and both relied heavily on persuasion and propaganda, though the ANC supplemented these with such political activities as petitions, mass demonstrations, and occasional strikes. Both were small and essentially powerless. Even in its prime in the 1920s and 1930s, the liberal movement, including the ANC, had no more than a few hundred activists. They published pamphlets, held seminars and organized conferences. To make their persuasions more effective, they sought whatever models they could find of the two races living together.

Two models were available to them. One was that of British Victorian liberalism, which was adopted mainly by the Cape liberals. Under British rule, Cape Africans had enjoyed limited suffrage, with those who met standards of education and property ownership permitted to vote. They also enjoyed greater freedom of expression than Africans in the Boer republics and even in the other British colony, Natal, where the government and the tiny white community carefully monitored the activities of the African majority. Only one African newspaper was published in Natal, several in the Cape. Cape Africans were also admitted to the local interracial Lovedale College, offering both educational opportunities for Africans and a certain amount of racial integration.

African liberals from Cape Province organized themselves and worked with sympathetic whites to gain an expanding role in what they believed was an evolving British system that could eventually result in a non-racial representative government.[4] In the pre-Union period, their most prominent spokesman was John Tengo Jabavu, whose independent black newspaper *Imvo Zabantsundu* (Native Opinion), founded in 1884 with white financing, served as a forum for African interests in the Cape Colony. John T. Jabavu put his energies behind securing the limited Cape franchise against incursions and used his influence and position as editor of the paper to prod white politicians to be responsive to African demands and to persuade Africans to support those who were. According to Sheridan Johns, 'As a spokesman for African interests in the Cape's pre-Union period, Jabavu was consistent both in his insistence that ... Africans possess the same rights as white voters and in his concern for a gradual but, as he hoped, irreversible advance of all Africans to the point where they could share his status as a "civilized British subject." '[5] A measure of his faith in eventual integration was his opposition to the South African Native Congress. In its stead, he founded the short-lived interracial South African Races Congress.

After the Union was established, his efforts were carried on by his eldest son, Davidson Don Jabavu, who, as President of the Cape Native Voters' Convention, similarly struggled to retain the limited Cape franchise for 'civilized' natives, with the hope of eventually having it extended to the rest of the Union. In the post-Union realities, the young Jabavu was more separatist than his father, more ready to work within all-native frameworks, and evidently less adamant about attaining racial equality. But, like his father, he still placed great store in the Cape's British liberal heritage. For many years, he urged natives to cooperate with Europeans, and when, in the course of time the Cape natives were reduced by legislation to the condition of the natives in the rest of the Union, it was to Britain that he turned for remedy.[6] In a 1932 pamphlet entitled 'Native Disabilities in South Africa', he calls for British support against the encroachments of the color bar, urges Britain to retain the colonies adjacent to the Union in order to protect the natives there from the oppression suffered by the natives in the rest of the Union, reminds Britain of its liberal tradition, and affirms: '[W]e still look to Britain as our fountain of justice and regard her as our permanent protector.'[7]

But Britain's acceptance of the principle of segregation in the 1910 unification treaty and its persistent refusal to intervene on behalf of the natives undermined most Africans' faith in Victorian liberalism. For some years, South Africa's liberals continued to court British protection. The African Native Congress sent various petitions and deputations to England asking for assistance against the policies of the Union government. But eventually, as S. M. Molema – who can be regarded as a spokesman for the South African intelligentsia after World War I – wrote in his book *The Bantu Past and Present*, Africans came to feel that: 'British liberalism is offering nothing to the Bantu of South Africa except such morbid creations and fancies as "the Native problem".'[8]

The model that remained was the United States: a multiracial society where different ethnic groups mingled to create one great nation. This model seemed viable because of America's apparent similarities to South Africa. Both countries had large black populations struggling to raise their level of achievement and attain the rights of full citizenship; and in both white habitation was accepted as permanent.[9] The white South African liberal Maurice Evans, who authored two scholarly volumes, *Black and White in South East Africa* (1911) and *Black and White in the Southern States* (1915), wrote that in some parts of the racially stratified states of South Carolina, Mississippi and Alabama, with their huge black populations, he felt as if he were back home in Natal.[10] The example of the United States was broad, flexible and amenable to different readings. Offering various models of racial relationships, it served liberals of various persuasions, all of whom seemed to find precisely the image they were looking for to hold up to South Africa.

One of the most active representatives of the separate-but-equal school is Pixley Ka I. Seme, who had studied at Columbia and Oxford universities. In 1903 he paid a visit to Tuskegee. This marked the starting point for many years of correspondence between him and the school's venerated founder, Booker T. Washington. In one of the first letters, Seme declared, 'We need your spirit in South Africa.'[11] What seems to have attracted Seme was the Booker T. Washington combination of insistence on eventual political rights on the one hand, and, on the other, a kind of black separatism, expressed both in his advocacy of black self-sufficiency and in his oft-quoted and oft-criticized dictum: 'In all things purely social we can be as separate as the fingers, yet one as the hands in all things essential to mutual progress.'[12]

Seme's racial philosophy is expressed in his 1906 article in the *African Abroad*: 'Men have tried to compare races on the basis of some equality. In all the works of nature, equality, if by it we mean identity, is an impossible dream! ... The races of mankind are composed of free and unique individuals. An attempt to compare them on the basis of equality can never be finally satisfactory. Each is self.'[13] This philosophy was probably behind Seme's establishment of the South African Native Congress, whose founding meeting in 1912 brought together local vigilance groups, chiefs, and other prominent Africans from throughout South Africa and the neighboring British territories.[14] When in the early 1930s the ANC was paralyzed by internal divisions, Seme blamed the situation on the lack of native unity and racial pride, which, he pointed out, was to be amply found among African-Americans and was the source of their strength:

My conviction is that here in Africa, as in America, the Africans should refuse to be divided. We need a strong body of men and women to give the leading daily thought and guidance to all our people in their daily duties and struggles as a nation. Such a leading voice can only be produced by a conference composed of the chosen leaders of the people come together for the purpose of building up the nation. ... I cannot ever forget the great vision of national power which I saw in Atlanta Georgia in 1907 when the late Dr. Booker T. Washington presided over the Annual Conference of the Negro Business League of America with delegates representing all Negro enterprises in that New World and representing 20 million Africans in the United States of America, the most advanced of my own race. ... We need more of what the American Negro calls 'Race Pride.' In that country you find coloured people most highly educated and efficient in the leading professions who cannot be distinguished from the white people, nevertheless refusing to be regarded as whites. The mothers are Negro African and they want to remain as Africans also. If our African people would only take a leaf from this book of Negro life in America, how much richer our people would be.[15]

Seme's statement bears all the marks of the African-American myth: the emphasis on the African origins and affinities of American blacks and the belief in their power. If to his American opponents Booker T. Washington represented excessive compromise with racial discrimination, to Seme he epitomized the power to be attained by black self-sufficiency, unity, and loyalty to racial identity. That American blacks were no more a monolithic group than the South African natives riven by tribal, regional and educational differences went by the wayside. What was important to Seme was the model and moral the image held for the blacks of his native land.

Other liberals found in the United States not so much an image of black power but rather an image of racial harmony, in which whites worked with blacks, assisted blacks, and, above all, did not shackle them with the restrictive regulations that made their lives a misery and was the source of endless, corrosive friction in South Africa. This image of America was geared to the country's whites who were fearful of being overwhelmed by the black majority, while the image of African-American solidarity was geared towards the Africans. D. D. T. Jabavu of the Cape, for all his British proclivities, drew upon that image of racial harmony. In 1926 he used the American example to support his arguments against incursions on the native franchise and other native rights in the Cape. Contending rather ingenuously from the platform of the Governor General's Native Conference (1925) that the native vote need not endanger continued white hegemony, he tried to convince his white hearers of this proposition by pointing to the example of the West Indies and the United States, where black people had, or supposedly had, the rights that South African natives were denied. The extracts from the conference proceedings summarize his argument as follows:

> The safest policy was to prove and convince the Natives of the justice of every proposal and give them liberty to develop to the best of their ability. The stopping of the franchise would be purely transient – it could not last. Their future generations would be in a position to insist upon fair play. If injustice were committed today, it would result in a legacy of discomfort, suspicion and ill will. In the West Indies white and black live happily together – there is no fear of the black man there. In America, negroes are living amicably with the whites with full opportunity to develop. If the Government wished white dominance to endure the best way was to give fair play to the black man.[16]

The argument is something of a medley, with images of racial integration and equal opportunity in the New World placed side by side with at least lip service to continued white dominance in South Africa. In other parts of his address, D. D. T. Jabavu grounds his somewhat dubious argument that the black franchise would not endanger white rule on the assumptions 1) that the black vote would remain very small, limited as it was by stringent property and education requirements, and 2) that the 'civilized' natives who would have the vote would know how to appreciate it and the whites who treated them justly. It is difficult to know to what extent the younger Jabavu had actually reconciled himself to white hegemony, so far from his father's vision of full integration. But what does emerge from the statement is the image of the New World where blacks are treated justly and the races can live together to the contentment of both – and the plea that the pattern be applied to South Africa.

A similar, though more hedged and qualified, image of racial harmony in America was evoked by Charles Loram, the so-called father of South African liberalism in the 1920s.[17] Firmly entrenched in the paternalistic school, Loram was concerned primarily with African welfare, with doing 'what good I can for the black folk'. But this good, as he saw it, was to be achieved within a framework of benevolent segregation, in which natives could aspire, at best, to becoming 'junior partners in the firm'.[18] Born in South Africa and educated at Cambridge University, he was exposed to American ideas as a young school inspector in Natal, where the American Zulu Mission played an active role in native education. In 1914 he received a scholarship from the Union government to study educational administration at Teachers College, Columbia University. By the time he returned to Natal, he had made America his model. In a speech probably delivered in the early 1920s, he declared that 'it is the United States with its sound basis of democracy, its sturdy insistence on local rights and its variety of school systems . . . which has most to teach us both in what to follow and what to avoid'.[19] Thus when in 1929 his liberal stand led to conflicts with the newly elected all-Nationalist government and he was fired from his position in the Native Affairs Commission, Loram moved to the United States – a move that followed naturally from his admiration for the American example. In 1931 he settled in as Sterling Professor of Education at Yale University, where he remained until his death in 1940.

Loram found in the greater United States an idealized, even idyllic, image of racial harmony akin to Jabavu's. Describing a personal visit to Hawaii in 1933, Loram expounded at length on how the different races lived in harmony on the island and held that pattern up as a model for South Africa:

> Never have I seen so many racial groups getting on so well together.
> . . . Except for the natural segregation possible in any country, all these

people are equal before the law and mix on terms of courtesy and
even friendship. ... All, irrespective of color or race, who satisfy the
conditions, are American citizens, all travel without restrictions on the
trains and trams, all mix in business and recreation, all go to the same
public schools, and all seem to get along well together. ... I wish that
those South Africans, not only the Negrophobes, but ordinary people
like you and me, who fear the race 'gogga' ['vermin' in Afrikaans] could
visit Hawaii and see how easily people of different races get on when
there is no tradition of race hatred, and where there is equality before
the law.[20]

This is a wistful, almost longing image of racial harmony posited on fellow feeling, the absence of a history of racial hatred, and equality before
the law. Loram himself evidently sensed the tenuousness and distance of
this ideal, noting in the next sentence that neither South Africa nor the
United States proper had enjoyed the necessary freedom from race hatred
in their pasts. Nonetheless, he held up the image not only as proof that
racial harmony is possible, but, like D. D. T. Jabavu, also as proof that it
is possible without endangering white culture, white safety, and white
hegemony: 'I know of course that conditions are different in South Africa,
and I have sympathy with those fine people who honestly fear that our
civilization may be swamped by the great mass of the Native peoples in
Africa, but I feel that they would be comforted, as I was, to see that this
need not be so ... and understand that the way to preserve white civilization is to spread it among the non-white groups.'[21] It was a soothing, com-
forting image directed to South African whites fearful of being swamped by
the native hordes. For all the differences between Hawaii and South Africa,
'this need not be so', Loram declares: South Africa's various races can
similarly live together on terms of courtesy, civility, and even friendship.
   Within the United States proper, Yale University provided Loram with
a similar image of racial harmony, equally idealized and just as unlikely
in South Africa. In a letter dated Christmas 1934, Loram notes, almost
proudly, that a native South African student of his, Z. K. Matthews (who
was to become President of the ANC between 1940 and 1949), 'lived in
the Hall of Graduate Studies on terms of perfect equality with the other
students and told me that never once was he discriminated against on the
grounds of his color'.[22] Yale, Loram writes, provides a milieu in which
people can relate to one another as human beings without regard to race:
'One of the best things about Yale is the way it disregards such accidentals
as color and bases its faculty and student opinion on the more substantial
grounds of scholarship, character, and behavior.'[23] Loram does not note that

the school's apparent freedom from prejudice rests on the elite, overwhelmingly white character of its student body and faculty, who, secure in their position, can readily extend a genteel and even warm acceptance to the academy's few highly select foreign students whom they greatly outnumber. Yale seems to have served Loram as a haven where his liberal vision of interracial harmony under white hegemony came as close to realization as possible.

The American racial harmony paradigm evoked by both Jabavu and Loram was surrounded by a vague aura of white goodwill. At the same time, South African liberals understood that racial harmony in the United States was inseparable from the existence there of a degree of social and political justice that was not available to the natives of their home country. Jabavu and Loram both stated as much. But it took the African physician Alfred Bitini Xuma, who came of age after the establishment of the Union, to emphasize this feature of the American model. Vice-President of interracial Joint Council of Johannesburg and President-General of the ANC between 1940 and 1949, Xuma seems to have had less faith than earlier South African liberals in the vagaries of goodwill. The United States he evoked for both the black and white audiences he addressed was less a place where well-meaning, well-educated people lived happily together whatever their race, than a place of just laws, which checked the power of whites to oppress blacks. The United States provided Xuma mainly with a constitutional model to hold up to his countrymen.

In his pained and poignant address entitled 'Bridging the Gap Between White and Black in South Africa', delivered before the Conference of European and Bantu Christian Student Associations at Fort Hare in 1930, Xuma argued that the gap between the races in South Africa could not be bridged so long as the blacks were legally deprived of the rights of full citizenship, and he held up the American Constitution as the model of everything that the Union's Constitution and laws were not. The South African Constitution reinstated the color bar and the laws based on it progressively stripped the native blacks of the franchise and other basic rights of citizenship, Xuma asserted. But American blacks are full and enfranchised citizens: 'If we compare certain portions of the constitution of the Union of South Africa with that of the United States of America, we find that the Constitution of the latter country was based on a code of morals and ethics recognizing liberties for all citizens of the country as expressed in the preamble and the XIVth and XVth amendments.' He went on to quote from the preamble to prove that it refers to all the people in the United States, including the former slaves, and from the two amendments to show that they, indeed, grant full citizenship and voting rights to all people regardless of color. To Xuma this meant that, for all the discrimination they suffered, African-Americans had basic rights and, moreover, grounds for hope that were denied to South African natives. 'Thus we see that whatever may be the practice in certain sections of the United States, the principles of liberty and justice is the foundation stone in the law of the land. It gives hope and citizenship rights to all alike.'[24]

Similarly, with regard to land. Citing the expulsions of Africans from their lands by the Union government and the constant harassment of the pass laws, Xuma observed that American blacks could own property, live where they pleased in the cities, and move about freely – all the things blacks could not do in South Africa:

> If we look into the United States land policy, or practice, we again find no comparison but a striking contrast to South African land policy. Land in city or country can be bought by any citizen of the United States. For instance, there are today over 1,000,000 Negro farmers most of whom own their land; others rent or plow on shares. These people were, only 70 years ago, so poor as slaves that they did not even own themselves. Today, some are landlords owning millions of acres with full title deeds to the land in the same way as any other American citizens. In the cities, the Negroes buy and reside on their own property in any part of the city, notwithstanding the fact that in certain sections individual Whites had protested.[25]

The picture is obviously idealized, with African-American land ownership greatly overestimated, the exploitation of sharecropping either glossed over or not comprehended, and the de facto ghettoization in American cities underplayed. But what was important for Xuma in the American constitutional model, and also to many western-educated Africans in other parts of the continent, was the principle that racial discrimination was not enshrined in federal law, as it was in South Africa's code of law. Federal law even protected American blacks from the prejudice of white individuals. Citing an American Supreme Court ruling that residential segregation is unconstitutional, Xuma exalts: 'Thus we see the striking contrast between a country whose foundation is principle and the other whose structure is expediency.'[26]

The racial unity, racial harmony and constitutional models were all highly idealized and highly theoretical. South African liberals also looked to America for more concrete ways of dealing with their country's racial problems, as well as for financial assistance in doing so. In particular, they sought models and aid in the fields of education, interracial understanding, and research that they thought could have practical uses.

EDUCATION: THE KEY TO INTEGRATION

Regardless of their race or the model they chose, all South African liberals regarded western education as the *sine qua non* to integration, after Christianity.[27] 'Our salvation, as a people, is in education and in that alone', proclaimed South African liberal John L. Dube.[28] Education was seen as the civilizing force which would, on the one hand, enable Africans to manage their own affairs in the modern world and, on the other hand, bring them up to the level of the whites. The assumption – or hope – was that the discrimination against blacks was based not on their race as such but on their cultural and educational inferiority. Once Africans lifted themselves up to the level of the whites and closed the gap, the liberals assumed, they would be accepted as partners in the South African enterprise. Thus, the future South African Nobel Peace Prize winner, Chief Albert Luthuli, wrote optimistically about his experience at Adams College in Natal in the 1920s: 'In the days when Professor Matthews and I were young teachers . . . it seemed mainly a matter of proving our ability and worth as citizens, and that did not seem impossible. We were, of course, aware of the existence of colour prejudice, but we did not dream that it would endure and intensify as it has.'[29] The assumption was behind the repeated liberal calls for greater government support for native education at every level.

In addition to church schools, the United States offered three different models of education for blacks: education in northern white schools; education in all-black academically oriented colleges, such as Atlanta, Fisk and Lincoln; and education in vocational schools using the Booker T. Washington model. Most of the South African liberals who looked to America for inspiration favored the third. As indicated in the previous chapter, the model permitted widely opposed interpretations. While Africans hoped to attain from its industrial and agricultural schools a high level of technical competence which would give them the skills with which to emulate whites, the Phelps-Stokes Commissions and the British colonial authorities saw such education as a means of providing Africans with horizontal mobility but preventing them from acquiring knowledge and skills that would enable, or worse, encourage them to challenge white hegemony, either in the economic or political arena. In South Africa, the liberals who espoused the idea of equal but separate co-existence could regard industrial education as a means of providing Africans with a modern trade or profession, which would allow them to rise above the position of unskilled laborers to which they had been relegated by whites. In other words, they could regard industrial education as a lever to self-sufficiency in a bi-racial society. For the paternalists on the other hand, the appeal of the Booker. T. Washington model would have been in the limited, purely functional training it offered. Industrial education could be a means of assuaging Africans' demands for better education while keeping them segregated and unequal in their rural communities.

John. L. Dube, the most prominent western-educated African in Natal in the early part of the twentieth century, provides an example for the first interpretation. Educated at Oberlin College in Ohio and the Union Missionary Training Institute in Brooklyn, Dube was the founder of the Zulu language newspaper *Langa Lase Natal*, and the first President-General of the South African Native Congress. His vision of racial relationships is suggested in a statement he made in 1914 as head of the Native Congress deputation sent to protest against the Native Land Act that had become law the previous year. His objection to the law, he made it very clear, was not that it segregated the races but that it deprived Africans of all independent means of supporting themselves and thereby forced them to serve as cheap labor for whites. The inequality of rights was abhorrent, but Africans made 'no protest against the principle of separation so far as it can be fairly and practically carried out', Dube declared.[30]

For Dube, as for Seme and others, Booker T. Washington was more than simply an educator. He was born into slavery and attained standing in America's interracial but bigoted society and was educating his people to do the same. Thus when Dube was elected to his post in the South African Native National Congress, he wrote in his letter of acceptance, on 2 February 1912, that 'for my patron saint I select that great and edifying man, Booker Washington', and expressed the wish that the black American leader 'were nigh to give us the help of his wise council!'.[31] Dube was so staunch an admirer that he was called 'South Africa's Booker T. Washington'.[32] In 1897 Dube visited Tuskegee for the specific purpose of learning enough about industrial education to apply the model to his native Natal. Addressing an audience of African-Americans, he said: 'I have come down to Tuskegee and Hampton to learn something of industrial education, for after working among my people in my own land, I find that the kind of work done at Hampton is the kind of work my people need.' The need, as he defined it, was much more far-reaching than the provision of limited, everyday skills to which Jones and the Phelps-Stokes Commission, along with his colleague in the liberal movement, Charles Loram, would later restrict it. Such education, as he saw it, was nothing less than the first step towards the Africans' reclamation of their country: 'Think what two such schools as Hampton and Tuskegee would do for our people', he went on to tell his African-American hearers. 'They would revolutionize the country, for the Zulus are intellectually and physically capable of the highest civilization . . . and the whites know that if we are educated as they are we shall rule the country.'[33]

On 8 August 1900, not long after he returned from America, he opened the Zulu Christian School, later renamed the Ohlange Institute, in Natal. Like Tuskegee, Ohlange combined academic and vocational subjects. The school had something of a dual character, in keeping with its founder's far-reaching aims. It was opened as a vocational training institution, presented itself as such to suspicious whites, and offered the requisite trade and homemaking courses, underpinned by a stern Calvinist morality and bourgeois ethos. At the same time, along with their vocational training and work on the school buildings and grounds, its students also took courses in the social sciences, literature and music; were prepared for admission to Fort Hare Native College; and were kept politically aware through political discussion and debate.[34] After World War I, commercial courses began to replace industrial ones, preparing the students for white collar jobs that were the privileged preserve of the settlers.[35]

Ohlange was an independent institution, run by South African natives. In this it emulated the all-black self-sufficiency of Tuskegee. Needless to say, the white community and the government of Natal viewed it as a challenge to their power and provided almost no financial support. In the hope of persuading them to adopt a more positive attitude to African education, Dube became active in numerous official and semi-official bodies connected with the education and social welfare of Africans, including the Natal Native Education Advisory Board, the Native Conference, the Natives Representative Council, and the Joint Council movement, which tried to promote racial harmony and dialogue.[36] These efforts did not achieve their end and Dube was compelled to apply abroad for financial support for his school. He sought funding in both Britain and the United States, but his efforts across the Atlantic were the more fruitful. Like African-Americans who obtained financing for Tuskegee and Hampton and other black educational institutions from the white community, Dube too turned to American whites.

Dube visited the United States a second time in 1896. A year later, he enrolled as a student at the Union Missionary Training Institute in Brooklyn where he made contact with a group of white Americans. In the early years of the twentieth century he used this connection to raise funds for his school in Natal. The group, called 'The American Committee', sent Dube household goods, farm tools, clothing, a printing press, iron bedsteads, schoolroom desks, books for the school library, tools for blacksmithing and carpentry shops, household utensils, and money. It built a men's dormitory in 1907, and between 1902 and 1910 provided funds for Ohlange students to study in the United States. In the winter of 1927 Dube travelled around the United States on a fundraising campaign and was successful in obtaining financial commitments from American donors, including $700 for a trades building.[37] Unlike the British, Dube's American donors permitted him to run his school with reasonable autonomy. Thus using an American model and relying largely on American funding, Dube was able to create and maintain a school that the scholar R. Hunt Davis, Jr has described as 'an example of Africans adapting black American educational concepts to further African self-sufficiency, not for the purpose of ultimate incorporation into the white dominated society but for the restoration of African nationhood'.[38]

The paternalistic interpretation of the Booker T. Washington model is exemplified by Charles Loram. Loram was a close associate of Thomas Jesse Jones. Like Jones, Loram had studied the applicability of the Tuskegee-Hampton model to South Africa. In 1917, the year Jones's report on black education in America was published, Loram published his own book based on his doctoral dissertation, 'The Education of the South African Native', with very similar ideas, which he had arrived at separately. Just as Jones was the natural choice to head the Phelps-Stokes Commission, so Loram was the natural choice of the Union government to accompany the commissions' tours of South Africa. Loram promulgated elementary school for all natives and was instrumental in promoting and eventually instituting the idea of government responsibility for native education at a time when many whites, from workers fearful of native competition through officials wary of the aspirations of educated Africans, objected to any education at all for Africans.[39] It is against this backdrop that Loram's admiration for President Franklin D. Roosevelt's firm support of the right of blacks to equal education, and criticism of the American educational system for neglecting black children, should be read: 'It is as if General Hertzog had said openly a year or so ago', exclaimed Loram, 'that the Nationalists in the Orange Free State were not doing enough for the education of the Natives.'[40] The statement, an indictment of Hertzog, is Loram's way of saying that if the American government can support black education, so can South African politicians.

At the same time, Loram presented education for the native not as an end in itself but as a way of reducing racial friction and perpetuating white power. 'The best hope for the solution of the problem of race adjustment in South Africa', declared Loram, '. . . lies in the education by the dominant whites of the black race in the light of its past history and institutions, its mental and moral make-up, and its political, social and economic future.'[41] It was an emaciated education, controlled by whites and adapted to the supposed limitations of the native, whom, throughout his writings, Loram referred to as 'primitive', 'retarded' and 'backward'.[42] 'The course of study should take into account the peculiar experiences of the Natives', expostulated Loram in *The Education of the South African Native*. 'From the beginning, the education given should be meaningful to the Natives, and to this end should lead up to the future occupations open to them.'[43] These occupations were largely manual and menial, and heavily agricultural.

Loram criticized native education in his home country as 'very much a bookish affair' and 'too academic and too little related to the everyday needs of the Africans'.[44] The criticism was consistent with contemporary views of much of missionary education, which was widely regarded as irrelevant to the lives and needs of African students. But the full import of his position is brought home in a rhetorical question he raised: 'Which is really more important in the African villages – practical hygiene or the ability to read? Elementary agriculture or geography? Wise recreation or arithmetic?' These questions are based on Jones's notion of the four essentials of black education: sanitation and health, agriculture and simple industry, the decencies and safeties of the home, and healthful recreation.[45] They are a far cry from Dube's interpretation of the Booker T. Washington model, as well as from the archetype itself, whose dignification of labor did not entail slighting the mind.

At both Tuskegee and Ohlange, industrial and agricultural education complemented and was complemented by basic academic studies. In Loram's conception they supplanted book learning. Early on in his career he urged the higher education of a select cadre of native leaders at Fort Hare Native College, but his reasoning was that if Africans could not obtain college training in their own country, where it could be properly supervised, they would seek it abroad, where it could not. On the whole, Loram was averse to academic studies for the bulk of South Africa's natives. He wished to reverse the academic emphasis of its schools for natives in favor of commercial and industrial training.[46]

At various stages in his career, he tried to put his preference into practice. As Chief Inspector of Native Education in Natal between 1917 and 1920, he dropped academic subjects such as algebra, geometry and translation from the curricula of the province's secondary schools, and substituted for them such subjects as hygiene and nature study, agriculture, woodwork, needlework, and domestic science.[47] From the mid-1920s, using his position on the South African Native Affairs Commission, he worked with Jones to institute the Jeanes Fund system in South Africa and other parts of the continent. Among the functions of the itinerant Jeanes supervisors, to Loram's mind, was to help rural teachers supplement the three R's with 'simple industrial work'.[48] His model for the system was the Penn School in an island off South Carolina, whose attraction was that its curriculum embodied Jones's four essentials. To promote the system, Loram arranged for South African educators, missionaries and government officials to visit Penn, distributed literature about Penn to persons involved in African education, and placed articles about the school in South African periodicals.[49]

Loram's efforts to subvert full education for natives were not as racist as they seem. His attitude probably stemmed at least in part from general British elitism. It should be remembered that higher education in Britain was limited and only a tiny proportion of students ever reached university in Loram's day. Nor were Loram's objections to higher education for Africans entirely consistent. Loram did not disallow the possibility that natives could join the elite, as is clear from his warm praise of Z. K. Matthews at Yale: 'Every one was struck by his poise, gentlemanly behavior and his ability. So successful was he that Yale University allowed him to complete all his Ph.D. courses and residential requirements in a year.'[50] In the same spirit Loram attempted to facilitate the M.A. studies in America of another African student, A. J. B. Desmore, principal of the Trafalgar Junior School at Cape Town. But such students were few and far between, and Loram seems not to have generalized from their example to the needs and abilities of other native students.[51] Loram's attitudes towards native education, as towards other aspects of the liberal ethos, were fraught with contradictions, born of the inherently opposing impulses of his desire to do and be good, on the one hand, and to retain power, on the other. A biographical essay of Charles Loram describes him as 'an educator and not-so-liberal liberal of British origin'.[52]

Cape liberals too adapted a version of the Booker T. Washington model, though not for many years. Initially they were wary of American education of any kind. They shared British skepticism about the merits of American schools, which they regarded as superficial, and they were especially dubious of the quality of African-American institutions.[53] More essentially, pre-Union Cape liberals were concerned that American-style schools run by and for blacks encouraged separatism and racial self-identification, impulses which could impede the full integration to which they aspired. For example, John T. Jabavu's newspaper *Imvo* roundly criticized the AME Church schools in the Cape for espousing racial segregation, which, it maintained, had no foundation in Christian doctrine and fed racial animosity.[54] Moreover, Cape liberals regarded higher education less as a means for attaining skills than as the vehicle for eventual full integration. To this end, they wanted Africans to be educated in the Cape itself along with whites. The Cape liberals' preferred alternative was thus the inter-racial Lovedale College in the Cape, run by their traditional allies, the white missionaries of the United Free Church of Scotland, who had done a great deal to promote native rights throughout the nineteenth century. Viewing Lovedale not only as an institution which would educate Africans to the level of whites, but also as a paradigm of integration for the rest of South African society, the liberals threw their support behind it.[55]

The Cape liberals' distrust of American education began to ease as their dreams for eventual integration waned. The elder Jabavu modified his opposition to black American education in 1903 when his son, Davidson Don, was rejected solely on racial grounds by Dale College, a high school in King Williamstown. That rejection undermined his advocacy of racial integration through education. Although he did not go so far as to send his son to America – he sent Davidson Don to complete his studies in England – the elder Jabavu was no longer opposed to Africans studying in America. Thus, he changed his negative attitude toward the Reverend Pambani Mzimba, who in 1898 had broken away from the United Free Church of Scotland in order to establish an all-black church of his own and, from 1901, had been sending Africans to study in the United States to provide it with native officers. The education in America that Jabavu now endorsed was at the all-black Lincoln University where Mzimba sent his students. He disregarded the criticism of his liberal opponents, who claimed in the *Cape Times* that his support of Mzimba was imbued with Ethiopianism.[56]

Further steps in the adoption of the American model were made in the course of the establishment of Fort Hare Native College. To meet the growing demand for higher education for natives, Cape liberals threw themselves into the campaign to establish a college for Africans at Fort Hare. The college would provide much-wanted educational opportunities for natives within South Africa. For Loram and other white liberals, this had the advantage of enabling white supervision. For John Tengo Jabavu and other non-white Cape liberals of his generation, it had the advantages of providing an alternative to higher education in America, where students could be exposed to undesirable influences, and of maintaining British values and associations.[57] During the more than a decade that it took to establish the college, John Tengo Jabavu put much of his energies and the support of his newspaper into making it a reality, going so far as to briefly back the 1913 Native Land Act in return for government support of the project.[58]

Fort Hare, built with the cooperation of the government and the active involvement of the United Free Church of Scotland, could be seen as a joint black-white enterprise, and John T. Jabavu originally expected that natives would have a greater say in the school's running than they were, in fact, ever allowed.[59] Yet as an all-native college, Fort Hare represented both a recognition of and a response to the incremental death of the Cape liberals' integrationist aspirations. The reality of segregation suddenly made the Booker T. Washington model, however interpreted, relevant to the Cape. Not long after the elder Jabavu became active in promoting Fort Hare, he began to publish praises of Booker T. Washington. A 1906 editorial in *Imvo* recommended the institution of Tuskegee-style practical education at Fort Hare and drew a highly favorable portrait of the American leader. In keeping with the Cape liberals' still pro-white sentiments and lingering hopes for eventual integration, the editorial commended, in addition to Washington's efforts to uplift his people, his devotion 'to the gigantic task of smoothing the relations between the whites and his race'. The editorial went on to contrast Washington's policies of racial reconciliation with the separatism of the AME Church.[60] This view of Booker T. Washington the reconciler is very different from Seme's view of Washington the separatist.

The reality of segregation also led to the introduction of Tuskegee-type vocational courses at Lovedale. The courses were first introduced by its principal James Stewart after his 1903 visit to Tuskegee. Since industrial education had great appeal among natives at this point in time, Stewart introduced the courses as a means of drawing Africans away from the competing AME Church and Mzimba's breakaway African church. His successor, the Reverend James Henderson, developed this policy in a further attempt to use the Booker T. Washington appeal to restore ebbing white missionary prestige. Interestingly, while Stewart's approach to the Tuskegee model was geared to promoting the creation of a fairly sophisticated class of independent African farmers, Henderson's, which coincided with and was later reinforced by Loram's, was aimed at preparing African farmer apprentices and industrial workers.[61]

Davidson Don Jabavu, like his father, also took up the Tuskegee banner. Jabavu visited Tuskegee in June 1913, with the aim, like Dube before him, of studying the applicability of its methods to South African natives. Asked by the Union of South Africa's Minister of Native Affairs to write a report on Tuskegee and its 'suitability to the conditions of the natives under the Union', he produced a 42-page document describing the Tuskegee Institute and making recommendations, including the experimental application of its combined industrial-academic curriculum in a few willing South

African institutions and the introduction of agricultural training with the help of imported Tuskegee graduates or of Bantus especially sent to Tuskegee for instruction.[62] Tuskegee in particular, and the American education available to blacks in general, provided D. D. T. Jabavu with a dual model of black self-sufficiency and intellectual capability on the one hand, and of white support for black advancement on the other. Much of Jabavu's report reads like a consciously balanced, somewhat methodical production, carefully covering the various aspects of the Tuskegee program, giving just due to its academic, industrial and agricultural studies, and to its research department.

But along with praising the school's industrial and agricultural syllabi, its work-study combination, and the fact that the students were paid for their labors, Jabavu takes pains to point out the school's intellectual virtues. Every student pursues academic studies, he is careful to state right from the beginning. He gives a list and synopsis of all of Washington's books and presents Tuskegee as proof that blacks are capable of attaining a respectable intellectual level on their own: 'The absence of white men, the successful administration of a purely Negro faculty in an intellectual village of this sort is not among the least significant phenomena [*sic*] of Tuskegee.' At the same time, he lauds the United States for providing the opportunities and support for such black self-actualization. Financially, he points out: 'The American Negroes are able to count largely on the generosity of white citizens for their institutions. While Tuskegee has to raise £30,000 yearly from the public, it has taken a decade to raise half the sum for the South African Native College.'[63] Moreover, he notes, though almost in passing, while South Africa has only one academic college open to blacks, African-Americans have the advantage of several such institutions as well as the possibility of being admitted to northern white universities. The message is clear. The dual image of black ability and white support in America underlies Jabavu's recommendation in the report for '[a]mpler provision for Native Higher Education' in South Africa.[64]

The various themes raised in the report are reiterated in 1920 in a paper entitled 'Native Educational Needs', in which D. D. T. Jabavu outlines, in order, the needs for academic, industrial, manual, agricultural and religious education for Africans. These aspects of native education are all of a piece and cannot be separated from one another. Although Jabavu comments favorably on Loram and makes such Loram-like statements as 'It [agriculture] is the most important thing in native life and therefore deserves a place in the school career of our boys', his interpretation of the Tuskegee model remains closer to Dube's. Under the heading 'Academic training',

D. D. T. Jabavu asserts that 'There is a need for secondary schools to feed the new Native College at Fort Hare' and that '[t]he college itself needs support in the way of scholarships and endowment if its development is not to be retarded'.[65] Under the heading 'Industrial training' he complains about 'the policy of our native industrial institutions that the native is to be trained not to be independent and to compete on equal terms with white artisans, but to fall somewhere short in this line', and holds up Tuskegee-style vocational training as the corrective that would enable native economic independence and competitive ability. 'Tuskegee and Hampton have much to teach us in this line', he affirms.[66]

Jabavu's strong advocacy of the Tuskegee educational model may have been related to his disillusion with the missionaries, in whom the previous generation of Cape liberals had placed their faith. Among the complaints that Jabavu outlines in his essay 'Native Unrest', read before the Natal Missionary Conference in 1920, was that unlike the dedicated and earnest missionaries of old who loved and understood the native, modern missionaries were cold and superior acting.[67] The Tuskegee educational model seems to have provided Jabavu with a black American alternative to the white missionary led program, which seemed no longer to have the Africans' best interests at heart.

During the same period, however, Jabavu also held up the Booker T. Washington model to rather different ends. The Tuskegee report and 'Native Educational Needs' had emphasized the dovetailing of academic and vocational educational training to the benefit of the native and held up the Tuskegee model as one that the South African government could and should adopt to that purpose. In his 1919 address to the Native Welfare Association in Johannesburg, Jabavu shifted his emphasis to the training of a native workforce that would benefit not only the natives but the country's whites. Beginning with an overview of the inefficiencies of native farming methods, for which he draws heavily on Loram's *Education of the South African Native*, he moves to the more general lack of training and motivation of the African laborer and in Loramesque fashion offers up the Booker T. Washington educational approach as what is needed to teach the natives to value work.

Most native schooling teaches Africans to despise labor, Jabavu contended, giving as an example his own alma mater, Lovedale, where the boys were forced to do demeaning and meaningless make-work like sweeping the school yard and breaking stones. The result was a contempt for manual labor and, ultimately, a poorly trained, poorly motivated native labor force. But at Tuskegee, 'boys receive pay for all manual labor and manual work is glorified per se, the outcome being that every Tuskegee boy seeks for renumerative employment'. And again: 'At Tuskegee, Alabama, I found that Booker T. Washington owed his phenomenal success as an educator and social reformer to the practical methods he applied in his school whereby he taught the American Negro the commercial value of manual work.' With such training, Jabavu holds, 'we shall have gone a long way to help employees of labor whether in mines, in municipalities, or in agriculture, as well as to render the Native a tremendous asset to the country's production'.[68] At the same time, he urged the adaptation of the modern agricultural techniques taught at Tuskegee and Hampton, using well-trained African-Americans brought in to teach the Africans.[69] D. D. T. Jabavu was convinced that modern agricultural technology brought over by African-Americans would work as a cure for the ills of African agriculture. Those ills, according to the scholar. Colin Bundy, were caused less by native lack of agricultural knowledge than by the restrictions imposed on independent native farmers to keep them from competing with whites and to ensure a constant supply of cheap African labor.[70]

The emphasis on the productive value of Tuskegee-style education was consistent with the topic of the address, which was not education as such but 'Natives in Agriculture', as well as with Booker T. Washington's own practical bent. Nor were all of its assertions new for Jabavu. But they seem strangely out of place for the man that Jabavu was: a university-educated African intellectual who was one of the first members of the classics faculty at Fort Hare, founded in 1916. The speech seems to reflect Jabavu's efforts to adjust, and to help his people adjust, to the ever-increasing restrictions placed on them by the Union government. In the Tuskegee report, Jabavu had included a brief character sketch of Booker T. Washington. After pointing out the great man's freedom from hatred towards whites, his realism, and his dedication to the educational and material needs of his people, Jabavu turns to the criticism of Washington by Du Bois and other northerners: that he compromised with discrimination. Jabavu's comments are somewhat double-edged: on the one hand, he acknowledges that Washington's avoidance of political issues limits the 'active guidance and concentration' he can provide in the political realm; on the other hand, he points out that conditions in the American South are very different from those in the North, from where Washington's critics came, and asserts that Washington is 'the right man for the peculiar conditions' there.[71] Jabavu's reductive application of the Tuskegee approach in 'Natives in Agriculture' seems to reflect his efforts to work for the interests of his people in a similarly oppressive environment, making the necessary compromises to do so. If to the elder Jabavu, Booker T. Washington was the great reconciler, for the younger Jabavu, caught in the tightening vise of the Union government, racial reconciliation must sometimes have seemed remote. What D. D. T. Jabavu felt was needed was a model figure who could maneuver, and teach Africans to maneuver, in the increasingly harsh conditions they faced.

Xuma, of the same generation as D. D. T. Jabavu, seems to have avoided the trap in which Jabavu apparently found himself by turning to what can be considered yet a different version of the American educational model: interracial academic education, which D. D. T. Jabavu mentioned in passing but never pressed in his Tuskegee report. Xuma spent over a decade studying, working and living in the United States. He went in 1912, as a not-so-young man of nineteen, to complete his high school studies at Tuskegee Institute, to which he was drawn, among other things, by the possibility of earning his keep in the process. Arriving penniless, he was taken into the home of Booker T. Washington, where, according to Washington's wife, he 'was just like one of the children in the house'.[72] Like Jabavu and many others before him, he apparently developed enormous respect for his mentor; in later years he frequently repeated Washington's maxims, 'Learn by doing' and 'It can be done', and also lived by them. Also like Jabavu and others, he was drawn to the potential that modern agricultural techniques taught at Tuskegee had for African farming. The title of the commencement address he gave at Tuskegee was 'The Clang of the Forge: Problems in Poultry Raising'.[73] Only for Xuma, Tuskegee was not an end but a beginning. From there, he went on to the University of Minnesota College of Agriculture, where he earned a B.Sc. in veterinary science, and then proceeded to obtain an M.D. with a specialization in obstetrics and gynecology from Northwestern University Medical School. When he returned to South Africa, he became, to use the words of the *Chicago Tribune*, 'the best physician in the territory, financially independent, his practice was principally among the prejudiced white South Africans'.[74]

His personal experience seems to have convinced him that natives did not require a special type of education, different from that given to whites, and, indeed, that there was no such thing as the native mentality that Loram assumed and D. D. T. Jabavu seemed to buy into. While Jabavu had emphasized the material gains that native education held out for both races, Xuma, setting the stakes much higher, stressed the role of education in providing the African leadership that in his view was essential to bridging the gap between the races: 'The educated African is our hope, our bridge. He is an asset that responsible and thinking White South Africa cannot afford either to ignore or to alienate without disastrous results in the long run.'[75] Education for leadership called for something different than Tuskegee-style training. In the same address in which he hailed the American constitutional model, Xuma urged a return to integrated, academically oriented education on the Cape model:

> in the Cape Colony, the earlier educational curriculum was identical for both Europeans and Bantu. Lovedale Mission Institution was opened with a class of 9 Europeans and of 11 Bantu students. . . . European and African students studied side by side. None seemed the worst for it. As a matter of fact, these generations of students produced some of the ablest and most prominent men in South Africa on both sides of the color line. The Africans suffered no disabilities by this arrangement. The Europeans lost nothing in prestige by it. They were all being prepared and trained to play their part as citizens in their common country. . . . [The native students] were primitive men so-called, not a day removed from savagery or from the life of barbarism, and yet side by side with White boys, they mastered the White man's education without special adaptation to Native mentality and needs and above all made the best use of their education for the good of their country.[76]

This description of natives and whites studying together at Lovedale, so different from Jabavu's picture of the school, makes no reference to America, but rather harkens back to the integrated Cape education of bygone times. But it may be suggested, though, that it was Xuma's long studies in the United States that enabled him to revive this image. It is a vision which was reluctantly relinquished by the elder Jabavu and which D. D. T. Jabavu let flag. How Xuma's American studies fed this vision of equal higher education for Africans can only be surmised. It was certainly nourished by the education, largely in white universities, that he received in the United States. But the younger Jabavu was similarly educated in white universities in Britain. Perhaps it was the education in liberty that the second generation of students in Africa received that made the difference. Whatever the inspiration, Xuma was an ideological kin to Faduma and to Faduma's mentor, Du Bois, who advocated high quality academic education for the purpose of training black leadership and meeting the intellectual and spiritual needs of blacks, which they insisted were no less than those of whites. Xuma's advocacy of equal education for whites and blacks, his refutation of the idea, adapted by D. D. T. Jabavu no less than by Loram, that natives have special educational needs, harken back to these men's insistence that the needs of black and white students are ultimately the same.

AMERICAN MODELS IN INTERRACIAL ORGANIZATIONS

American models also inspired interracial organizations that grew up in South Africa in the 1920s. One type consisted of what might be classified as welfare cum dialogue organizations, modeled on the interracial organizations that developed in the United States, and especially in the South, during and after World War I to reduce racial tension and smooth the way to interracial cooperation. In 1921, the idea of such organizations was adapted to South Africa at the suggestion of Thomas Jesse Jones and James Aggrey. During their visit to the region with the Phelps-Stokes Education Commission, the considerable native discontent in the country boiled over into bloody clashes between Africans and police in Bloemfontein, Port Elizabeth and other towns.[77] Drawing on their knowledge of the interracial organizations established in communities in the southern United States, Jones and Aggrey suggested forming similar groups in South Africa, where Africans and whites could work together to find practical means of increasing racial understanding.[78]

Their suggestion led to the formation in Johannesburg in 1921 of the first Joint Council of Europeans and Africans, where western-educated Africans and Europeans came together to discuss everyday matters. The Joint Councils were mainly occupied with African social-welfare issues, as well as with cultivating interracial cooperation. For instance, of nine points listed on the agenda of a meeting of the Executive Committee of the Johannesburg Joint Council of Europeans and Africans, dated 7 June 1937, five concerned African social and welfare activities; one, African education; one, race relations; and two, the council's internal matters.[79] The Johannesburg Joint Council was a precursor to similar councils elsewhere in the country. Branches were set up in other parts of Transvaal, in Natal, and also in the Cape, where its interracial format was consistent with the Cape liberals' ideals.

The councils were an expression of liberal optimism, of the belief that goodwill and understanding between the races would lead to an improvement in the lot of the African. This is the spirit in which the Reverend Abner Mtimkulu, in the *Cape Times* of 30 May 1924, noted that 'The Welfare Societies and the joint council have supplied a long-felt need and should bridge the gulf between Europeans and natives; should educate public opinion of their wants and needs, and create confidence by assisting them.'[80] The Joint Council movement seemed to flourish. In 1926 the various councils were joined under the title of the Federated Joint Councils and Welfare Societies.[81] In 1927, the Phelps-Stokes Fund contributed $2,000 to help finance the movement, and in 1928 the Carnegie Corporation donated $3,750 to the movement to be spent on welfare work among Africans over a five-year period.[82] The financial aid of these American foundations helped the movement expand. By 1934, there were about thirty Joint Councils in various parts of South Africa.

One of the major achievements of the Joint Council movement was the introduction of liberal ideas to broader segments of white South African society. In 1923, and again in 1927, black and white leaders from all areas of the Union met for the European Bantu Conference, held under the aegis of the Federal Council of the Dutch Reformed Churches. The first such interracial meetings on a nationwide scale in the history of the Union, the conferences evoked great enthusiasm among the supporters of an interracial society. Remarkably, the conferences were initiated and run by Afrikaners, who of all the whites in the country offered the strongest opposition to equal co-existence of the races. These conferences served as a public forum where Africans articulated their main grievances concerning the Land Act of 1913, restrictions on Africans in urban areas, and the lack of African political representation. These grievances found their way to the conferences' resolutions. Neither the resolutions nor the discussions which preceded them were specifically political, but they 'tended to support those who were arguing for a sharp reversal of government policy away from the accelerating trend to segregation'.[83] South African liberals welcomed the Dutch Reformed Churches' initiatives. Professor Edgar Brookes, historian and white liberal activist, called the 1923 conference 'one of the turning points in the history of Race Relations in South Africa'.[84]

The Joint Council movement took root in South Africa at about the same time as a wave of Garveyism struck the Cape Peninsula with the opening of four branches of the UNIA. Supporters of the Garveyite movement were articulate in raising their voices against the liberal efforts to bring together whites and Africans. For instance, James Thaele, an African from the Cape who had returned from the United States in the early 1920s imbued with UNIA ideology, bitterly attacked the 1923 conference organized by the Federal Council of the Dutch Reformed Churches when he stated that the meeting and other similar attempts at dialogue were an exercise in white hypocrisy. In an article in the *Workers' Herald* he appealed, in Garveyist fashion, 'to the racial consciousness of the radical aboriginal to use all the means to rouse the African race to wake from their long sleep of many decades'.[85] The influence of the UNIA waned until by 1924 the South African branches folded.[86] James Thaele, for instance, left his radical stand and joined the ranks of the liberals.[87] An official report of the Union government stated that 'American Negro Propaganda', as the South African Native Affairs Commission dubbed Garveyism, had some influence in Cape Town and Johannesburg, 'but the results achieved do not seem to have justified the promoters in the belief that the Bantu of the Union would welcome salvation for their race under a regime imported from the Western Continent'.[88]

The Joint Council movement continued its activities after the dissolution of the UNIA branches; however, it became clear to the liberal leaders that the effectiveness of the Joint Councils and the Dutch Reformed Churches' conferences was limited. The conferences were isolated events; and although the Joint Councils were ongoing, neither of these frameworks had much impact on the Union governments, which proceeded virtually unperturbed with their systematic curtailment of native rights. To deal with this reality, the intellectually minded liberals who led the Joint Council movement turned not to political activity, but to research. In May 1929 several leaders in the Joint Council movement, among them Loram, Rheinallt Jones, the Johannesburg accountant Howard Pim, the historian Edgar Brookes, and D. D. T. Jabavu, met at the Johannesburg home of the Reverend Ray E. Phillips of the American Board of Commissioners for Foreign Missions. They established the South African Institute of Race Relations (SAIRR) with Loram as chairman, Pim as treasurer, and Rheinallt Jones as secretary and advisor on race relations.[89]

The Institute, which became a center for black and white liberal activists, aimed to support the Joint Councils' and other welfare activities by underpinning them with a foundation of research in race relations. It was expected that the Institute's empirical research would be applied by the floundering welfare organizations and, moreover, be used to increase awareness among South African whites of the need for racial harmony. An early SAIRR publication cites its objectives as gathering and publishing information on the conditions of disadvantaged groups in the Union of South Africa, raising public awareness of the need for racial harmony, and promoting interracial understanding. The Institute espoused such principles as racial tolerance, the dignity of all persons regardless of color, and the right of all to fully develop their innate potential.[90]

Loram was one of the main activists in the Institute. It was often called 'Loram's midwife'.[91] He was so convinced of the need for such a research institute that in 1933, shortly after he arrived at Yale, he established the Department of Race Relations at the graduate school there. As head of the department, Loram extended the research activities of the SAIRR to the United States. His intentions are clearly set forth in a 1933 letter to his friends back home, retrospectively explaining his decision to move to the United States after he was fired from the Native Affairs Commission: '[I] realized two things: the first was that this question of racial adjustment was a world problem and that the one way to influence South Africa was to show her that she was not playing a lone hand. The second was that I personally could not do much more, but that I might help to conduct research into the matter and to train others to carry on my work.'[92] For all his idyllic visions of racial relations in Hawaii and at Yale, Loram saw the United States as a place with similar racial problems to South Africa's. It is this similarity that made the United States, to his mind, the ideal locale for studying racial relations and for training disciples to carry on his liberal efforts in his home country. From the Department of Race Relations, Loram carried out research and conducted courses on race relations for Africans, colonial government officials, and missionaries. As part of this work, he organized tours for his students to visit the southern states to observe, it may be presumed, 'what to follow and what to avoid'. The American South provided him with examples of both. In his letters from America, he notes such negative things as racial discrimination in tourist homes and hotels, which made it difficult for him to find lodging with his black students when they toured the South, and the diversion by local councils in the southern states of funds earmarked for black education to white schools.[93]

On the positive side, he found in the South examples of African-American educational institutions and of a variety of interracial organizations engaged in good works on behalf of the black population. His letters are sprinkled with observations as to what might be adapted to South Africa and what not.[94] In his activities at Yale, Loram expressed not only his own hopes for learning from the good and bad examples of the southern states, but the view of the SAIRR liberals in general, who regarded the American South as a huge laboratory and training ground in which they and their countrymen could study the situation, progress and problems of black Americans, with the aim of applying their findings to South Africa. The concept is aptly expressed in the statement by Robert R. Moton, Booker T. Washington's successor as the head of Tuskegee: 'The United States is God's great laboratory for testing whether the white and black races can live side by side. If they can do so in America, they can do so anywhere.'[95] South African liberals believed that the American experience could serve them in their efforts to establish an interracial society in their own country. Thus, in April 1933, the SAIRR sent A. J. B. Desmore for a year of special study in the United States, whose purpose Rheinhallt Jones defined as follows: 'If he could be put under someone like [Thomas J.] Woofter [of the University of North Carolina] and could train him on methods of investigation and shown some different investigations at work in addition to seeing something generally of Negro life in America, I believe that when he returned to South Africa we could use him very considerably.'[96] Three years later, at the end of 1936, when Rheinhallt Jones presented his credentials as a representative of South African natives to the South African Senate, Loram insisted that he travel around the American South to obtain 'an insight into the American Negro situation which would be of immense value to you in your future work'.[97]

From his position at Yale, Loram thus also served as a contact and liaison for the SAIRR. In his letters to Rheinallt Jones, he provided practical information about Yale and other American universities to which the Institute sent South African students, including information about courses, requirements, scholarships and work opportunities. He served as academic advisor and as a mentor to South African students at Yale. And he sent back assessments of such students to the Institute, with the idea that they could be harnessed to the cause of racial harmony on their return to their home country. For example, in his letter to Rheinallt Jones dated 8 May 1934, Loram offers Yale scholarships to two South Africans and recommends the native South African, Z. K. Matthews, who was studying under him at Yale, to the SAIRR, with the idea that Matthews could be useful to the liberal cause: 'In this connection I am sure you will be interested in a first rate study that has been done by Z. K. Matthews under my direction. . . . I think he is quite the ablest South African Native I know and is destined to play an important part in South African affairs. Do keep in touch with him and give him the benefit of your counsel.'[98] For the liberals, study in the United States was a means rather than an end. As Loram put it in a letter in 1935: 'I think you will agree with me that our concern should not be so much the aspirations of students as with the work they can do and the influence they can use when they return to their own people.'[99]

The United States served the SAIRR not only as a research laboratory and source of ideas for ways in which the races could live together, but also as a major source of funding, much as it did Dube's Ohlange Institute and the Joint Council movement. This American funding was vital. The liberal institutions were non-profit and voluntary, but the tiny liberal movement lacked a local middle-class base to which it could appeal for support in South Africa itself.[100] In the main, the SAIRR was funded by the Phelps-Stokes Fund and the Carnegie Corporation, which pledged £3,750 for the start-up of the Institute, with occasional assistance from other American foundations. Loram had maintained a close working relationship with the Phelps-Stokes Fund and with its educational director Thomas Jesse Jones ever since 1920, when he had served as the Union of South Africa's representative on the Phelps-Stokes Education Commissions. In 1924 he was appointed the Fund's representative in the Union of South Africa. When he moved to the United States in 1931, he effectively became the liaison between the SAIRR and the Fund. Among other things, the Phelps-Stokes Fund helped to finance Rheinhallt Jones's study tour of the American South; and it recompensed Edgar Brookes for the six months' salary he lost when he left his position as lecturer at the University of Pretoria to raise funds for the SAIRR.[101]

In the first ten years of the SAIRR activities, the Institute received $20,000 from the Carnegie Corporation and $10,000 from the Phelps-Stokes Fund.[102] In addition to direct financial assistance, the SAIRR was able to rely on the Phelps-Stokes Fund for indirect assistance in funding joint educational projects for South Africans. With financial help from the Phelps-Stokes and other American funds, Loram was able to organize seminars, in 1934, 1935 and 1936, in which visitors and students from the Union of South Africa met with American experts to discuss ways of promoting racial harmony.[103] The largest event of this kind was a seminar entitled 'The Education of Negroes and the Native African' at Chapel Hill, North Carolina, on 1 September 1937, where ten South African and ten British colonial authorities on African education met with American directors of education to discuss this topic. The seminar was followed by a month's tour of the southern states.[104] The close cooperation between the Phelps-Stokes Fund and the SAIRR brought Rheinhallt Jones to compare the Institute's activities in South Africa with the work done by the Phelps-Stokes Fund in the United States. Like the Phelps-Stokes Fund, the Institute, he implied, was at the vanguard of the development of black education and welfare in South Africa.[105]

For about twenty years, liberal organizations and institutions in South Africa thus found both ideological and instrumental support in the United States. The financial support went entirely to the liberals' educational, social and cultural bodies, not to the politically oriented ANC. The bulk of the American financing came to an end by 1940. The failure of Jesse Jones's educational policies and the death of Loram in 1940, one year after he had been appointed a trustee of the Phelps-Stokes Fund, virtually put an end to the Fund's activities in and for South Africa.

THE INADEQUACY OF AMERICAN MODELS

The South African liberal movement succeeded in fostering some cooperation between whites and Africans, but it never brought about a fundamental change in their country's policy of racial segregation and oppression. For all its activity, the movement remained too small, too divided, and, above all, too much before its time to turn its ideas into reality. By the late 1930s, all but the liberals' academic activity had come to an end. The Joint Councils were disbanded and the ANC had not yet recovered from the disarray into which it had fallen by 1930. The American model, which seemed so promising, was never really applicable to South Africa. The large black population in the southern States seemed to parallel South Africa's demographic composition. South African liberals were inspired both by the educational, economic and legal struggle of American blacks to attain equality and by what they saw as the readiness of American whites to grant it. Nonetheless, America was fundamentally different from South Africa.

The crucial difference was that while blacks were a minority in the United States, they were a huge majority in South Africa. This demographic difference meant that the US federal government could express support of racial equality and integration without apprehension of a serious threat to its largely white character, while the South African government and most of the country's white population, frightened of being overwhelmed by the native masses, required the tool of racial discrimination to preserve white dominance. For most South African whites, and perhaps for most American whites too, the real issue at the time was not whether and how blacks and whites could live together in peace, but how whites could preserve their privileged status in a bi-racial society. Xuma's call for the adaptation of the American constitutional model and even D. D. T. Jabavu's less articulated plea for native civil rights inevitably fell on deaf ears. Even within the liberal movement itself, the whites in the paternalistic school did not envision entirely giving up their privileged status in the foreseeable future.

If the federal model was a vain hope, the model of the southern states was largely a fiction. In the American South, where the demographic realities of large black population concentrations were closer to those of South Africa, African-Americans were segregated, disenfranchised and subjected to endless other forms of legal discrimination. The liberals' assumption that they could learn from the southern states what to copy and what to avoid in racial relations were, from the beginning, ill-founded. The supposition depended on emphasizing the differences between South Africa and the American South, where the liberals found isolated examples of racial cooperation, and on downplaying the sad similarities. This imbalance runs through Loram's work. The radical Garveyite model also failed. From the beginning, it had less support among the natives than the liberal model, and unlike the latter, had no white support at all. Even in the ANC, the radical Garvey supporters constituted only a tiny minority.

South African liberals adapted the African-American myth despite their awareness of American realities, for they had little else on which to pin their hopes. Neither their own country nor England provided any model at all of racial harmony. Their mythologized image of black–white relations in the United States provided them with the inspiration to work towards a more equitable and just future and the hope that such a future was indeed attainable. But it did not provide a viable paradigm for change.

Conclusion

The term African-American myth has been used in this book to refer to the welter of images and conceptions in Africa concerning African-Americans and the country they lived in. The United States occupied a unique place in the minds of Africans. More than any other country in the New World, the United States fired the imagination of Africans, who believed it to be a land of unlimited opportunity for people in general and for members of the black race in particular. That positive picture of the United States issued in a similarly positive image of the African-Americans who lived there. The positive image of the American blacks was inseparable from the image of the country itself. Landmarks in the history of the United States, events that related specifically to the black community, white American leaders who seemed to favor black development and equality, and black American celebrities – all these provided kindling that kept the flame of the American myth burning in Africa. Africans perceived African-Americans to have advantages which they themselves, subject as they were to colonial or white minority rule, only dreamed of. Blacks in America were free citizens. As Africans saw it, the federal government pursued a policy of equal rights for blacks, opposing the discriminatory regulations enacted by southern states. Large portions of the American white community openly supported black initiatives and donated money to black colleges. African-Americans, not unlike whites, had their own celebrities: Paul Robeson and Booker T. Washington were equally admired by blacks and whites. All these things were regarded as tremendous advantages. All of them went into the making of the American myth in Africa.

It was Africans who created and spread the myth. Americans, black no less than white, were almost entirely passive. The vast majority of the black community in the United States turned a cold shoulder on their 'motherland'. Black American advocates of the back-to-Africa movement, such as Bishop Turner, were unable to generate a mass emigration movement. Most of the black American missionaries who served in Africa worked to spread the gospel and convert the African heathens, and were not interested in spreading the American myth. Booker T. Washington and W. E. B. Du Bois, who greatly inspired the Africans, believed that African-Americans had to take their proper place in America and opposed the idea of mass black American migration to Africa.

The fact that the American myth was an African creation explains why it spread the length and breadth of Africa. No external propaganda, however

176

well-planned, orchestrated or applied, could be dispersed as widely or penetrate different cultural strata as thoroughly as the home-grown myth. The fact that the myth was created and disseminated by Africans also explains why it was part and parcel of African responses to the colonial situation. The African-American myth was behind the creation of various millenarian and political movements, the founding of separatist African churches, and the establishment of a new educational system.

The African-American myth was upheld by extremely different types of personalities, from different social and ethnic groups, in different parts of Africa, under widely different cultural and political situations. Edward Wilmot Blyden of West Africa and Tomo Nyirenda of East-Central Africa represented not only different geographical regions, but also different cultural and religious approaches. Blyden was an eloquent spokesman for western-educated Africans devoted to the idea of regeneration of Africans along western lines. Nyirenda, also devoted to the salvation of his country, believed in returning to traditional African ways. Blyden believed that the lives of Africans could be bettered only through the adoption of Christianity and western culture. Nyirenda chose an eschatological approach and belief in metaphysical power to bring his people a better future. Yet the two men shared a common faith in the African-American model. Blyden believed that African-Americans would help Africans take their place among the nations of the world. Nyirenda, like other Watch Tower preachers, was convinced that African-Americans would come to help Africans overturn colonialism and restore Africa to its glories prior to the European conquest.

James Kwegyir Aggrey, an African from the Gold Coast, studied and worked in the United States. Charles Templeman Loram was reared and educated in Britain and Natal. Aggrey decided to return permanently to Africa, while Loram left South Africa and took up residence in the United States. Aggrey believed that European tutelage was indispensable for African progress. However, he saw the tutelage as temporary and emphasized the African right to self-expression and self-esteem. Loram, a South African liberal of the paternalistic school, believed that Africans would always need whites to show them the way. Yet despite their different backgrounds and outlooks, both Aggrey and Loram were staunch believers in the African-American educational model and worked hard to institute it in Africa.

John Chilembwe from Nyasaland and John Dube from Natal were clergymen who acquired their religious educations in the United States and then struggled for African equality in their native lands. In 1915, frustrated in his aims, Chilembwe led a violent rebellion against the British authorities.

John Dube chose a constitutional approach. Each of them believed in his own political way, but both looked to America for inspiration and guidance. Chilembwe modeled himself on the American abolitionist hero John Brown, while Dube was a devoted disciple of Booker T. Washington.

Blaise Diagne, a black French official who was a staunch believer in the superiority of the French culture, labored to extend the French assimilationist policy all over Francophone Africa. Touvelou-Houenou, although a black Frenchman, opposed the assimilationist approach of the black French officials and believed in African political and economic autonomy apart from France. Yet to promote their opposing ways, each of them found an ally among the African-Americans. Diagne associated himself for a while with the pan-African movement of W. E. B. Du Bois, while Touvelou-Houenou sought ties with the black nationalist movement of Marcus Garvey.

Like all myths, the African-American myth seemed to provide a solution for almost any problem. It offered total salvation in East-Central and Southern Africa, a model for race integration in South Africa, and an example for an educational system in West Africa. It was this flexibility and inclusiveness that gave the myth its broad appeal in Africa and that drew such a large variety of adherents.

Of equal importance, their reliance on African-Americans as saviours, as an avant-garde, or as models to imitate also provided a handy way for the African leaders to shunt responsibility and to foist off the blame for failures on their American brethren. For instance, in 1899 the Vicar Bishop Dwane accused the AME Church leaders of causing the break between the Ethiopian Church and the black American church. In 1920, when black French officials concluded that their partnership in the pan-African movement would not serve their purpose, their leader, Blaise Diagne, avowed that Du Bois 'became . . . our enemy'. The heavy dependence of the apocalyptic prophecies in East-Central and Southern Africa on black Americans meant that their inevitable failure to materialize could also be blamed on black Americans. In fact, in 1926 in Transkei, when eschatological expectations that Aggrey would bring about a miracle remained unfulfilled, the millenarian leader Wellington of the Zulu ethnic group claimed that Aggrey 'had been bought by the Whites'.

The African-American myth also evoked strong opposition. The objectors had to battle on two fronts. The first was against the advocates of the African-American model. Thus, members of the NCBWA attacked members of the UNIA branches in West Africa in newspapers and public forums. Some Cape liberals raised their voices against the black American vocational curriculum that was supported by other liberals. The second front was against African-Americans. The advocates of the African avant-garde openly disparaged blacks in America. They went so far as to regard them as political enemies, while they saw the colonial rulers as the Africans' true partners. It is paradoxical that up to World War II, African nationalists never openly demanded the abolition of foreign rule or the withdrawal of the colonial powers, but did publicly oppose and reject their own brethren from the New World.

Race and race identity were issues that concerned both the advocates and the opponents of the African-American model. The issue was not initially an African one, but rather brought in by whites. During most of the nineteenth century, western-educated Africans in the British domains were relatively well accepted. Avenues to educational, economic and social advancement were relatively open to them, and they saw themselves as belonging to the same class and culture as the British in their midst. In the last decades of the century, however, the avenues to advancement for Africans were blocked as a result of newly instituted racist policies, and race, which had hardly been an issue till then, became a major concern. Western-educated Africans discovered the potential embodied in racial solidarity with their brethren in the New World and emphasized the bond. The social, economic and political achievements of the African-Americans provided them with the proof they needed that, contrary to what their white detractors maintained, blacks were inherently equal to whites. The racial bond thus became a core element in their belief in and promulgation of the African-American myth.

Race worked in other ways as well. It was the basis for the promotion of the vocational curriculum. The whole idea of adopting Booker T. Washington's educational philosophy throughout Africa, for black students of all abilities and inclinations, stemmed from the assumption that what worked for black people on one side of the ocean would work for members of the race on the other side. The same logic was behind the activities of the South African liberals, who sought to adopt features of the black–white relationship in America. In a very different way, race was the basis for the conviction of the African messianic and millenarian sects that American blacks would come to liberate them from the white oppressor.

Race, which was the cornerstone for advocates of the African-American myth, was a stumbling block for its opponents. The latter could deny neither the fact that Africans and African-Americans belonged to the same race nor that, in comparison to themselves, black Americans had achieved relatively high social, economic and political status. These facts seemed to undermine their claim that Africans, not African-Americans, should lead Africa into the future. The opponents of the African-American myth based their position in favor of an African avant-garde on two major claims. One was that blacks in America were a different breed: 'black white men' who had lost everything they ever had in common with Africans. The other claim was that black Africans were, in fact, superior to black Americans: 'the native African ... has accomplished more with his five talents singlehanded and alone than the American Negro has with his ten talents and the financial aid of a great body of the dominant race in this country [the United States]'. This line of argument both sullied the American myth and raised the indigenous Africans above African-Americans. At the same time, race was at the heart of the ambivalence that the opponents of the African-American myth demonstrated. It was virtually impossible for them not to be excited by Garvey's Black Star Line and to dream of its commercial advantages for Africans.

After World War I, the dispute over the African-American myth focused on its political ramifications. The upheavals caused by the war raised the level of political awareness in both Africa and America and led African-Americans, for the first time in history, to come forward with concrete political solutions to what they perceived to be the problems of the entire black race. W. E. B. Du Bois's pan-African movement appealed to both Anglophone and Francophone Africans, though it never really moved from Europe, where all but one of the pan-African congresses were held, to Africa itself. Garvey's militaristic UNIA, for a brief spate, had a much wider and deeper grip in Africa. Yet his vision of an African government all over the black continent was mocked as ridiculous and unrealistic by his opponents, and by the 1930s hardly a trace of the UNIA was left in Africa.

The course of the African-American myth in Africa was fraught with irony. In the last decades of the nineteenth century the advocates of the African-American avant-garde actively sought black American volunteers to come and take the lead in regenerating the black continent, and there was virtually no organized opposition to their efforts. But African-Americans did not come. They did not have the mass-member organizations which would have been necessary to recruit them under the back-to-Africa banner. The AME Church and AME Zion Church, the largest African-American organizations, had no political ambitions and confined their work to spreading the gospel and converting the Africans. After World War I, conditions changed and there were black Americans who seemed to be ready to answer the call for help. The UNIA rallied hundreds of thousands of African-Americans under the back-to-Africa slogan, founded a shipping line to bring them over, and went so far as to send a contingent of settlers to Liberia. But it was in the same years that the opposition to the African-American myth in West Africa became organized as the NCBWA and eventually supplanted the UNIA branches in Africa. The biggest irony of all, of course, is that whatever the Africans and African-Americans might have wanted to do, there is no way that the colonial powers would ever have permitted the dream to become reality.

The African-American myth was a powerful presence throughout Africa and could boast a large number of promulgators and believers. Nevertheless, its advocates were not able to get a single program off the ground. Neither politically, economically, educationally nor socially did the African-American model successfully take root in African soil. Nor was the cause the extensive African opposition it provoked. The main reason was that whenever the model was put to the test, it did not work. The Booker T. Washington educational approach, as it was implemented in most of Africa, proved unsuited to African conditions. South African liberals were unable to put into effect any social or economic schemes based on the African-American model. The salvation promised by the millenarian movements never materialized. American blacks never emigrated to Africa in large numbers. But, like other myths, the power of the African-American myth did not depend on empirical success. For all the myth's failures on the ground, America and African-Americans remained for Africans objects of admiration and models for emulation.

Notes

Introduction

1. St Clair Drake, 'Negro Americans and the Africa Interest', in *The American Negro Reference Book*, ed. John P. Davis (Englewood Cliffs, N.J.: Prentice-Hall, 1966), 664.
2. George A. Shepperson, 'Notes on Negro American Influences on the Emergence of African Nationalism', *Journal of African History* 1, no. 2 (1960): 299.
3. Nnamdi Azikiwe, *My Odyssey: An Autobiography* (New York: Praeger, 1970), 196.
4. Mark Schorer, 'The Necessity of Myth', in *Myth and Mythmaking*, ed. Henry A. Murray (Boston: Beacon Press, 1968), 355.
5. For example, Andrew Lang analyzes myth's relationship to ritual and religion in his two volumes, *Myth, Ritual and Religion* (New York: AMS Press, 1968); Adrian Cunningham edited a volume which deals with myth and meaning, *The Theory of Myth: Six Studies* (London: Sheed and Ward, 1973); myth and culture are treated in Leszek Kolakowski, *The Presence of Myth* (Chicago: University of Chicago Press, 1989); Stephen H. Daniel approaches myth in relation to modern philosophy in his work, *Myth and Modern Philosophy* (Philadelphia: Temple University Press, 1990); the relationship between myth and the modern human sciences is the subject of Joseph Mali's study, *The Rehabilitation of Myth: Vico's 'New Science'* (Cambridge: Cambridge University Press, 1992).
6. The following is a sample of research dealing with various aspects of African-American and African relations: Adelaide Cromwell Hill and Martin Kilson, eds, *Apropos of Africa: Sentiments of Negro American Leaders on Africa from the 1800's to the 1950's* (London: Frank Cass, 1969). Bernard Magubane, *The American Negro's Conception of Africa: A Study in the Ideology of Pride and Prejudice* (Los Angeles: University of California Press, 1967). Charles Alvis Bodie, 'The Images of Africa in the Black American Press, 1890–1930' (Ph.D. diss., Indiana University, 1975). Codjo Achode, 'The Negro Renaissance from America Back to Africa: A Study of the Harlem Renaissance as a Black and African Movement' (Ph.D. diss., University of Pennsylvania, 1986). Dennis Hickey and Kenneth C. Wylie, *An Enchanting Darkness: The American Vision of Africa in the Twentieth Century* (East Lansing: Michigan State University Press, 1993). Donald Franklin Roth, '"Grace Not Race" Southern Negro Church Leaders, Black Identity, and Missions to West Africa, 1865–1919' (Ph.D. diss., University of Texas at Austin, 1975). Edwin S. Redkey, *Black Exodus: Black Nationalist and Back-to-Africa Movements, 1890–1910* (New Haven: Yale University Press, 1969). Elliott P. Skinner, *Afro-Americans and Africa: The Continuing Dialectic* (New York: Columbia University Press, 1973). Felix N. Okoye, *The American Image of Africa: Myth and Reality* (Buffalo: Black Academy Press, 1971). Josephine Moraa Moikobu, *Blood and Flesh: Black*

American and African Identifications (Westport, Conn.: Greenwood Press, 1981). Okon Edet Uya, ed., *Black Brotherhood: Afro-Americans and Africa* (Lexington, Mass.: D. C. Heath, 1971). Milfred C. Fierce, 'African-American Interest in Africa and Interaction with West Africa: The Origins of the Pan-African Idea in the United States, 1900–1919' (Ph.D. diss., Columbia University, 1976). Pearl T. Robinson and Elliott P. Skinner, eds, *Transformation and Resiliency in Africa as Seen by Afro-American Scholars* (Washington, D.C.: Howard University Press, 1983). Presence Africaine, *Africa Seen by American Negroes* (New York: Presence Africaine, 1958). Wilber Christian Harr, 'The Negro as an American Protestant Missionary in Africa' (Ph.D. diss., University of Chicago, 1945). William B. Helmreich, ed., *Afro-Americans and Africa: Black Nationalism at the Crossroads* (Westport, Conn.: Greenwood Press, 1977). William R. Scott, 'A Study of Afro-American and Ethiopian Relations, 1896–1941' (Ph.D. diss., Princeton University, 1971).

7. George A. Shepperson, 'Notes on Negro American Influences', 299–312; 'External Factors in the Development of African Nationalism, with Particular Reference to British Central Africa', in *African Politics and Society: Basic Issues and Problems of Government and Development*, ed. Irving Leonard Markovitz (New York: Free Press, 1970), 179–98; 'Pan-Africanism and "Pan-Africanism": Some Historical Notes', *Phylon* 23, no. 4 (Winter 1962): 346–57; 'Abolitionism and African Political Thought', *Transition* 3, no. 12 (1964): 22–6; 'The African Abroad or the African Diaspora', paper presented at the International African History Conference, Tanzania, 1965.

8. George Shepperson and Thomas Price, *Independent African: John Chilembwe and the Origins, Setting and Significance of the Nyasaland Native Rising in 1915* (Edinburgh: Edinburgh University Press, 1958).

9. Edward H. Berman, 'Education in Africa and America: A History of the Phelps-Stokes Fund, 1911–1945' (Ed.D. diss., Columbia University, 1970). J. Ayodele Langley, *Pan-Africanism and Nationalism in West Africa, 1900–1945: A Study in Ideology and Social Classes* (Oxford: Clarendon Press, 1978). John W. Cell, *The Highest Stage of White Supremacy: The Origins of Segregation in South Africa and the American South* (Cambridge: Cambridge University Press, 1982). Kenneth James King, *Pan-Africanism and Education: A Study of Race, Philanthropy and Education in the Southern States of America and East Africa* (Oxford: Clarendon Press, 1971).

10. Probably the only exception is an unpublished paper by T. O. Ranger, 'The Myth of the Afro-American in East-Central Africa, 1900–1939' (African Studies Center, University of California, Los Angeles, April 1971, mimeographed).

1 The Shape and Shaping of the African-American Myth

1. Kenneth King, 'Early Pan-African Politicians in East Africa', *Mawazo* 2, no. 1 (June 1969): 4.

2. In September 1921, Kamulegeya corresponded with participants of the Negro Farmers Conference held in Tuskegee and urged them to strengthen their ties with the Africans in Africa. Ibid., 5.

3. Quoted in Kings M. Phiri, 'Afro-American Influence in Colonial Malawi,

1891–1945: A Case Study of the Interaction between Africa and Africans of the Diaspora', in *Global Dimensions of the African Diaspora*, ed. Joseph E. Harris (Washington, D.C.: Howard University Press, 1982), 261.

4. Quoted in Ibid., 262.
5. Stephen Ward Angell, *Bishop Henry McNeal Turner and African-American Religion in the South* (Knoxville: University of Tennessee Press, 1992), 225.
6. Joyce Cary, *The Case For African Freedom and Other Writings on Africa* (Austin: University of Texas Press, 1962), 20–1.
7. Kenneth King, 'Early Pan-African Politicians', 8.
8. Amy Jacques Garvey, *Garvey and Garveyism* (New York: Octagon Books, 1978), 273–4.
9. John Runcie, 'The Influence of Marcus Garvey and the Universal Negro Improvement Association in Sierra Leone', *Africana Research Bulletin* 12, no. 3. (June 1983): 10.
10. Tony Martin, *Race First: The Ideological and Organizational Struggles of Marcus Garvey and the Universal Negro Improvement Association* (Westport, Conn.: Greenwood Press, 1976), 116–17.
11. Quoted in Frederick German Detweiler, *The Negro Press in the United States* (College Park, Md.: McGrath Publishing, 1968), 16.
12. R. C. F. Maugham, British Consul-General in Dakar, Senegal, to George Curzon, Principal Secretary of State for Foreign Affairs of Great Britain, 17 August 1922, as published under the title, 'The Influence of Marcus Garvey on Africa', *Science and Society* 32, no. 1 (Winter 1968): 322.
13. George A. Shepperson, 'External Factors in the Development of African Nationalism, with Particular Reference to British Central Africa', in *African Politics and Society: Basic Issues and Problems of Government and Development*, ed. Irving Leonard Markovitz (New York: Free Press, 1970), 196.
14. J. Mutero Chirenje, 'The Afro-American Factor in Southern African Ethiopianism, 1890–1906', *in Profiles of Self-Determination: African Responses to European Colonialism in Southern Africa, 1652–Present*, ed. David Chanaiwa (Northridge: California State University Foundation, 1976), 251.
15. Manning Marable, 'Ambiguous Legacy: Tuskegee's "Missionary" Impulse and Africa During the Moton Administration, 1915–1935', in *Black Americans and the Missionary Movement in Africa*, ed. Sylvia M. Jacobs (Westport, Conn: Greenwood Press, 1982), 82.
16. *Crisis*, edited by W. E. B. Du Bois, was the organ of the NAACP. King, 'Early Pan-African Politicians', 4, 6.
17. Quoted in Detweiler, *The Negro Press*, 16.
18. T. O. Ranger, 'The Myth of the Afro-American in East-Central Africa, 1900–1939' (African Studies Center, University of California, Los Angeles, April 1971, mimeographed), 2.
19. 'Our Petition to Government', *Sierra Leone Weekly News*, 6 May 1939, 9.
20. Tom Mboya, 'Our Revolutionary Tradition: An African View', *Current History* (Dec. 1956): 346.
21. Ezekiel Mphahlele, B. Enwonwu and T. O. Oruwariye, 'Comments on AMSAC Pan-Africanism Conference', in *Readings in African Political Thought*, ed. Gideon-Cyrus M. Mutiso and S. W. Rohio (London: Heinemann, 1975), 71.
22. 'The Position of the Negro in America by a Negro', *Sierra Leone Weekly News*, 12 May 1900, 4.

23. 'West African Colonial Attitude Toward Americans', *Lagos Weekly Record*, 15 March 1913.
24. Quoted in W. C. Wilcox, 'John L. Dube: the Booker T. Washington of the Zulus', *Missionary Review of the World* 22, no. 12 (Dec. 1909): 916.
25. George Shepperson, *Myth and Reality in Malawi* (Evanston, Ill.: Northwestern University Press, 1966), 9. It is interesting to note that African-American missionaries did not share that opinion. The official publication of the black denomination, the National Baptist Convention, United States, which operated in Nyasaland, lamented the low salaries and poor equipment provided for their missionaries. C. C. Adams and Marshall A. Talley, *Negro Baptists and Foreign Missions* (Philadelphia: The Foreign Mission Board of the National Baptist Convention, USA, Inc., 1944), 53.
26. Quoted in Kenneth P. Lohrentz, 'Joseph Booth, Charles Domingo, and the Seventh Day Baptists in Northern Nyasaland, 1910–1912', *Journal of African History* 12, no. 3 (1971): 471.
27. 'Professor Booker T. Washington', *Lagos Standard*, 28 October 1903, 5.
28. Wilcox, 'John L. Dube', 915.
29. Orishatuke Faduma, 'The Lure to America', *Sierra Leone Weekly News*, 11 August 1928, 8.
30. George Simeon Mwase, *Strike a Blow and Die: A Narrative of Race Relations in Colonial Africa*, ed. with an introduction by Robert I. Rotberg (Cambridge, Mass.: Harvard University Press, 1967), 69–70.
31. D. D. T. Jabavu, 'Native Unrest Its Cause and Cure', in *The Black Problem: Papers and Addresses on Various Native Problems* (Lovedale: Lovedale Institution Press, 1920), 4.
32. Nnamdi Azikiwe, *My Odyssey: An Autobiography* (New York: Praeger, 1970), 196.
33. *Sierra Leone Weekly News*, 1 August 1908, 2.
34. Edward W. Blyden, *The African Problem and Other Discourses, Delivered in America in 1890* (London: W. B. Whittingham, 1890), 14–15.
35. 'President Roosevelt and his Appointment of Negroes to Office in the United States', *Lagos Standard*, 27 May 1903.
36. 'Rise and Progress of the Negro in America', *Sierra Leone Weekly News*, 15 November 1930, 7.
37. D. D. T. Jabavu, 'Natives and Agriculture', in *The Black Problem: Papers and Addresses on Various Native Problems* (Lovedale: Lovedale Institution Press, 1920), 102–3.
38. John V. Taylor and Dorothea A. Lehmann, *Christians of the Copperbelt: The Growth of the Church in Northern Rhodesia* (London: SCM Press, 1961), 237.
39. 'Life in the United States of America', *Sierra Leone Weekly News*, 1 August 1908, 2.
40. 'Rise and Progress of the Negro in America', *Sierra Leone Weekly News*, 15 November 1930, 7.
41. Wulf Sachs, *Black Anger: The Mind of an African Negro Revealed by Psychoanalysis*, 2nd edn (New York: Greenwood Press, 1968), 80.
42. Kimpianga Mahania, 'The Presence of Black Americans in Lower Congo from 1878 to 1921', in *Global Dimensions of the African Diaspora*, ed. Joseph E. Harris (Washington, D.C.: Howard University Press, 1982), 270.

43. Quoted in George A. Shepperson, 'Ethiopianism and African Nationalism', *Phylon* 14, no. 1 (1953): 15.

44. Editorial, 'The Color Question in the United States', *Sierra Leone Weekly News*, 21 February 1903, 4.

45. 'President Roosevelt and the American Negro', *Sierra Leone Weekly News*, 14 February 1908, 5.

46. Thoodore Roosevelt, *American Ideals and Other Essays, Social and Political* (New York: Knickerbocker Press, 1970), 272–3.

47. 'President Taft Advocates Higher Education for Coloured Americans', *Sierra Leone Weekly News*, 16 April 1910, 8.

48. 'The New Status of the Negro in America', *Sierra Leone Weekly News*, 3 April 1909, 6.

49. Ibid. The capital letters and italics are from the source.

50. George F. Ketcham, 'The New Negro', *Sierre Leone Weekly News*, 2 August 1930, 10.

51. 'The African Methodist Episcopal Church – Centennial Celebration', *Sierra Leone Weekly News*, 25 March 1916, 5. The AME Church was founded in 1816 in Philadelphia by free blacks in reaction to racial discrimination by American society in general and the Methodist church in particular. Four years later, in New York, different groups of free blacks united and established another independent black church, the African Methodist Episcopal Zion Church. Although the difference between the two bodies was negligible, they maintained their independence. Both churches supported the Abolitionist movement and condemned racial discrimination in the United States. They established and maintained elementary and higher educational institutions for American blacks. These activities aroused political feelings among blacks and helped create a black intellectual elite.

52. Raffaele Pettazzoni, 'The Truth of Myth', in *Sacred Narrative: Readings in the Theory of Myth*, ed. Alan Dundes (Berkeley: University of California Press, 1984), 98.

53. 'The Negro Problem in America', *Lagos Standard*, 3 June 1903.

54. 'The Negro in Civilization', *Sierra Leone Weekly News*, 7 November 1908, 4.

55. O. T. Nana, 'The Negro Problem', *Sierra Leone Weekly News*, 22 July 1911, 5.

56. E. A. Ayandele, *The Missionary Impact on Modern Nigeria, 1842–1914: A Political and Social Analysis* (New York: Humanities Press, 1967), 194. African missionaries in the Niger Delta referred to the inferior status of African-Americans. In 1891, an outburst of anti-European feeling spread among the Christian communities in West Africa in reaction to the Church Missionary Society's decision to fire black missionaries, who were under the supervision of the first black Bishop Samuel Crowther, the head of the Niger Mission. African missionaries stoked the animosity of the Africans with stories describing the evils committed by the white man in America against the black community there. Ibid., 217.

57. Quoted in Mercer Cook and Stephen E. Henderson, *The Militant Black Writer in Africa and the United States* (Madison: University of Wisconsin Press, 1969), 37.

58. Ibid.

59. Robert Rotberg, 'Psychological Stress and the Question of Identity: Chilembwe's Revolt Reconsidered', in *Protest and Power in Black Africa*, ed. Robert I. Rotberg and Ali A. Mazrui (New York: Oxford University Press, 1970), 356.
60. Edwin W. Smith, *Aggrey of Africa: A Study in Black and White* (New York: Doubleday, Doran, 1929), 214–15.
61. 'Negroes Still Serfs, Says Du Bois', *Lagos Daily News*, 30 December 1931, 3.
62. J. Mutero Chirenje, *Ethiopianism and Afro-Americans in Southern Africa, 1883–1916* (Baton Rouge: Louisiana State University Press, 1987), 19.
63. Baker J. Cauthen and others, eds, *Advance: A History of Southern Baptist Foreign Missions* (Nashville, Tenn.: Broadman Press, 1970), 145. It is significant that the official publication of the Southern Baptist Convention does not supply the whole story of the schism. Compare with Ayandele, *The Missionary Impact*, 198–200.
64. Quoted in J. Tremayne Copplestone, *History of Methodist Missions*, vol. 4 (New York: Board of Global Ministries of United Methodist Church, 1973), 548.
65. Ibid., 552–3, 562, 563, 565. A schism occurred not only in American white-dominated churches, but also in an African-American church. In 1899, leaders of the Ethiopian Church of South Africa who had affiliated with the AME Church one year earlier decided to break away from the African-American church. Their decision followed a dispute over budget and educational policy, as will be elaborated on later in this chapter.
66. Claude Levi-Strauss, *Structural Anthropology* (New York: Basic Books, 1963), 229.
67. Geoffrey Stephen Kirk, *Myth: Its Meaning and Functions in Ancient and Other Cultures* (Cambridge: Cambridge University Press, 1970), 258.
68. Quoted in Clement T. Keto, 'Black Americans and South Africa, 1890–1910', *A Current Bibliography on African Affairs* 5, no. 6 (1972): 387–8.
69. 'The Jubilee Singers', *Imvo Zabantsundu*, 16 October 1890, quoted in Chirenje, *Ethiopianism*, 36.
70. Ibid., 58–9.
71. J. E. Kunnie, 'Black Churches in the United States and South Africa: Similarities and Differences', in *Afro-Christianity at the Grassroots: Its Dynamics and Strategies*, ed. G. C. Oosthuizen, M. C. Kitshoff and S. W. D. Dube (Leiden: E. J. Brill, 1994), 87.
72. Quoted in Chirenje, *Ethiopianism*, 63.
73. Angell, *Bishop Henry McNeal Turner*, 234.
74. Daniel Thwaite, *The Seething African Pot: A Study of Black Nationalism, 1882–1935* (London: Constable, 1936), 36–7.
75. Angell, *Bishop Henry McNeal Turner*, 229.
76. Ibid., 230.
77. Chirenje, *Ethiopianism*, 64.
78. Richard R. Wright Jr, *Eighty-seven Years Behind the Black Curtain: An Autobiography* (Philadelphia: Rare Book, 1965), 241.
79. Amos Jerome White and Luella White, *Dawn in Bantuland: An African Experiment, or an Account of Missionary Experiences and Observations in South Africa* (Boston: Christopher Publishing, 1953), 231.
80. Wright, *Eighty-seven Years*, 232.

81. Walton Johnson, 'The Africanization of a Mission Church: The African Methodist Episcopal Church in Zambia', in *African Christianity: Patterns of Religious Continuity*, ed. George Bond and others (New York: Academic Press, 1979), 92.

82. Milfred C. Fierce, *The Pan-African Idea in the United States, 1900–1919: African-American Interest in Africa and Interaction with West Africa* (New York: Garland Publishing, 1993), 107; 'The African Methodist Episcopal Zion Church on the Gold Coast', *Gold Coast Aborigines*, 19 November 1898, 2–3.

83. 'The African Methodist Episcopal Zion Church On The Gold Coast', *Gold Coast Chronicle*, 10 May 1901, 3.

84. 'The African Methodist Episcopal Zion Church', *Gold Coast Aborigines*, 25 February 1899, 3.

85. 'The African Methodist Episcopal Zion Church on the Gold Coast', *Gold Coast Chronicle*, 10 May 1901, 3.

86. David Kimble, *A Political History of Ghana: the Rise of Gold Coast Nationalism, 1850–1928* (London: Clarendon Press, 1963), 163.

87. 'The African Methodist Episcopal Zion Church', *Gold Coast Aborigines*, 25 February 1899, 3.

88. Shepperson, *Myth and Reality*, 9, 10.

89. Hampton Thomas Medford, *Zion Methodism Abroad: Giving the Rise and Progress of the A.M.E. Zion Church on its Foreign Fields* (Washington, D.C.: n.p., 1937), 36.

90. T. O. Ranger, 'The "Ethiopian" Episode in Barotseland, 1900–1905', *Rhodes-Livingstone Journal* 37 (June 1965): 32.

91. Walton R. Johnson, 'The AME Church and Ethiopianism in South Africa', *Journal of Southern African Affairs* 3, no. 2 (April 1978): 212.

92. R. Hunt Davis Jr, 'The Black American Education Component in African Responses to Colonialism in South Africa (ca. 1890–1914)', *Journal of Southern African Affairs* 3, no. 1 (January 1978): 75.

93. Quoted in Ibid.

94. Richard David Ralston, 'A Second Middle Passage: African Student Sojourns in the United States During the Colonial Period and Their Influence upon the Character of African Leadership' (Ph.D. diss., University of California at Los Angeles, 1972), 65.

95. Davis, 'The Black American Education Component', 75.

96. Johnson, 'The AME Church', 213–14.

97. 'Anniversary of the A.M.E.Z.C. Kwitta', *Gold Coast Chronicle*, 12 May 1900, 2; Medford, *Zion Methodism Abroad*, 115.

98. 'The African Methodist Episcopal Zion Church on the Gold Coast', *Gold Coast Aborigines*, 19 November 1898, 3.

99. *Gold Coast Aborigines*, 26 November 1898, 4.

100. Samuel B. Coles, *Preacher with a Plow* (Boston: Houghton Mifflin Co., 1957), 11.

101. Ibid., 217–18.

102. Quoted in Tony Martin, *The Pan-African Connection: From Slavery to Garvey and Beyond* (Dover, Mass.: Majority Press, 1983), 35.

103. Clinton Caldwell Boone, *Congo as I Saw It* (New York: J. J. Little and Ives, 1927), 58.

104. Alexander Walters, *My Life and Work* (New York: Fleming H. Revell, 1917), 172.
105. Garvey's UNIA has been described as a quasi-religious organization. Nonetheless, Garvey insisted on keeping it open to Christians of all denominations as well as to non-Christians. His insistence led to a rift between the UNIA and the African Orthodox Church initially formed under its aegis. Randall K. Burkett, *Garveyism as a Religious Movement: The Institutionalization of a Black Civil Religion* (Metuchen, N.J.: Scarecrow Press, 1978), 71, 195. Martin, *Race First*, 70–2.
106. Booker T. Washington, *Up From Slavery: An Autobiography* (Williamstown: Corner House Publishers, 1971), 154–5.
107. Booker T. Washington became a celebrity in many parts of the world. His educational philosophy attracted people in India, Sri Lanka and Japan, as well as the Caribbean Islands and South America. Louis R. Harlan, *Booker T. Washington, The Wizard of Tuskegee, 1901–1915*, vol. 2 (New York: Oxford University Press, 1983), 278.
108. Ibid., 267.
109. Quoted in Louis R. Harlan, 'Booker T. Washington and the White Man's Burden', *American Historical Review* 71, no. 2 (January 1966): 442.
110. 'Death of Booker T. Washington', *Sierra Leone Weekly News*, 18 December 1915.
111. 'Professor Booker T. Washington and Negro Education in America', *Lagos Weekly Record*, 20 August 1898.
112. Erasmus W. B. Cole, 'The Mabala Devil of Yore – Now a Metamorphosed Personality', *Sierra Leone Weekly News*, 31 December 1917, 10.
113. Quoted in Marable, 'Ambiguous Legacy', 82.
114. D. D. T. Jabavu, 'Native Educational Needs', in *The Black Problem: Papers and Addresses on Various Native Problems* (Lovedale: Lovedale Institution Press, 1920), 94.
115. 'The Negro in Conference at Tuskegee Institute', *African Times and Orient Review*, July 1912, 11.
116. Reverend F. A. Pinanko, 'An Address Delivered at the International Conference on the Negro, Held at Tuskegee, Alabama', *Gold Coast Nation*, supplement, 6 February 1913, 223.
117. John Henrik Clarke, *Africans at the Crossroads: Notes for an African World Revolution* (Trenton, N.J.: Africa World Press, 1991), 88.
118. Dennis Hickey and Kenneth C. Wylie, *An Enchanting Darkness: The American Vision of Africa in the Twentieth Century* (East Lansing: Michigan State University Press, 1993), 260.
119. Elton C. Fax, *Garvey: The Story of a Pioneer Black Nationalist* (New York: Dodd, Mead, 1972), 39–44.
120. E. David Cronon, *Black Moses: The Story of Marcus Garvey and the Universal Negro Improvement Association* (Madison: University of Wisconsin Press, 1987), 16, 18.
121. Edwin S. Redkey, 'The Flowering of Black Nationalism: Henry McNeal Turner and Marcus Garvey', in *Key Issues in the Afro-American Experience*, ed. Nathan I. Huggins, Martin Kilson and Daniel M. Fox (New York: Harcourt, Brace, Jovanovich, 1971), 2:117.
122. Ali A. Mazrui estimates that at one stage the number of UNIA supporters

and members together reached six million. Ali A. Mazrui, 'The World Economy and the African/Afro-American Connection', in *Dynamics of the African/Afro-American Connection: From Dependency to Self-Reliance*, ed. Adelaide M. Cromwell (Washington, D.C.: Howard University Press, 1987), 42–3.

123. Ronald Walters claims that Garvey's economic vision was entirely directed toward redeeming Africa and Africans. Ronald W. Walters, *Pan Africanism in the African Diaspora: An Analysis of Modern Afrocentric Political Movements* (Detroit: Wayne State University Press, 1993), 50.

124. 'Pan-Negroism of Marcus Garvey', *Nigerian Pioneer*, 22 October 1920, 5.

125. *Gold Coast Independent*, 22 October 1921. Quoted in Kimble, *A Political History of Ghana*, 543.

126. 'Reflections, Observations and Criticisms', *Sierra Leone Weekly News*, 24 January 1920, 6.

127. 'The U.N.I.A. Convention Held in America During the Month of August, 1920', *Colonial and Provincial Reporter*, 18 September 1920, 8.

128. 'The Universal Negro Improvement Association of America: What it Means to the Negro!', *Colonial and Provincial Reporter*, 7 August 1920, 3.

129. 'The U.N.I.A. Convention Held in America During the Month of August, 1920', *Colonial and Provincial Reporter*, 18 September 1920, 4.

130. 'Copy of Report Read by the Assistant General Secretary, Westward Charter, Freetown, Sierra Leone', *Negro World*, 12 November 1922.

131. Cronon, *Black Moses*, 64, 66, 67.

132. Kimble, *A Political History of Ghana*, 543.

133. 'The Hon. Marcus Garvey, President of Africa', *African Political Organization*, 25 February 1922, 10, file: South Africa: A Collection of Miscellaneous Documents, 1902–1963, microfilm reel 12, archives, Hoover Institution on War, Revolution and Peace, Stanford, California.

134. Marcus Garvey's article appeared in *Negro World*, 5 July 1919, reprinted by *Times of Nigeria*, 3–24 November 1919, 7.

135. Announcement, *Sierra Leone Weekly News*, 10 July 1920, 12.

136. 'The New Black Star Liner', *West Africa Mail and Trade Gazette*, 24 September 1921, 2.

137. Emily Christmas Kinch presentation at the UNIA Annual Meeting, New York, 20 June 1920, Robert A. Hill, ed., *The Marcus Garvey and Universal Negro Improvement Association Papers, 27 August 1919–31 August 1920*, vol. 2 (Berkeley: University of California Press, 1983), 387.

138. Bernard Magubane, *The Ties That Bind: African-American Consciousness of Africa* (Trenton, N.J.: Africa World Press, 1989), 89.

139. To the Editor of the Negro Wordl [*sic*], 'Conditions in Sierra Leone', *Negro World*, 21 March 1921.

140. 'Benjamin Majafi to S.A. Haynes, President of the Pittsburgh division of the UNIA, 8 March 1927', *Negro World*, 30 April 1927, 5.

141. 'The Trial of Marcus Garvey', *Gold Coast Leader*, 18 August 1923, 4.

142. 'Mr. Marryshow and Marcus Garvey', *Gold Coast Leader*, 12 January 1924. Albert T. Marryshow, a black pan-African activist from Grenada, represented the British colony of Grenada at the London session of the Second Pan-African Congress, 1921, where he strongly advocated black participation in the government of the island. In 1935 he acted as a deputy chairman

of the International African Friends of Abyssinia. Imanuel Geiss, *The Pan-African Movement: A History of Pan-Africanism in America, Europe and Africa* (New York: Africana Publishing, 1974), 244, 354–5.

143. Quoted in Amy Jacques Garvey, *Black Power in America: Marcus Garvey's Impact on Jamaica and Africa: The Power of the Human Spirit* (Kingston, Jam.: Amy Jacques Garvey, 1968), 29. Peter Abrahams, from Pietersburg in Transvaal, South Africa, a poet and author, was deeply influenced by black American writers and singers, and published poems in African newspapers, as well as three books. Tim Couzens, '"Moralizing Leisure Time": The Trans-Atlantic Connection and Black Johannesburg, 1918–1936', in *Industrialisation and Social Change in South Africa: African Class Formation, Culture, and Consciousness, 1870–1930*, ed. Shula Marks and Richard Rathbone (New York: Longman, 1982), 327–9.

144. Smith, *Aggrey of Africa*, 178.
145. 'The Life of Aggrey', *Sierra Leone Weekly News*, 27 April 1929, 4.
146. Kwame Nkrumah, *Ghana: The Autobiography of Kwame Nkrumah* (London: Thomas Nelson and Sons, 1957), 14.
147. Walton Johnson, *Worship and Freedom: A Black American Church in Zambia* (New York: Africana Publishing, 1977), 15.
148. Quoted in Smith, *Aggrey of Africa*, 156.
149. 'West Africa and the Education Commission – American Experts Begin their Mission: Sierra Leone's Welcome', *African World*, Special West African Monthly Supplement, no. 48, 30 October 1920, 13.
150. Quoted in King, 'Early Pan-African Politicians', 9.
151. Smith, *Aggrey of Africa*, 219.
152. *Pretoria News*, n.d.
153. 'Governor Addresses the Missionary Conference', *Rhodesia Herald*, 6 June 1924, 20–1.
154. Smith, *Aggrey of Africa*, 217.
155. 'Native Education – The Phelps-Stokes Education Commission', *Rhodesia Herald*, 6 June 1924, 14.
156. Smith, *Aggrey of Africa*, 288.
157. The allegory of the eagle is described at length in Ibid., 135–7.
158. Carlos I. H. Nelson, 'Kwame Nkrumah: A Study of his Intellectual Development in the United States, 1935–1945' (Ph.D. diss., Temple University, 1985), 51–2.
159. Smith, *Aggrey of Africa*, 135–6.
160. 'Is the Negro Coming?', *Lagos Weekly Record*, 7 April 1917, 4.
161. 'Professor Aggrey Wins Great Distinction in Scholastic Affairs', *Nigerian Pioneer*, no. 362, 17 December 1920, 6a.
162. 'The Life of Aggrey', *Sierra Leone Weekly News*, 27 April 1929, 4.
163. Harry Levin, 'Some Meanings of Myth', in *Myth and Mythmaking*, ed. Henry A. Murray (Boston: Beacon Press, 1968), 105.
164. Jerome S. Bruner, 'Myth and Identity', in Ibid., 276.

2 African Millenarianism and the African-American Myth

1. William Bascom, 'African Culture and the Missionary', *Civilisations* 3, no. 4 (1953): 500–1.

2. Quoted in Wulf Sachs, *Black Anger: The Mind of an African Negro Revealed by Psychoanalysis*, 2nd edn (New York: Greenwood Press, 1968), 106.

3. T. O. Ranger, *The African Voice in Southern Rhodesia, 1898–1930* (Evanston, Ill.: Northwestern University Press, 1970), 199.

4. Robert I. Rotberg, *The Rise of Nationalism in Central Africa: The Making of Malawi and Zambia, 1873–1964* (Cambridge, Mass.: Harvard University Press, 1965), 137.

5. Michael Barkun, *Disaster and the Millennium* (Syracuse: Syracuse University Press, 1986), 35.

6. Richard Gray points to the social importance of tiny sects of African Christians, which he calls 'small nuclei of believers'. Richard Gray, 'Popular Theologies in Africa: A Report on a Workshop on Small Christian Communities in Southern Africa', *African Affairs* 85 (January 1986): 50–1.

7. R. Bastide, 'Messianism and Social and Economic Development', in *Social Change: The Colonial Situation*, ed. Immanuel Wallerstein (New York: John Wiley and Sons, 1966), 470.

8. The Watch Tower was first established as a corporation under the title The Zion's Watch Tower Society in 1884. The title was changed in 1909 to The People's Pulpit Association. Later, the organization took the title The Watch Tower Bible and Tract Society, which served as its official name. From 1931, it was also known as Jehovah's Witnesses. Herbert Hewitt Stroup, *The Jehovah's Witnesses* (New York: Russell and Russell, 1967), 4.

9. Thomas Hodgkin, *Nationalism in Colonial Africa* (New York: New York University Press, 1962), 102.

10. Richard Gray, *Black Christians and White Missionaries* (New Haven: Yale University Press, 1990), 107.

11. Quoted in Tony Hodges, *Jehovah's Witnesses in Africa* (London: Minority Rights Group, 1985), 7.

12. Efraim Andersson, *Messianic Popular Movements in the Lower Congo* (Uppsala, Sweden: Studia Ethnographica Upsaliensia, 1958), 62.

13. Quoted in Ian Linden and Jane Linden, *Catholics, Peasants, and Chewa Resistance in Nyasaland, 1889–1939* (Berkeley: University of California Press, 1974), 93.

14. Rotberg, *The Rise of Nationalism*, 138.

15. Hodges, *Jehovah's Witnesses*, 7.

16. Rotberg, *The Rise of Nationalism*, 66–7.

17. Quoted in ibid.

18. Gray, *Black Christians*, 107–8.

19. Andrew D. Roberts, 'The Lumpa Church of Alice Lenshina', in *Protest and Power in Black Africa*, ed. Robert I. Rotberg and Ali A. Mazrui (New York: Oxford University Press, 1970), 520–1.

20. John S. Mbiti, *African Religions and Philosophy* (London: Heinemann, 1989), 195.

21. Hodges, *Jehovah's Witnesses*, 7.

22. F. Deaville Walker, *The Day of the Harvest in the White Fields of West Africa* (London: Cargate Press, n.d.), 7; Christine Heward, 'The Rise of Alice Lenshina', *New Society* 4, no. 98 (13 August 1964): 6.

23. Quoted in Randall K. Burkett, *Garveyism as a Religious Movement: The*

Institutionalization of a Black Civil Religion (Metuchen, N.J.: Scarecrow Press, 1978), 63.

24. Ibid.
25. E. David Cronon, *Black Moses: The Story of Marcus Garvey and the Universal Negro Improvement Association* (Madison: University of Wisconsin Press, 1987), 63–4.
26. J. Barnard Belman, 'Garvey "Great King" in South Africa', *Negro World*, 24 October 1925, file: UNIA, Garveyism in South Africa, no. 1, Marcus Garvey, Papers, African Studies Center, University of California, Los Angeles (hereafter cited as Marcus Garvey Papers).
27. Robert Edgar, 'Garveyism in Africa: Dr. Wellington and the American Movement in the Transkei', *Ufahamah* 6, no. 3 (1976): 35–6.
28. W. Ozmond, Divisional Criminal Investigation Officer, Kimberly Division, to the Commissioner, South African Police, Pretoria, 9 August 1928, S.4/19/28, file: UNIA, Garveyism in South Africa, no. 2., Marcus Garvey Papers.
29. Quoted in Rotberg, *The Rise of Nationalism*, 141.
30. Quoted in Ibid.
31. James R. Hooker, 'Witnesses and Watchtower in the Rhodesias and Nyasaland', *Journal of African History* 6, no. 1 (1965): 100.
32. Griffith Quick, 'Some Aspects of the African Watch Tower Movement in Northern Rhodesia', *International Review of Missions* 29, no. 114 (April 1940): 218.
33. Quoted in Edgar, 'Garveyism in Africa', 39. It is interesting to mention that the same idea that African-Americans would be the avant-garde in the liberation of Africa prevailed at the same time among UNIA supporters in the United States. Dennis Hickey and Kenneth C. Wylie, *An Enchanting Darkness: The American Vision of Africa in the Twentieth Century* (East Lansing: Michigan State University Press, 1993), 261.
34. Quoted in Ranger, *The African Voice*, 205.
35. Edgar, 'Garveyism in Africa', 38. The source for these rumors was the UNIA Black Star Line. The stories of a shipping line owned by black Americans and the messianic hopes which it generated were not limited to East-Central or Southern Africa. In Nigeria, there were similar rumors that a ship commanded by a black captain and black officers was carrying armed black Americans coming to free the Africans from the British yoke. Joyce Cary, *The Case For African Freedom and Other Writings on Africa* (Austin: University of Texas Press, 1962), 20–1.
36. Quoted in George Shepperson, 'Nyasaland and the Millennium', in *Black Africa, Its Peoples and Their Cultures Today*, ed. John Middleton (London: Macmillan, 1970), 235.
37. Ranger, *The African Voice*, 205.
38. Quoted in Rotberg, *The Rise of Nationalism*, 140–1.
39. Edgar, 'Garveyism in Africa', 41.
40. Ibid.
41. T. O. Ranger, 'The Myth of the Afro-American in East-Central Africa, 1900–1939' (African Studies Center, University of California, Los Angeles, April 1971, mimeographed), 14.
42. Andersson, *Messianic Popular Movements*, 256.

43. The Providence Industrial Mission was established with the help of two African-American missionaries of the National Baptist Convention Foreign Missions: Emma B. Delaney and Reverend L. N. Cheek. Milfred C. Fierce, *The Pan-African Idea in the United States, 1900–1919: African-American Interest in Africa and Interaction with West Africa* (New York: Garland Publishing, 1993), 105.

44. Linden, *Catholics, Peasants*, 94. Karonga was a battleground between colonial British forces that came from Nyasaland and German forces that were stationed in German East Africa, today Tanzania. Unlike West and Southern Africa where the Allies occupied the German colonies until 1916, the fighting in East Africa continued until the end of World War I when Imperial Germany was defeated.

45. Quoted in Ibid., 95.

46. Ibid.

47. George Simeon Mwase, *Strike a Blow and Die: A Narrative of Race Relations in Colonial Africa*, ed. with an introduction by Robert I. Rotberg (Cambridge, Mass.: Harvard University Press, 1967), 36.

48. Robert Rotberg, who discovered Mwase's manuscript in the Malawian archives in 1962, attributed to the manuscript a high degree of authenticity and accuracy. In his article, 'Psychological Stress and the Question of Identity: Chilembwe's Revolt Reconsidered', Rotberg accepts Mwase's view that Chilembwe was seeking martyrdom when he led his rebellion in 1915. Robert I. Rotberg, 'Psychological Stress and the Question of Identity: Chilembwe's Revolt Reconsidered', in *Protest and Power in Black Africa*, ed. Robert I. Rotberg and Ali A. Mazrui (New York: Oxford University Press, 1970), 337–73.

    Jane and Ian Linden and George Shepperson cast doubts on the validity of Mwase's diary as a reliable source. Jane Linden and Ian Linden, 'John Chilembwe and the New Jerusalem', *Journal of African History* 12, no. 4 (1971): 631–2; George Shepperson, 'The Place of John Chilembwe in Malawi Historiography', in *The Early History of Malawi*, ed. Bridglal Pachai (Evanston, Ill.: Northwestern University Press, 1972), 417.

49. George A. Shepperson, 'External Factors in the Development of African Nationalism, with Particular Reference to British Central Africa', in *African Politics and Society: Basic Issues and Problems of Government and Development*, ed. Irving Leonard Markovitz (New York: Free Press, 1970), 195.

50. Shepperson, 'Nyasaland and the Millennium', 236.

51. Edwin W. Smith, *Aggrey of Africa: A Study in Black and White* (New York: Doubleday, Doran, 1929), 181.

52. George Shepperson, *Myth and Reality in Malawi* (Evanston, Ill.: Northwestern University Press, 1966), 11.

53. Smith, *Aggrey of Africa*, 215.

54. Ibid., 207.

55. Shepperson, 'Nyasaland and the Millennium', 235.

56. Quoted in Smith, *Aggrey of Africa*, 181.

57. Ibid., 181–2.

58. Jeanne Maquet-Tombu, *Le Siecle marche. Recit Historique* (Brussels: Office de Publicite, 1936), 205.

59. R. C. Taderera, sworn statement, no. X101, Gutu, 22 October 1932, F. H.

Lemon, Justice of the Peace, file: AMEC in Zimbabwe, NAR, S1542/m8A, Marcus Garvey Papers.

60. Superintendent of Natives' Office to Chief Native Commissioner, 4 August 1932, 4061, 1, file: AMEC in Zimbabwe, NAR, S1542/m8A, Marcus Garvey Papers.
61. When these events took place, the AME Church bishopric in the region was vacant and was expected to be filled by Reverend Dr Sims who was to arrive in Cape Town from America at the end of January 1933. AME Church officials in Cape Town denied any connection between the black American church and the millenarian movement. Chief Native Commissioner, report, 19 December 1932, 2, file: AMEC in Zimbabwe, NAR, S1542/m8A, Marcus Garvey Papers.
62. Superintendent of Natives' Office to Chief Native Commissioner, 4 August 1932, 4061, 3, file: AMEC in Zimbabwe, NAR, S1542/m8A, Marcus Garvey Papers.
63. Vittorio Lanternari, *The Religions of the Oppressed: A Study of Modern Messianic Cults* (New York: Alfred A. Knopf, 1963), 30.
64. Michel Merlier, *Le Congo de la colonisation belge a l'independance* (Paris: Francois Maspero, 1962), 240.
65. Ranger, *The African Voice*, 204.
66. Bruce Fetter, ed., *Colonial Rule in Africa: Readings from Primary Sources* (Madison: University of Wisconsin Press, 1979), 135.
67. T. O. Ranger, 'The Mwana Lesa Movement of 1925', in *Themes in the Christian History of Central Africa*, ed. T. O. Ranger and John Weller (Berkeley: University of California Press, 1975), 57.

3 African Cultural Nationalism: Contrasting Views of the African-American Myth

1. Elliott P. Skinner, 'Personal Networks and Institutional Linkages in the Global System', in *Dynamics of the African/Afro-American Connection: From Dependency to Self-Reliance*, ed. Adelaide M. Cromwell (Washington, D.C.: Howard University Press, 1987), 16.
2. Quoted in J. B. Webster, 'Political Activity in British West Africa, 1900–1940', in *History of West Africa*, ed. J. F. A. Ajayi and Michael Crowder (London: Longman, 1974), 2: 569.
3. Leo Spitzer, *The Creoles of Sierra Leone: Responses to Colonialism, 1870–1945* (Madison: University of Wisconsin Press, 1974), 43–4.
4. A. E. Afigbo, 'The Establishment of Colonial Rule, 1900–1918', in *History of West Africa*, vol. 2, ed. J. F. A. Ajayi and Michael Crowder (London: Longman, 1974), 441.
5. Webster, 'Political Activity', 569.
6. From 1840 until 1870, the decline in mortality rate from fevers in the tropics varied from 61 per cent to 90 per cent. Quinine, the first 'wonder drug', contributed to this decline. Philip Curtin, *Death by Migration: Europe's Encounter with the Tropical World in the Nineteenth Century* (Cambridge: Cambridge University Press, 1989), 62.
7. Spitzer, *The Creoles of Sierra Leone*, 65.
8. E. A. Ayandele, *Holy Johnson: Pioneer of African Nationalism, 1836–1917*

(London: Frank Cass, 1970), 179. Henry Carr, a leading western-educated African in Lagos, was one of the main advocates of the Booker T. Washington educational philosophy. See Chapter 5.

9. Spitzer, *The Creoles of Sierra Leone*, 64.

10. Edward W. Blyden, 'Ethiopia Stretching Out Her Hands Unto God: or Africa's Service to the World', in *Readings in African Political Thought*, ed. Gideon-Cyrus M. Mutiso and S. W. Rohio (London: Heinemann, 1975), 8.

11. Quoted in Francis Agbodeka, 'The Fanti Confederacy, 1865–1869: An Enquiry Into the Origins, Nature and Extent of an Early West African Protest Movement', *Transactions of the Historical Society of Ghana* 7 (1964): 96.

12. Ayandele, *Holy Johnson*, 178.

13. Quoted in David Kimble, *A Political History of Ghana: The Rise of Gold Coast Nationalism, 1850–1928* (London: Clarendon Press, 1963), 91.

14. Quoted in St Clair Drake, *The Redemption of Africa and Black Religion* (Chicago: Third World Press, 1970), 57.

15. Lecture by Kwamankra, quoted in Casely Hayford, *Ethiopia Unbound: Studies in Race Emancipation* (London: C. M. Phillips, 1911), 194.

16. Rina Lee Okonkwo, 'The Emergence of Nationalism in British West Africa, 1912–1940' (Ph.D. diss., City University of New York, 1980), 188, 193, 194, 199.

17. Hayford, *Ethiopia Unbound*, 173–4.

18. O. T. Nana, 'The Negro Problem', *Sierra Leone Weekly News*, 22 July 1911, 5.

19. Okonkwo, 'The Emergence of Nationalism', 95.

20. Samuel Rohdie, 'The Gold Coast Aborigines Abroad', *Journal of African History* 6, no. 3, (1965): 389–90.

21. O. T. Nana, 'The Negro Problem', *Sierra Leone Weekly News*, 22 July 1911, 5.

22. Quoted in Robert W. July, *The Origins of Modern African Thought: Its Development in West Africa During the Nineteenth and Twentieth Centuries* (London: Faber and Faber, 1968), 343.

23. Spitzer, *The Creoles of Sierra Leone*, 116–17.

24. Ibid., 151.

25. E. A. Ayandele, *A Visionary of the African Church: Mojola Agbebi, 1860–1917* (Nairobi: East African Publishing House, 1971), 13–14.

26. Edward W. Blyden, 'Africa and the Africans', in *Readings in African Political Thought*, ed. Gideon-Cyrus M. Mutiso and S. W. Rohio (London: Heinemann, 1975), 17.

27. J. Ayodele Langley used the term 'Afro-American school of thought' to describe the bulk of pan-African ideas that emerged in the United States at the turn of the century and its influence on western-educated Africans. Langley does not discuss how western-educated Africans made use of Negro Americans to support their own doctrine for the regeneration of Africa. J. Ayodele Langley, *Pan-Africanism and Nationalism in West Africa, 1900–1945: A Study in Ideology and Social Classes* (Oxford: Clarendon Press, 1978), 35–9.

28. Walter L. Williams, *Black Americans and the Evangelization of Africa, 1877–1900* (Madison: University of Wisconsin Press, 1982), 98.

29. Ayandele, *Holy Johnson*, 353–4, 203.

30. Edward W. Blyden, *The African Problem and other Discourses, Delivered in America in 1890* (London: W. B. Whittingham, 1890), 1, 11.
31. Ibid., 14.
32. Ibid., 11.
33. Quoted in Drake, *The Redemption of Africa*, 63.
34. Quoted in V. Y. Mudimbe, *The Invention of Africa: Gnosis, Philosophy, and the Order of Knowledge* (Bloomington: Indiana University Press, 1988), 98.
35. Blyden, *The African Problem*, 2.
36. 'The Afro-Americans at Victoria Park', *Sierra Leone Weekly News*, 23 January 1915, 6.
37. 'The Negro Problem in America', *Lagos Standard*, 3 June 1903.
38. John T. Marcus, 'The World Impact of the West: The Mystique and the Sense of Participation in History', in *Myth and Mythmaking*, ed. Henry A. Murray (Boston: Beacon Press, 1968), 222.
39. 'Racial Unity', *Gold Coast Leader*, 24–31 July 1920, 5.
40. Reverend John A. Gregg, 'Africa and a Way Out', *AME Church Review* 37, no. 4 (April 1921): 213.
41. Quoted in Kenneth King, 'James E. K. Aggrey: Collaborator, Nationalist, Pan-African', *Canadian Journal of African Studies* 3, no. 3, (Fall 1970): 516.
42. Kimpianga Mahaniah, 'The Presence of Black Americans in Lower Congo from 1878 to 1921', in *Global Dimensions of the African Diaspora*, ed. Joseph E. Harris (Washington, D.C.: Howard University Press, 1982), 270.
43. Blyden, *The African Problem*, 14.
44. Robert W. July, 'Nineteenth-Century Negritude: Edward W. Blyden', *Journal of African History* 5, no. 1 (1964): 76–7.
45. Ayandele, *Holy Johnson*, 353.
46. Quoted in Mudimbe, *The Invention of Africa*, 113.
47. Rina Lee Okonkwo, 'Orishatukeh Faduma: A Man of Two Worlds', *Journal of Negro History* 68, no. 1 (Winter 1983): 27.
48. Hollis R. Lynch, 'Edward W. Blyden: Pioneer West African Nationalist', *Journal of African History* 6, no. 3 (1965): 387.
49. Blyden, 'Ethiopia Stretching Out', 6–7.
50. Ayandele, *Holy Johnson*, 240.
51. Bishop H. M. Turner, 'The American Negro and the Fatherland', in *Africa and the American Negro: Addresses and Proceedings of the Congress on Africa . . . December 13–15, 1895*, ed. John Wesley Bowen (Miami: Mnemosyne Publishing, 1969), 195.
52. Alexander Walters, *My Life and Work* (New York, Fleming H. Revell, 1917), 172.
53. David H. Anthony, 'Max Yergan in South Africa: From Evangelical Pan-Africanist to Revolutionary Socialist', *African Studies Review* 34, no. 2 (Sept. 1991): 27, 31.
54. Blyden, besides his vigorous campaign for the African-American avant-garde, expressed differing and even opposite opinions. See, for example, July, 'Nineteenth-Century Negritude', 79–86. E. A. Ayandele, who read all the printed works as well as many unpublished official letters of Blyden, cast light on that phenomenon. Ayandele refers to Blyden as 'master of

realism; for him there could be no question of sticking to principles'. Ayandele concluded that Blyden was characterized by 'consistent inconsistencies'. Ayandele, *Holy Johnson*, 62, n 30. That inconsistent behavior does not diminish Blyden's leading role in supporting African-American avant-garde theory.

55. O. Faduma, 'What the African Movement Stands For', *Sierra Leone Weekly News*, 3 October 1914, 6–7.

56. Pierre Daye, 'Le mouvement pan-negre', *Le Flambeau* 3 (May–Aug. 1921): 368, 372.

57. Tony Martin, *Race First: The Ideological and Organizational Struggles of Marcus Garvey and the Universal Negro Improvement Association* (Westport, Conn.: Greenwood Press, 1976), 113.

58. 'Farewell to Delegates to League of Nations', Report from the UNIA Convention, New York, 22 August 1922, Robert A. Hill, ed., *The Marcus Garvey and Universal Negro Improvement Association Papers, 1 September 1921– 2 September 1922*, vol. 4 (Berkeley: University of California Press, 1985), 947.

59. E. U. Essien-Udom, 'The Relationship of Afro-Americans to African Nationalism', *Freedomways* 2, no. 4 (Fall 1962): 397.

60. Amy Jacques Garvey, ed., *Philosophy and Opinions of Marcus Garvey: or Africa for the Africans*, 2nd edn, 2 vols (London: Frank Cass, 1967), 363, 376–377.

61. Hayford, *Ethiopia Unbound*, 172–3.

62. Ayandele, *A Visionary*, 27.

63. 'American Negroes and Africa', *Lagos Weekly Record*, 5 July 1899.

64. 'More on Ethiopianism', *Central African Times*, 25 May 1901, 9.

65. Hayford, *Ethiopia Unbound*, 180–2.

66. *Lagos Weekly Record*, 31 October 1914.

67. S. Y. Boadi-Siaw, 'Brazilian Returnees of West Africa', in *Global Dimensions of the African Diaspora*, ed. Joseph E. Harris (Washington, D.C.: Howard University Press, 1982), 291; Akintola J. G. Wyse, 'The Sierra Leone Krios: A Reappraisal from the Perspective of the African Diaspora', in Ibid., 325.

68. Mojola Agbebi, 'Lecture on Liberia', *Lagos Weekly Record*, 13 October 1894, 2.

69. Kobina Sekyi, 'Our White Friends', *Gold Coast Leader*, 18 November 1922, 6.

70. Kimble, *A Political History of Ghana*, 355.

71. G. M. Haliburton, *The Prophet Harris: A Study of an African Prophet and his Mass Movement in the Ivory Coast and the Gold Coast, 1913–1915* (London: Longman, 1971), 83–4.

72. Hayford, *Ethiopia Unbound*, 170.

73. Kimble, *A Political History of Ghana*, 332, 341, 350–1.

74. Blyden, *The African Problem*, 2; Hayford, *Ethiopia Unbound*, 173.

75. Kimble, *A Political History of Ghana*, 138.

76. Ayandele, *Holy Johnson*, 353, 288–9.

77. Veronika Gorog-Karady, 'Stereotypes ethniques et domination coloniale: l'image du Blanc dans la litterature orale africaine', *Cahiers d'Etudes Africaines* 15, no. 4 (1975): 635–47.

78. Rohdie, 'The Gold Coast Aborigines Abroad', 389.

79. 'At the Headquarters, Accra', *Gold Coast Leader*, 13 January 1906, 4.
80. Quoted in A. Adu Boahen, *African Perspectives on Colonialism* (Baltimore: Johns Hopkins University Press, 1987), 20.
81. Africanus B. Horton, *Letters on the Political Condition of the Gold Coast* (London: Frank Cass, 1970), iii.
82. July, *The Origins of Modern African Thought*, 447.
83. Casely Hayford, *The Truth about the West African Land Question* (New York: Negro Universities Press, 1969), 99.
84. Lynch, 'Edward W. Blyden', 379.
85. Mudimbe, *The Invention of Africa*, 102–3.
86.· O. T. Nana, 'The Negro Problem', *Sierra Leone Weekly News*, 2 July 1911, 5.
87. 'The Relation of the Negro in Exile to Africa', *Lagos Weekly Record*, 2 June 1900.
88. Hayford, *Ethiopia Unbound*, 171.
89. Okonkwo, 'The Emergence of Nationalism', 196.

4 African-American Models in African Politics

1. C. W. Farquhar, 'Monsieur Blaise Diagne', *Sierra Leone Weekly News*, 11 January 1919, 8.
2. Quoted in 'Sir H. H. Johnston and the Pan-African Congress', *West Africa*, 10 September 1921, 1054. *West Africa* was established in London in 1917, reflecting West African commercial interests. It was directed at Europeans, but soon became popular among western-educated Africans. J. Ayodele Langley, *Pan-Africanism and Nationalism in West Africa, 1900–1945: A Study in Ideology and Social Classes* (Oxford: Clarendon Press, 1978), 255, n 56.
3. John Runcie, 'The Influence of Marcus Garvey and the Universal Negro Improvement Association in Sierra Leone', *Africana Research Bulletin* 12, no. 3. (June 1983): 5, 16.
4. Tony Martin, *The Pan-African Connection: From Slavery to Garvey and Beyond* (Dover, Mass.: The Majority Press, 1983), 134–5.
5. Rina Lee Okonkwo, 'The Garvey Movement in British West Africa', *Journal of African History* 21, no. 1 (1980): 110.
6. *Sierra Leone Weekly News*, 10 July 1920, 12; 'Universal Negro Improvement Association and African Communities' League, Lagos Branch, Notice to the General Public', *Lagos Weekly Record*, 25 September 1920, 6.
7. 'The Proposed Technical and Industrial School for Girls, A Reply to Ma Mashado', *Sierra Leone Weekly News*, 19 June 1920, 9.
8. 'The Marcus Garvey Movement', *Times of Nigeria*, 21 May 1920, 5.
9. David Levering Lewis, *W. E. B. Du Bois: Biography of a Race, 1868–1919* (New York: Henry Holt, 1993), 316, 399, 439.
10. W. E. B. Du Bois, *Dusk of Dawn: An Essay Toward an Autobiography of a Race Concept* (New York: Schocken Books, 1968), 116–17.
11. W. E. B. Du Bois, 'To the Nations of the World', address of the Pan-African Congress (Leaflet, London, 1900), also in *The Afro-Americans: Selected Documents*, ed. John H. Bracey Jr, August Meier and Elliott Rudwick (Boston: Allyn and Bacon, 1972), 388.
12. Milfred C. Fierce, 'African-American Interest in Africa and Interaction with West Africa: The Origins of the Pan-African Idea in the United States,

1900–1919' (Ph.D. diss., Columbia University, 1976), 280. For a thorough discussion of Du Bois's complex attitude towards World War I and the role of blacks in it, see Wilson Jeremiah Moses, *The Golden Age of Black Nationalism, 1850–1925* (New York: Oxford University Press, 1988), 220–50.

13. Elliott P. Skinner, *African Americans and U.S. Policy Toward Africa, 1850–1924: In Defense of Black Nationality* (Washington: Howard University Press, 1992), 396.

14. Quoted in Judge McCants Stewart, 'A Proposed Pan African Conference', *West Africa*, 12 February 1919, 7. For Du Bois's preparation to organize the congress, see Lewis, *W. E. B. Du Bois: Biography of a Race, 1868–1919*, 561–3.

15. 'The Pan African Conference', *Gold Coast Leader*, Cape Coast, 12 July 1919, 3.

16. B. Diagne and W. E. B. Du Bois, 'The Pan African Congress', *Sierra Leone Weekly News*, 14 June 1919, 7.

17. 'The Pan African Conference', *Gold Coast Leader*, Cape Coast, 12 July 1919, 3.

18. *West Africa*, 20 August 1921.

19. *West Africa*, 8 October 1921, 12.

20. Isaac Beton, a teacher and publisher, taught at a lycée in Paris and published the journal *Imperium, Revue Coloniale Francaise*. The Pan-African Association was created following the resolution of the Second Pan-African Congress in 1921 to carry out the various decisions adopted by the congress. Imanuel Geiss, *The Pan-African Movement: A History of Pan-Africanism in America, Europe and Africa* (New York: Africana Publishing, 1974), 248, 250.

21. Actually, the Second Pan-African Congress of 1921 was dominated by Du Bois who organized and financed the meetings with the help of contributions from the black community in the United States. 'West Africa and the Pan-African Congress', *African World*, Special West African Monthly Supplement, no. 59, 30 September 1921, 11.

22. Geiss, *The Pan-African Movement*, 250.

23. Editorial Notes, *Gold Coast Leader*, 14 August 1920.

24. 'The Congress in Paris', *African World*, Special West African Monthly Supplement, no. 59, 30 September 1921, 17. It is of interest to note that during the 1920s and 1930s the African-Americans were seen as a vanguard by communist leaders as well, who assigned them the task of spreading communism and organizing communist activities among Africans in Africa. James R. Hooker, *Black Revolutionary: George Padmore's Path from Communism to Pan-Africanism* (New York: Praeger, 1967), 9–10.

25. *West Africa*, 8 October 1921.

26. 'West Africa and the Pan-African Congress', *African World*, Special West African Monthly Supplement, no. 59, 30 September 1921, 15.

27. Martin Kilson, 'The National Congress of British West Africa, 1918–1935', in *Protest and Power in Black Africa*, ed. Robert I. Rotberg and Ali A. Mazrui (New York: Oxford University Press, 1970), 572.

28. David Kimble, *A Political History of Ghana: The Rise of Gold Coast Nationalism 1850–1928* (London: Clarendon Press, 1963), 381, 383–4.

29. Robert W. July, *The Origins of Modern African Thought: Its Development*

in West Africa During the Nineteenth and Twentieth Centuries (London: Faber and Faber, 1968), 445–6.

30. Kimble, *A Political History of Ghana*, 385–6.
31. The only positive reference to the black American educational system was at the Bathurst Session of the NCBWA, December 1925–January 1926, where a decision was made to set up National Schools in West Africa, modelled on the Tuskegee Institute. Langley, *Pan-Africanism and Nationalism*, 147.
32. Geiss, *The Pan-African Movement*, 240–1.
33. Langley, *Pan-Africanism and Nationalism*, 77–8.
34. Langley devotes a whole chapter to the formation and activities of the various branches of the NCBWA in his comprehensive research. Ibid., 134–94.
35. Quoted in Leo Spitzer, *The Creoles of Sierra Leone: Responses to Colonialism, 1870–1945* (Madison: Wisconsin University Press, 1974), 174.
36. Quoted in Langley, *Pan-Africanism and Nationalism*, 133.
37. 'Pan-African Congress', Editorial, *Gold Coast Leader*, 12 July 1919, 3. Quoted in Okonkwo, 'The Garvey Movement', 109–10.
38. Quoted in Kimble, *A Political History of Ghana*, 542.
39. Editorial Notes, *Gold Coast Leader*, 18 December 1920.
40. 'What We Think', *African World*, 14 August 1920, 73.
41. Kobina Sekyi, *Gold Coast Leader*, 18 November 1922, 6.
42. 'Marcus Garvey's Pipe Dream', *Nigerian Pioneer*, 17 December 1920, 5.
43. Margaret Priestley, *West African Trade and Coast Society: A Family Study* (London: Oxford University Press, 1969), 173.
44. Spitzer, *The Creoles of Sierra Leone*, 173.
45. 'Marcus Garvey and His African Problems', *Sierra Leone Weekly News*, 13 November 1920, 8. Langley analyzes the moderate and liberal nationalism of the NCBWA activists. Langley, *Pan-Africanism and Nationalism*, 113–20.
46. 'Marcus Garvey's Pipe Dream', *Nigerian Pioneer*, 17 December 1920, 5.
47. Ibid.
48. 'Marcus Garvey and His African Problems', *Sierra Leone Weekly News*, 13 November 1920, 8.
49. 'Comments of the West African Press. African Evolution', *West Africa*, 27 November 1920, 1496.
50. 'Pan-Negroism of Marcus Garvey II', *Nigerian Pioneer*, 29 October 1920, 5.
51. 'Marcus Garvey's Pipe Dream', *Nigerian Pioneer*, 17 December 1920, 5.
52. 'Marcus Garvey and His African Problems', *Sierra Leone Weekly News*, 13 November 1920, 8.
53. Quoted in Letter to the Editor, J. G. Campbell, *Times of Nigeria*, 24 May 1920, 4. J. G. Campbell was one of the architects of the National Congress policy that rejected Garvey's political scheme while accepting commercial contact with the UNIA. In a personal letter to the editor of *Times of Nigeria*, Campbell explains that policy and quotes Resolution 5. Campbell's quotation contains grammatical errors and is incomplete.
54. Langley, *Pan-Africanism and Nationalism*, 103.
55. Ibid., 102–3.
56. 'Universal Negro Improvement Association and African Communities' League, Lagos Branch, Notice to the General Public', *Lagos Weekly Record*, 25 September 1920, 6.

57. 'The Universal Negro Improvement Association', *Lagos Weekly Record*, 27 November 1920, 5.
58. Kobina Sekyi, *Gold Coast Leader*, 18 November 1922, 6.
59. J. B. Webster, 'Political Activity in British West Africa, 1900–1940', in *History of West Africa*, ed. J. F. A. Ajayi and Michael Crowder (London: Longman, 1974) 2:581.
60. Harold R. Isaacs, 'Dubois and Africa', *Race: The Journal of the Institute of Race Relations* 2, no. 1 (Nov. 1960): 13.
61. 'The Pan African Conference', *Gold Coast Leader*, 12 July 1919, 3; Lewis, W. E. B. *Du Bois: Biography of a Race, 1868–1919*, 567.
62. The two leading positions of the executive committee, president and secretary, were divided between Diagne and Du Bois respectively, and both signed a conference report. B. Diagne and W. E. B. Du Bois, 'The Pan African Congress', *Sierra Leone Weekly News*, 14 June 1919, 7. Diagne and Du Bois also divided between themselves the leading positions of the executive committee which was set up by the congress. David Levering Lewis, ed., *W. E. B. Du Bois: A Reader* (New York: Henry Holt, 1995), 670.
63. Garvey's biographer, E. David Cronon, referred to Du Bois as 'Garvey's old enemy'. E. David Cronon, *Black Moses: The Story of Marcus Garvey and the Universal Negro Improvement Association* (Madison: University of Wisconsin Press, 1987), 130. George Padmore, a black contemporary of the two, notes: 'Common ground between them, there was none. Their concepts of political philosophies and economic systems were diametrically opposed.' George Padmore, *Pan-Africanism or Communism* (London: Doubleday, 1971), 84. Wilson Jeremiah Moses points to the public mudslinging they both engaged in. Wilson Jeremiah Moses, *Black Messiahs and Uncle Toms: Social and Literary Manipulations of a Religious Myth* (University Park: Pennsylvania State University Press, 1982), 130.
64. Diagne to Garvey, 3 July 1921, quoted in Henri Charpin, 'La question noire', *La Revue Indigene* 18 (Nov.–Dec. 1922): 281. A magazine bearing a similar title, *Revue Indigene*, was established in 1927 in Haiti by a group of black Francophone intellectuals who returned from Paris where they had become imbued with pan-African nationalist ideas. Geiss, *The Pan-African Movement*, 316–17.
65. Diagne's letter quoted in Charpin, 'La question noire', 279.
66. Ibid.
67. Quoted in Ibid.
68. Hans Kohn and Wallace Sokolsky, *African Nationalism in the Twentieth Century* (Princeton, N.J.: D. Van Nostrand, 1965), 126.
69. Geiss, *The Pan-African Movement*, 239.
70. Langley, *Pan-Africanism and Nationalism*, 64–5.
71. Maurice Delafosse, 'Le Congres Panafricain', *Bulletin du Comite de l'afrique Francaise* (March–April 1919): supplement 55.
72. 'West Africa and the Pan-African Congress', *African World*, Special West African Monthly Supplement, no. 59, 30 September 1921, xv.
73. 'M. Diagne, depute du Senegal et president du Congres pannoir le dit aux lecteurs de la Nation Belge, Paris, 22 Septembre', *La Nation Belge*, 24 September 1921.
74. Ibid.

75. Elliott M. Rudwick, *W. E. B. Du Bois: Propagandist of the Negro Protest* (New York: Atheneum, 1968), 224.
76. Diagne to Garvey, quoted in Charpin, 'La question noire', 281.
77. Lewis, *W. E. B. Du Bois: A Reader*, 663–4.
78. Robert Broadhurst, 'The Second Pan African Congress', *Sierra Leone Weekly News*, 5 November 1921, 149; W. E. B. Du Bois, 'Africa and the American Negro Intelligentsia', *Presence Africaine* 5 (1955–6): 42–3.
79. Pierre Daye, 'Le mouvement pan negre', *Le Flambeau* 3 (May–August 1921): 370–1.
80. Charpin, 'La question noire', 282.
81. Ibid., 282–5.
82. Daye, 'Le mouvement pan negre', 372.
83. *Neptune*, 14 June 1921, quoted in Padmore, *Pan-Africanism or Communism*, 110–11; Langley, *Pan-Africanism and Nationalism*, 82, n 16.
84. 'Au Congres Pan-Noir "L'Afrique aux African" a dit Marcus Garvey, "Langage de bolchevik!" replique M. Diagne', *Depeche Coloniale et Maritime*, 6 September 1921.
85. 'M. Diagne, depute du Senegal et president du Congres pannoir le dit aux lecteurs de la Nation Belge, Paris, 22 Septembre', *La Nation Belge*, 24 September 1921.
86. Quoted in Charpin, 'La question noire', 279.
87. J. Suret-Canale, 'Un pionnier meconnu du mouvement democratique et national en Afrique', *Etudes Dahomeennes*, no. 3 (December 1964): 10.
88. Du Bois's contribution to the congresses is beyond question; however, he used to overemphasize the importance of his own role and influence. Thus he claimed to be the initiator of the Mandate system. See Du Bois, 'Africa and the American Negro Intelligentsia', 42. Du Bois used various organs of the NAACP, such as *Crisis* and annual reports, to paint a rosy picture of the pan-African movement. Referring to the First Pan-African Congress, Du Bois stated in *Crisis* that the entire press of the world had approved the congress resolutions. The *Tenth Annual Report*, which he himself probably wrote, describes how the leaders of the world, Lloyd George, Georges Clemenceau, besides representatives of Belgium, Portugal and the United States, expressed their support for the congress. Rudwick, *W. E. B. Du Bois: Propagandist*, 213–14. Du Bois often diminished the roles played by other pan-African activists. For instance, he refrained from mentioning Sylvester Williams, who was the initiator and coordinator of the 1900 Pan-African Conference, and referred to him as a 'black West Indian barrister, practising in London'. Isaacs, 'Du Bois and Africa', 19.
89. Langley, *Pan-Africanism and Nationalism*, 312–13.
90. Imanuel Geiss was the first scholar to publish comprehensive research on the political pan-Africanism of various groups in France after World War I, in his volume, *The Pan-African Movement*, which first appeared in German under the title, *Panafrikanismus-Zur Geschichte der Dekolonisation*, Frankfurt A/M, 1968. In 1969 J. Ayodele Langley published his work on the subject: 'Pan-Africanism in Paris, 1924–36', *Journal of Modern African Studies* 7, no. 1 (1969) that preceded his book, *Pan-Africanism and Nationalism in West Africa 1900–1945*.
91. Langley, *Pan-Africanism and Nationalism*, 291.

92. Quoted in Hooker, *Black Revolutionary*, 39–40.
93. Iheanachor Egonu, '"Les Continents" and the Francophone Pan Negro Movement', *Phylon* 42, no. 3 (Fall 1981): 246.
94. Geiss, *The Pan-African Movement*, 310.
95. Langley, 'Pan-Africanism in Paris, 1924–36', 73.
96. Ibrahima B. Kake, 'The Impact of Afro-Americans on French-Speaking Black-Africans, 1919–1945', in *Global Dimensions of the African Diaspora*, ed. Joseph E. Harris (Washington, D.C.: Howard University Press, 1982), 206.
97. Geiss, *The Pan-African Movement*, 309.
98. Kojo Touvalou-Houenou, 'Paris, Couer de la Race Noire', *Les Continents*, 1 October 1924, 1; Egonu, 'Les Continents', 247–8.
99. Cronon, *Black Moses*, 146–7.
100. When Garvey visited Paris, the two main activists of national pan-Africanism, Touvalou-Houenou and Lamine Senghor, were not there to welcome him. Touvalou-Houenou was in Dahomey and Lamine Senghor had died in 1927. However, the work of pan-Africanism and nationalism was carried on by other prominent Francophone Africans including Tiemoho Garan-Kouyate from the French Sudan and Emile Faure, a Senegalese engineer. Their ideas were published by two newspapers carrying the same title, *La Race Negre*. Geiss, *The Pan-African Movement*, 311.
101. Cronon, *Black Moses*, 145, 147, 150.
102. Roi Ottley, *No Green Pastures* (New York: Charles Scribner's Sons, 1951), 108.
103. 'French Garvey Now in Paris', *Baltimore Afro-American*, 9 May 1924, 1.
104. Kake, 'The Impact of Afro-Americans', 205.
105. *Negro World*, 11 August 1928, 1.
106. Garvey's speech before his Paris audience was published in the Paris edition of the *Chicago Tribune* and only later reprinted in *Negro World*, 27 October 1928, 5.
107. Ibid. Garvey's new attitude could also be attributed to his political decline. As mentioned earlier, his European tour was a failure. His plan to establish a new strong base for the UNIA in Europe went awry. Even before his visit to Paris, Garvey mentioned the possibility of cooperation with the colonial powers. On 6 June 1928, in a speech at Royal Albert Hall, London, Garvey declared that the UNIA would be satisfied if the various colonial powers would allocate to black rule only part of Africa under their control. He even hinted that the UNIA would be content to accept the less desirable parts of the black continent. Cronon, *Black Moses*, 145.
108. Bernard Magubane, *The Ties That Bind: African-American Consciousness of Africa* (Trenton, N.J.: Africa World Press, 1989), 109. There was a tendency to present the Harlem Renaissance as a white creation. For the debate over that issue, see Charles T. Davis, *Black is the Color of the Cosmos: Essays on Afro-American Literature and Culture, 1942–1981*, ed. Henry Louis Gates Jr (Washington: Howard University Press, 1989), 68.
109. Nathan Irvin Huggins, *Harlem Renaissance* (New York: Oxford University Press, 1971), 59–60.
110. Ibid., 79–80.
111. Leopold Senghor, 'What is Negritude?', in *Readings in African Political*

Thought, ed. Gideon-Cyrus M. Mutiso and S. W. Rohio (London: Heinemann, 1975), 83.

112. Sulayman S. Nyang, *Islam, Christianity and African Identity* (Brattleboro, Vt.: Amana Books, 1984), 79.

113. Codjo Achode, 'The Negro Renaissance from America Back to Africa: A Study of the Harlem Renaissance as a Black and African Movement' (Ph.D. diss., University of Pennsylvania, 1986), 253–4.

114. Cary D. Wintz, *Black Culture and the Harlem Renaissance* (Houston, Tex.: Rice University Press, 1988), 228–9.

115. Huggins, *Harlem Renaissance*, 178, 188.

116. Wintz, *Black Culture*, 229.

117. Jacques Louis Hymans, 'French Influences on Leopold Senghor's Theory of Negritude, 1928–48', *Race: The Journal of the Institute of Race Relations* 7, no. 4 (April 1966): 366–7; St Clair Drake, '"Hide my Face?" On Pan-Africanism and Negritude', in *The Making of Black America: Essays in Negro Life and History*, vol. 1, ed. August Meier and Elliott Rudwick (New York: Atheneum, 1969), 72.

118. This, of course, does not deny the other roots of the Harlem Renaissance, as discussed by David Levering Lewis in *When Harlem Was in Vogue* (New York: Oxford University Press, 1989).

119. Quoted in St Clair Drake, 'Negro Americans and the Africa Interest', in *The American Negro Reference Book*, ed. John P. Davis (Englewood Cliffs, N.J.: Prentice-Hall, 1966), 688.

5 Africans and African-American Educational Models

1. For instance, in missionary schools operating in various parts of Africa there was a total of 137,000 African students by 1894. In the same year in one Marina highlands region of Madagascar, the proportion of young people attending missionary schools was similar to that in western Europe at the same time. Philip Curtin, et al., eds, *African History* (London: Longman, 1978), 414.

2. Where Africans were able to choose between religious and secular education, they usually preferred the latter. A case in point is the Grammar School in Freetown. When that secular school was founded in 1845, it drew students from the religious Fourah Bay Institution, established in 1827, where enrollment declined to the point that the religious institution was closed temporarily in 1859. E. A. Ayandele, *Holy Johnson: Pioneer of African Nationalism, 1836–1917* (London: Frank Cass, 1970), 71.

3. Quoted in J. Mutero Chirenje, *Ethiopianism and Afro-Americans in Southern Africa, 1883–1916* (Baton Rouge: Louisiana State University Press, 1987), 119.

4. 'The African Methodist Episcopal Zion Church on the Gold Coast', *Gold Coast Chronicle*, 5 July 1901, 2.

5. *Gold Coast Times*, 16 February 1924, 4.

6. Hamidou Cheikh Kane, *L'Aventure Ambigue Recit* (Paris: Union Generale D'editions, 1961), 47.

7. Laing Gray Cowan, James O'Connell and David G. Scanlon, eds, *Education and Nation-Building in Africa* (New York: F. A. Praeger, 1965), 28.

8. 'The Cause of Education', *Nigerian Pioneer*, 5 November 1920, 5.
9. Quoted in Chirenje, *Ethiopianism*, 118.
10. Edward H. Berman, 'Education in Africa and America: A History of the Phelps-Stokes Fund, 1911–1945' (Ed.D. diss., Columbia University, 1970), 121.
11. Veronika Gorog-Karady, 'Stereotypes ethniques et domination coloniale: l'image du Blanc dans la litterature orale africaine', *Cahiers d'Etudes Africaines* 15, no. 4 (1975): 637–8.
12. 'American Negroes and Africa', *Lagos Weekly Record*, 5 July 1899.
13. 'Industrial Education a Pressing Need', *Colonial and Provincial Reporter*, 2 October 1920, 7.
14. M. Mokete Manoedi, *Garvey and Africa* (New York: The New York Age Press, [192?]), 6–7.
15. Quoted in Mercer Cook and Stephen E. Henderson, *The Militant Black Writer in Africa and the United States* (Madison: University of Wisconsin Press, 1969), 31.
16. The three R's is a common expression for the basic educational skills: reading, writing and arithmetic.
17. 'Dr. Booker T. Washington in England', *Lagos Weekly Record*, 11 February 1911.
18. E. G. Granville Sutton, 'Booker T. Washington – An Appreciation', *Times of Nigeria*, 1–8 February 1916, 4.
19. Thomas Sowell, *Ethnic America: A History* (New York: Basic Books, 1981), 203.
20. John McCracken, *Politics and Christianity in Malawi, 1875–1940: The Impact of the Livingstonia Mission in the Northern Province* (London: Cambridge University Press, 1971), 214.
21. Donald Franklin Roth, ' "Grace Not Race" Southern Negro Church Leaders, Black Identity, and Missions to West Africa 1865–1919' (Ph.D. diss., University of Texas, 1975), 278.
22. Coles graduated from Talladega College with an A.B. in sciences. He used his agricultural-vocational knowledge during his service in Angola. Samuel B. Coles, *Preacher with a Plow* (Boston: Houghton Mifflin, 1957), 44–6, 52–3, 64.
23. James N. Calloway, 'Tuskegee Cotton-Planters in Africa', *Outlook*, 29 March 1902, 772; St Clair Drake, 'Negro Americans and the Africa Interest', in *The American Negro Reference Book*, ed. John P. Davis (Englewood Cliffs, N.J.: Prentice-Hall, 1966), 681; Booker T. Washington, 'The Successful Training of the Negro', *Sierra Leone Weekly News*, 18 May 1905, 3.
24. Hoffman also served as sanitation commissioner for the city of Abekuta and conducted agricultural experiments in Egba, Yorubaland. During his work in Nigeria from 1903 to 1908 he developed a new strain of cotton which was to become a major export crop by the 1920s. Manning Marable, 'Ambiguous Legacy: Tuskegee's "Missionary" Impulse and Africa During the Moton Administration, 1915–1935', in *Black Americans and the Missionary Movement in Africa*, ed. Sylvia M. Jacobs (Westport, Conn: Greenwood Press, 1982), 86.
25. Drake, 'Negro Americans', 682.
26. R. Hunt Davis Jr, 'The Black American Education Component in African

Responses to Colonialism in South Africa (ca. 1890–1914)', *Journal of Southern African Affairs* 3, no. 1 (Jan. 1978): 68.

27. T. O. Ranger, 'The "Ethiopian" Episode in Barotseland, 1900–1905', *Rhodes-Livingston Journal* 37 (June 1965): 30.

28. Marable, 'Ambiguous Legacy', 82.

29. Ayandele mentions that the CMS was ready to undertake the project of a West African University even before Blyden and Johnson raised the notion. The notion was never fulfilled because it was impractical. Ayandele, *Holy Johnson*, 72–3.

30. J. Ayodele Langley, *Pan-Africanism and Nationalism in West Africa, 1900– 1945: A Study in Ideology and Social Classes* (Oxford: Clarendon Press, 1978), 128–9. It is interesting to mention that the NCBWA policy of rejecting the African-American model was ignored during the third session held in Bathurst, December 1925–January 1926. The various delegations recommended the establishment of National Schools modelled on Booker T. Washington's Tuskegee Institute. Ibid., 147. The change in policy could be attributed to the effect of the Phelps-Stokes Education Commission which completed its second tour in Africa in 1924.

31. Harry Johnston, 'African Teachers and their Education: The Continent's Need for Native Universities', *African World* Special West African Supplement, no. 46, 28 August 1920, iii.

32. Johnston was sympathetic to the African cause. For instance, he was clearly against the slave trade and the trade in alcohol; in his opinion, the European slave traders ruined African societies 'from Cape Verde to the Niger Delta' and 'distilled spirit' was used by the European traders as inducement for African chiefs to become slave-traders. His sympathy toward Liberia, the first black republic in Africa, is expressed in his two-volume work entitled *Liberia* (1906; reprint, New York: Negro Universities Press, 1969). Johnston was one of the few Britains who openly supported the Republic of Liberia in its border disputes with Britain and France. Chapter 14 of the second volume is devoted to the border disputes. See also, C. Abayomi Cassell, *Liberia: History of the First African Republic* (New York: Fountainhead Publishers, 1970), 6–7, 101, 319–20.

33. John Tengo Jabavu became the spokesman for the group as editor for the newspaper *Imvo Zabantsundu* (Native Opinion) which he founded in 1884. Chirenje, *Ethiopianism*, 128.

34. W. E. B. Du Bois, *The Souls of Black Folk: Essays and Sketches* (New York: Fawcett Publications, 1970), 42.

35. David Levering Lewis, *W. E. B. Du Bois: Biography of a Race, 1868–1919* (New York: Henry Holt, 1993), 73, 548–9. Du Bois, like Booker T. Washington, had to defend education for blacks against charges by fearful whites that it would lead to dissatisfaction and agitation, and he took pains to do so. Moreover, according to Wilson Moses, Du Bois himself distrusted the mob. Wilson Jeremiah Moses, *The Golden Age of Black Nationalism 1850–1925* (New York: Oxford University Press, 1988), 140.

36. Du Bois, *The Souls of Black Folk*, 48.

37. Ibid., 77–8.

38. Ibid., 65, 79.

39. O. Faduma, 'Drawbacks and Successes of Missionary Work in Africa', *Sierra Leone Weekly News*, 20 April 1918, 18.

40. Ibid.
41. O. Faduma, 'Negro Development – Its Phases', *Sierra Leone Weekly News*, 24 September 1921.
42. Ibid.
43. O. Faduma, 'Negro Development – Its Phases', *Sierra Leone Weekly News*, 1 October 1921.
44. Ibid.
45. O. Faduma, 'Negro Development – Its Phases', *Sierra Leone Weekly News*, 24 September 1921.
46. David G. Scanlon, ed., *Church, State, and Education in Africa* (New York: Teacher's College Press, 1966), 15.
47. Berman, 'Education in Africa and America: A History of the Phelps-Stokes Fund, 1911–1945', 121–3.
48. Kenneth James King, *Pan-Africanism and Education: A Study of Race, Philanthropy and Education in the Southern States of America and East Africa* (Oxford: Clarendon Press, 1971), 51, 56. Thomas Jesse Jones, who headed the commissions, acknowledges Oldham's role in establishing and supporting the First Phelps-Stokes Education Commission. Thomas Jesse Jones, *Education in Africa: A Study of West, South, and Equatorial Africa by the African Education Commission, under the Auspices of the Phelps-Stokes Fund and Foreign Mission Societies of North America and Europe* (New York: Phelps-Stokes Fund, 1922), xxii.
49. Pierre Bovet, 'Education as Viewed by the Phelps-Stokes Commissions', *International Review of Missions* 15, no. 59 (July 1926): 483.
50. King, *Pan-Africanism and Education*, 35–6.
51. Edward H. Berman, 'Tuskegee in Africa', *Journal of Negro Education* 41, no. 2 (Spring 1972): 103; King, *Pan-Africanism and Education*, 121.
52. Jones, *Education in Africa*, 52–4.
53. In 1929 the Phelps-Stokes Fund published a circular entitled 'Information for Africans Planning to Study in the United States of America'. Paragraph 7 advises that the letter of application 'should be accompanied by recommendations (a) from a European or American missionary, preferably one engaged in education; (b) from a government official, preferably in the educational service'. James Hardy Dillard, Thomas Jesse Jones, and others, *Twenty Year Report of the Phelps-Stokes Fund 1911–1931* (New York: Phelps-Stokes Fund, 1932), 26.
54. Jones, *Education in Africa*, 80.
55. As already mentioned, Jones's educational ideas were not exceptional in his time. His recommendations were widely accepted, mainly by missionary educators. Pierre Bovet praised Jones's educational philosophy in an article published in 1926. Bovet, 'Education', 483, 492.
56. Edward H. Berman, 'Educational Colonialism in Africa: The Role of American Foundations, 1910–1945', in *Philanthropy and Cultural Imperialism: The Foundations at Home and Abroad*, ed. Robert F. Arnove (Boston: G. K. Hall, 1980), 188.
57. Quoted in Berman, 'Education in Africa and America: A History of the Phelps-Stokes Fund, 1911–1945', 144.
58. K. J. King, 'The American Negro as Missionary to East Africa: A Critical Aspect of African Evangelism', *African Historical Studies* 3, no. 1 (1970): 11.

59. Bridglal Pachai, *Malawi, the History of the Nation* (London: Longman Group, 1973), 222.
60. R. C. F. Maugham, British Consul-General in Dakar, Senegal, to George Curzon, Principal Secretary of State for Foreign Affairs of Great Britain, 17 August 1922, as published under the title, 'The Influence of Marcus Garvey on Africa', *Science and Society* 32, no. 1 (Winter 1968): 321.
61. King, 'The American Negro as Missionary', 11.
62. Quoted in Roderick J. Macdonald, 'Rev. Dr. Daniel Sharpe Malekebu and the Providence Industrial Mission, 1926–39: An Appreciation', in *From Nyasaland to Malawi: Studies in Colonial History* (Nairobi: East African Publishing House, 1975), 218.
63. Nnamdi Azikiwe, *My Odyssey: An Autobiography* (New York: Praeger, 1970), 181.
64. *Gold Coast Leader*, 17 December 1927, quoted in Tony Martin, *Race First: The Ideological and Organizational Struggles of Marcus Garvey and the Universal Negro Improvement Association* (Westport, Conn.: Greenwood Press, 1976), 114.
65. Richard David Ralston, 'A Second Middle Passage: African Student Sojourns in the United States During the Colonial Period and Their Influence upon the Character of African Leadership' (Ph.D. diss., University of California at Los Angeles, 1972), 86.
66. K. A. B. Jones-Quartey, 'Ghana', in *As Others See Us: The United States through Foreign Eyes*, ed. Franz M. Joseph (Princeton: Princeton University Press, 1959), 244–5. Jones-Quartey, a native of the Gold Coast, acquired his early education in West Africa. From 1934 to 1937, he was employed as a reporter and assistant editor of the *African Morning Post*, Accra, under Nnamdi Azikiwe. From 1937 to 1946, he studied at Lincoln and Columbia universities in the United States. When he returned to the Gold Coast, he was appointed Deputy Director, Department of Extra-Mural Studies, University College, Ghana. Among his publications is K. A. B. Jones-Quartey, *A Life of Azikiwe* (Baltimore, Md.: Penguin Books, 1965).
67. Jesse Jones, 'American Education in Africa', memorandum, 1934, H. P. Stokes Series, Schomburg Center for Research in Black Culture, New York Public Library (hereafter cited as Stokes Series).
68. Berman, 'Educational Colonialism in Africa', 186–7.
69. King, *Pan-Africanism and Education*, 213.
70. Adelaide Casely Hayford, 'Industrial Education: A Pressing Need', *Colonial and Provincial Reporter*, 28 October 1920, 7.
71. 'Mr. Carr's Speech at The Dinner Given by the Reform Club the Phelps-Stokes Education Commission', *Nigerian Pioneer*, 3 December 1920, 6. Henry Carr was described by E. A. Ayandele as 'one of the best minds of his age', an educationist who had 'no equal in West Africa'. Carr was well-off, his father-in-law was Henry Robbin, the wealthiest man in Abeokuta and he held important positions in the church and colonial administration, among them: first secretary of the Lagos Church Missions (1883–1900); founder and member of the Board of Education of the CMS (1886–1900); member of the Legislative Council, Lagos Colony (1886–1894); chief clerk, Lagos Colony (1889–1893); inspector of schools in the colonies (almost continuously from 1891 to 1909); and chairman of a committee whose aim

was to convince the British government to establish industrial education in Nigeria. Ayandele, *Holy Johnson*, 70, 85, 176.

72. 'The Phelps-Stokes Commission: Its Mission and Purpose', *Lagos Weekly Record*, 13 November 1920, 5.

73. Quoted in Berman, 'Education in Africa and America: A History of the Phelps-Stokes Fund, 1911–1945', 164. Charles Loram was heavily involved with African educational matters in South Africa. See Chapter 6.

74. Quoted in Kenneth King, 'Early Pan-African Politicians in East Africa', *Mawazo* 2, no. 1 (June 1969): 9.

75. Quoted in King, *Pan-Africanism and Education*, 233.

76. Jesse Jones to Handley Hooper, 20 December 1926, Stokes Series.

77. Dillard, *Twenty Year Report*, 21–2.

78. Margaret F. Grant, 'Jeanes Teachers in Central Africa', n.d., Stokes Series.

79. H. S. Keigwin to Jesse Jones, Easter Day, 1926; Keigwin to Jones, 21 June 1926, Stokes Series.

80. Quoted in 'Our American Cousins as Our Teachers', *Sierra Leone Weekly News*, 26 May 1928, 9 (italics in original).

81. Quoted in King, *Pan-Africanism and Education*, 206.

82. W. H. Seaton to Jesse Jones, 25 October 1930, Stokes Series.

83. Margaret F. Grant, 'Jeanes Teachers in Central Africa', n.d., Stokes Series.

84. Native teachers to J. W. C. Dougall, July 1926, Stokes Series.

85. Oldham to Jones, 16 March 1927, Stokes Series.

86. L. A. Roy to Thomas Jesse Jones, 10 August 1927, Stokes Series.

87. Jesse Jones to Anson Phelps-Stokes, 23 August 1927, Stokes Series.

88. Ibid.

89. Berman, 'Education in Africa and America: A History of the Phelps-Stokes Fund, 1911–1945', 280–1.

90. Ibid., 281.

91. Ita to Jones, 22 March 1934, Stokes Series; Berman, 'Education in Africa and America: A History of the Phelps-Stokes Fund, 1911–1945', 281.

92. James S. Coleman, *Nigeria: Background to Nationalism* (Berkeley: University of California Press, 1958), 219–20.

93. Berman, 'Education in Africa and America: A History of the Phelps-Stokes Fund, 1911–1945', 283–4.

94. It is interesting to mention that Kalibala, who was scheduled to play an important role on behalf of the Phelps-Stokes Fund, was granted a sum of $400, while other African students who applied for financial aid but were not favored by the fund, such as Emmet Harmon from Liberia and Nnamdi Azikiwe from Nigeria, received more moderate funding, $100 and $25 respectively. L. A. Roy to Anson Phelp Stokes, 17 August 1934, Stokes Series; King, *Pan-Africanism and Education*, 242.

95. T. O. Ranger, *The African Voice in Southern Rhodesia, 1898–1930* (Evanston, Ill.: Northwestern University Press, 1970), 195–6.

96. Coles, *Preacher with a Plow*, 19–20.

97. Berman, 'Education in Africa and America: A History of the Phelps-Stokes Fund, 1911–1945', 282–3.

98. A case in point is Osam Pinanko (Frank Arthur), from the Gold Coast, a schoolmate of Aggrey's at Livingstone College who was sent back in 1903 to Cape Coast as an ordained minister where he served as a presiding elder

of the AME Zion Church and was in charge of the development of the area's churches and educational systems. William J. Walls, *The African Methodist Episcopal Zion Church: Reality of the Black Church* (Charlotte, N.C.: A.M.E. Zion Publishing House, 1974), 236, 239.

99. Ibid., 229. The difficulties of raising money for missionary activities in the United States and abroad are described in detail in Ibid., 374–87.
100. Quoted in Emmett J. Scott, 'Tuskegee in Africa and Africa at Tuskegee', Manuscript in the Washington Papers Container 334, Library of Congress, Washington, D.C., n.d., 2.
101. King, *Pan-Africanism and Education*, 233.
102. Peter Mbiyu Koinange, *The People of Kenya Speak for Themselves* (Detroit: Kenya Publication Fund, 1955), 25–30.
103. Jesse Jones to Ernest Riggs, 22 September 1928, Stokes Series.
104. Charles Loram to J. D. Rheinallt Jones, 19 October 1933, correspondence with African Students Overseas 1933, AD 843/RY/Kb3.3, South African Institute of Race Relations, education, Gen. African Students Overseas, Catalog: Records of the SAIRR, part 2, University of Witwatersrand, Johannesburg, South Africa.
105. L. A. Roy to Dr Phelps-Stokes, memorandum, 17 August 1934, Stokes Series.
106. L. A. Roy to Jesse Jones, 11 August 1924, Stokes Series.
107. Banda had the opportunity to hear Aggrey's address in 1921 in South Africa, three years prior to Aggrey's visit to Banda's homeland, Nyasaland. In 1923 Banda established contact with Bishop L. T. Vernon, AME Church representative in the Union, and asked his help for an opportunity to study in the United States. With the help of the bishop, Banda went to America in July 1925. Kings M. Phiri, 'Afro-American Influence in Colonial Malawi, 1891–1945: A Case Study of the Interaction between Africa and Africans of the Diaspora', in *Global Dimensions of the African Diaspora*, ed. Joseph E. Harris (Washington, D.C.: Howard University Press, 1982), 260.
108. Thomas C. Howard, 'Black American Missionary Influence on the Origins of University Education in West Africa', in *Black Americans and the Missionary Movement in Africa*, ed. Sylvia M. Jacobs (Westport, Conn.: Greenwood Press, 1982), 98.
109. Aggrey gave Azikiwe the book, *Negro Education: A Study of the Private and Higher Schools for Coloured People in the United States*, which provided the necessary contacts for education in America. Vincent C. Ikeotuonye, *Zik of New Africa* (London: Macmillan, 1961), 38, 29.
110. Kwame Nkrumah, *Ghana: The Autobiography of Kwame Nkrumah* (London: Thomas Nelson and Sons, 1957), 15.
111. Kenneth King, 'James E. K. Aggrey: Collaborator, Nationalist, Pan-African', *Canadian Journal of African Studies* 3, no. 3 (Fall 1970): 528.
112. The division between the first and second generations of western-educated Africans is drawn by James Coleman, who uses World War I as the dividing line. Coleman, *Nigeria*, 147. World War I can also be used to define the two generations of American-educated Africans.
113. Data available on 68 Africans who studied in the United States between 1870 and 1900 shows that most of them were converts who were sent to the United States by African-American missions to be trained as missionaries.

Walter Williams, *Black Americans and the Evangelization of Africa, 1877–1900* (Madison: University of Wisconsin Press, 1982), 145–6.

114. George Shepperson and Thomas Price, *Independent African: John Chilembwe and the Origins, Setting and Significance of the Nyasaland Native Rising of 1915* (Edinburgh: Edinburgh University Press, 1958), 146.

115. Jones-Quartey, 'Ghana', 241–2.

116. Azikiwe, *My Odyssey*, 78, 82–4.

117. Martin Kilson, 'The Emergent Elites of Black Africa, 1900 to 1960', in *Colonialism in Africa, 1870–1960*, vol. 2, ed. L. H. Gann and Peter Duignan (Cambridge: Cambridge University Press, 1970), 355, 378.

118. Azikiwe, *My Odyssey*, 32–3.

119. Ibid., 34–5.

120. A. G. Fraser, newsletter no. 19, November 1926, 3–4, Stokes Series.

121. Quoted in Cook and Henderson, *The Militant Black Writer*, 32.

122. Azikiwe, *My Odyssey*, 213.

123. Ibid., 217.

124. Ibid., 280.

125. Jones-Quartey, 'Ghana', 252–3.

126. Quoted in Beaulah M. Flournoy, 'The Relationship of the African Methodist Church to Its South African Members, 1896–1906', *Journal of African Studies* 2, no. 4 (Winter 1975/76): 531.

127. Quoted in King, 'Early Pan-African Politicians', 7.

128. Okechukwu Ikejiani, 'Nigeria's Made-in-America Revolution', *Magazine Digest* (Jan. 1946): 57.

129. Nnamdi Azikiwe, *Zik: A Selection from the Speeches of Nnamdi Azikiwe* (London: Cambridge University Press, 1961), 61.

130. Azikiwe, *My Odyssey*, 174.

131. Akwasi B. Assensoh, 'Kwame Nkrumah of Ghana: His Formative Years and the Shaping of His Nationalism and Pan-Africanism, 1935–1948' (Ph.D. diss., New York University, 1984), 3. Quoted in John Henrik Clarke, *Africans at the Crossroads: Notes for an African World Revolution* (Trenton, N.J.: Africa World Press, 1991), 196.

132. Berman, 'Education in Africa and America: A History of the Phelps-Stokes Fund, 1911–1945', 286.

133. The attraction of the African-American academic curriculum is illustrated in 1933 when I. Clements Muwamba, one of the African trade union leaders in Northern Rhodesia, urged his fellow Africans to pursue education as a means for elevating their socio-economic status as black Americans had done ever since their emancipation. Walton Johnson, *Worship and Freedom: A Black American Church in Zambia* (New York: Africana Publishing, 1977), 15.

134. O. Faduma, 'African Negro Education', *Sierra Leone Weekly News*, 31 August 1918.

135. Quoted in Richard D. Ralston, 'Political Change in Colonial African Leadership (ca. 1914–ca. 1945): American and Afro-American Influences', *Ufahamu* 4, no. 1 (Spring 1973): 90.

136. Jones-Quartey, *A Life of Azikiwe*, 25–7.

137. Azikiwe, *My Odyssey*, 84–5.

138. Ibid., 275.

139. Coleman, *Nigeria*, 244. It is interesting to compare the political activism of

the American-educated West Africans with the attitude of activists in the liberal movement in the Union of South Africa who were attracted by the Booker T. Washington educational philosophy precisely because it was apolitical. This point will be discussed further in Chapter 6.

140. Quoted in Ralston, 'A Second Middle Passage', 87.
141. Horace Mann Bond, 'Forming African Youth, A Philosophy of Education', in *Africa Seen by American Negroes*, ed. Presence Africaine (New York: Presence Africaine, 1958), 260–1.
142. Ikejiani, 'Nigeria's Made-in-America Revolution', 58.
143. Hollis R. Lynch, 'Pan-African Responses in the United States to British Colonial Rule in Africa in the 1940's', in *The Transfer of Power in Africa: Decolonization 1940–1960*, ed. Prosser Gifford and William R. Louis (New Haven: Yale University Press, 1982), 70.
144. Kwame Nkrumah, *Ghana*, 48.
145. John Henrik Clarke points out that Nkrumah, during his years in power, employed more African-Americans than all the other African heads of state combined. Clarke, *Africans at the Crossroads*, 113.
146. *Pretoria News*, n.d.
147. Quoted in Edwin W. Smith, *Aggrey of Africa: A Study in Black and White* (New York: Doubleday, Doran, 1929), 249.
148. Aggrey intended in his dissertation to prove that Great Britain was active in cooperating with Africa and that British colonial rule fostered cooperation between Africans and Europeans. Ibid., 271.

6 The South African Liberal Movement and the Model of the American South

1. H. J. Simons and R. E. Simons, *Class and Colour in South Africa, 1850–1950* (Middlesex: Penguin Books, 1969), 51.
2. The formation and activities of the liberal movement are somewhat obscure because of the problem of defining the term 'liberal' in the class society that existed in South Africa. The small size of the movement also makes research on its activities difficult. Thus, Shula Marks cautiously confines the terms 'liberal attempt' and 'racial harmony' in quotation marks. John W. Cell referred to white liberalism in South Africa as the 'liberal dilemma'. Shula Marks, 'The Ambiguities of Dependence: John Dube of Natal', *Journal of Southern African Studies* 1, no. 2 (April 1975): 163; John W. Cell, *The Highest Stage of White Supremacy: The Origins of Segregation in South Africa and the American South* (Cambridge: Cambridge University Press, 1982), 227.
3. All these organizations were established after World War I by whites and Africans who cooperated to increase understanding between the two races. In addition, liberals established newspapers such as *Umteteli wa Bantu* in 1920, whose stated aim was 'to educate white and black and to point out their respective and their common duties'. Tim Couzens, '"Moralizing Leisure Time": The Trans-Atlantic Connection and Black Johannesburg, 1918–1936', in *Industrialisation and Social Change in South Africa African Class Formation, Culture, and Consciousness, 1870–1930*, ed. Shula Marks and Richard Rathbone (London: Longman, 1982), 318–19.
4. Sheridan Johns III, *Protest and Hope, 1882–1934*, vol. 1 of *From Protest*

  to Challenge: A Documentary History of African Politics in South Africa,
  1882–1964, ed. Thomas Karis and Gwendolyn M. Carter (Stanford: Hoover
  Institution Press, 1972), 8.

5. Ibid., 6.

6. Proceedings and Resolutions of the Non-European Conference, June 1927
  [Extracts], document 44, ibid., 258.

7. D. D. T. Jabavu, *'Native Disabilities in South Africa* (Lovedale: Lovedale
  Institution Press, 1932), 16–18.

8. Quoted in Paul B. Rich, *White Power and the Liberal Conscience: Racial
  Segregation and South African Liberalism, 1921–1960* (Manchester: Manchester University Press, 1984), 18–19.

9. A. P. Walshe, 'Black American Thought and African Political Attitudes in
  South Africa', *Review of Politics* 32 (January 1970): 53–4.

10. Cell, *The Highest Stage,* 31.

11. Quoted in William Manning Marable, 'African Nationalist: The Life of
  John Langalibalele Dube' (Ph.D. diss., University of Maryland, 1976), 244.

12. Booker T. Washington, *Up From Slavery: An Autobiography* (Williamstown:
  Corner House Publishers, 1971), 221–2.

13. Pixley ka Isaka Seme, 'The Regeneration of Africa', *The African Abroad,*
  5 April 1906, document 20, Sheridan Johns III, *Protest and Hope,* 69.

14. Ibid., 61.

15. Pixley ka Isaka Seme, 'The African National Congress – Is it Dead?', 1932
  [Extract], document 481, ibid., 313–15.

16. Proceedings and Resolutions of the Governor-General's Native Conference,
  1926 [Extracts], document 39d, ibid., 184.

17. Rich, *White Power,* 17.

18. Quoted in R. Hunt Davis Jr, 'Charles T. Loram and an American Model for
  African Education in South Africa', *African Studies Review* 19, no. 2 (September 1976): 88, 90. Loram's paternalism in regard to education is clearly
  evident in his writings. However, his position on political matters, such as
  enfranchisement and civil rights for Africans, is more difficult to detect.

19. Quoted in Marable, 'African Nationalist', 300.

20. Loram News, no. 4, October 1933, Charles Loram, Correspondence, Records
  of the South African Institute of Race Relations, University of Witwatersrand,
  Johannesburg, South Africa (hereafter cited as Loram Correspondence).

21. Ibid.

22. Loram News, no. 5, Christmas 1934, Loram Correspondence.

23. Ibid.

24. A. B. Xuma, 'Bridging the Gap Between White and Black in South Africa',
  Address, Conference of European and Bantu Christian Student Associations
  at Fort Hare, 27 June–3 July 1930 [Extracts], Document 41d, Johns, *Protest
  and Hope,* 221.

25. Ibid., 222.

26. Ibid.

27. South African liberals with deep religious backgrounds, such as Reverend
  John Dube, emphasized the role of Christianity in the process of civilization. In that matter as well, the African-American was a model to emulate.
  'From a Christian standpoint the black man of America is highly favored
  above his African cousin in that he is born into and is reared and lives in

Gospel light . . .', and the result was 'The children of American negroes have advantages of some of the best schools in the country, while the African children are taught to believe in idols and superstition.' John L. Dube, 'Are Negroes Better Off in Africa?', *Missionary Review of the World* 17, no. 8 (August 1904): 583.

28. Quoted in R. Hunt Davis, 'John L. Dube: A South African Exponent of Booker T. Washington', *Journal of African Studies* 2, no. 4 (1975/76): 514.

29. Quoted in Ken Smith, *The Changing Past: Trends in South African Historical Writing* (Athens: Ohio University Press, 1988), 134.

30. John L. Dube, President, South African Native National Congress, to the Prime Minister, Petition, 14 February 1914, Document 25, Johns, *Protest and Hope*, 84–6.

31. Quoted in Davis, 'John L. Dube', 497–8.

32. G. Gerhart and T. Karis, eds, *Political Profiles, 1882–1964*, vol. 4 of *From Protest to Challenge: A Documentary History of African Politics in South Africa, 1882–1964*, ed. T. Karis and G. Carter (Stanford: Hoover Institution Press, 1977), 24.

33. John L. Dube, 'Need of Industrial Education in Africa', *Southern Workman* 27, no. 7 (July 1897): 141–2.

34. Marable, 'African Nationalist', 142–52.

35. R. Hunt Davis Jr, 'The Black American Education Component in African Responses to Colonialism in South Africa (ca. 1890–1914)', *Journal of Southern African Affairs* 3, no. 1 (January 1978): 76.

36. Marks, 'The Ambiguities of Dependence', 165, 174; Davis, 'John L. Dube', 524–6.

37. Besides financial support from the United States, Dube relied on the support of the English Committee for Ohlange under the chairmanship of Viscount Buxton. Marable, 'African Nationalist', 105, 165–8, 326.

38. Davis, 'The Black American Education Component', 76.

39. Marable, 'African Nationalist', 302.

40. Loram News, No. 5, Christmas 1934, Loram Correspondence.

41. Quoted in Davis, 'John L. Dube', 517.

42. Davis, 'Charles T. Loram', 91, n 13.

43. Quoted in Edward H. Berman, 'Tuskegee in Africa', *Journal of Negro Education* 41, no. 2 (Spring 1972): 102.

44. Quoted in Davis, 'Charles T. Loram', 91.

45. Quoted in Ibid.

46. Ibid., 92.

47. Ibid.

48. Ibid., 94.

49. Ibid., 94–5.

50. Loram News, No. 5, Christmas 1934, Loram Correspondence.

51. Loram to Reinhallt Jones, 25 January 1934, Loram Correspondence.

52. Swanson, 'Charles T. Loram Biographical Essay', Carter-Karis Collection, microfilm reel 14a, 2:XT8:96/1,2.

53. J. Mutero Chirenje, *Ethiopianism and Afro-Americans in Southern Africa, 1883–1916* (Baton Rouge: Louisiana State University Press, 1987), 124–5.

54. Ibid., 64.

55. Smith, *The Changing Past*, 32, 134.

56. Chirenje, *Ethiopianism*, 124.
57. Ibid., 126.
58. Paul B. Rich, 'The Appeals of Tuskegee: James Henderson, Lovedale, and the Fortunes of South African Liberalism, 1906–1930', *International Journal of African Historical Studies* 20, no. 2 (1987): 275.
59. Ibid., 278.
60. Quoted in Chirenje, *Ethiopianism*, 131–2.
61. Rich, 'The Appeals of Tuskegee', 274–5, 277.
62. D. D. T. Jabavu, 'Booker T. Washington His Methods Applied to South Africa', in *The Black Problem: Papers and Addresses on Various Native Problems* (Lovedale: Lovedale Institution Press, 1920), 25–6, 43.
63. Ibid., 58, 60.
64. Ibid., 38, 57.
65. D. D. T. Jabavu, 'Native Educational Needs', in *The Black Problem: Papers and Addresses on Various Native Problems* (Lovedale: Lovedale Institution Press, 1920), 93–4.
66. Ibid., 93.
67. Johns, *Protest and Hope*, 118–25.
68. D. D. T. Jabavu, 'Natives and Agriculture', in *The Black Problem: Papers and Addresses on Various Native Problems* (Lovedale: Lovedale Institution Press, 1920), 101, 103.
69. Jabavu, 'Native Educational Needs', 94.
70. Colin Bundy, *The Rise and Fall of the South African Peasantry* (London: Heinemann, 1979), 113, 115, 127, 135.
71. Jabavu, 'Booker T. Washington', 63–4.
72. Richard D. Ralston, 'American Episodes in the Making of an African Leader: A Case Study of Alfred B. Xuma (1893–1962)', *International Journal Of African Historical Studies* 6, no. 1 (1973): 75–6.
73. Ibid., 78.
74. *Chicago Tribune*, March 1946.
75. A. B. Xuma, 'Bridging the Gap Between White and Black in South Africa', Address at the Conference of European and Bantu Christian Student Associations at Fort Hare, 27 June–3 July 1930 [Extracts], Document 41d, Johns, *Protest and Hope*, 227.
76. Ibid., 223–4.
77. Edward H. Berman, 'Education in Africa and America: A History of the Phelps-Stokes Fund, 1911–1945' (Ed.D. diss., Columbia University, 1970), 159–60.
78. It is worth noting that the idea of interracial meetings was initiated by members of the American Zulu Mission. Already in 1883, they arranged an interdenominational meeting of black and white ministers in Pietermaritzburg. At that meeting, a concrete plan for interdenominational cooperation was agreed upon. Clement Tsehloane Keto, 'American Involvement in South Africa, 1870–1915: The Role of Americans in the Creation of Modern South Africa' (Ph.D. diss., Georgetown University, 1972), 142.
79. Errol Byrne, *The First Liberal Rheinallt Jones* (Johannnesburg: Angel Press, 1990), 22–4.
80. Reverend Abner Mtimkulu, 'The Native Problem', *Cape Times*, 30 May 1924, Document 41c, Johns, *Protest and Hope*, 216.

81. Berman, 'Education in Africa and America: A History of the Phelps-Stokes Fund, 1911–1945', 236; Quintin Whyte, 'Interracial Cooperation', in *Handbook on Race Relations in South Africa*, ed. Ellen Hellmann (Cape Town: Oxford University Press, 1949), 653.
82. Berman, 'Education in Africa and America: A History of the Phelps-Stokes Fund, 1911–1945', 238.
83. Johns, *Protest and Hope*, 151.
84. Edgar H. Brookes, *The Colour Problems of South Africa: Being the Phelps-Stokes Lectures, 1933, Delivered at the University of Cape Town* (Westport, Conn.: Negro University Press, 1970), 15–16.
85. James S. Thaele, 'Christianity, Basis of Native Policy?', *Workers' Herald*, 21 December 1923, Document 41b, Johns, *Protest and Hope*, 215, 150.
86. Walshe, 'Black American Thought', 62.
87. Johns, *Protest and Hope*, 150.
88. Report of the Native Affairs Department for the Years 1919 to 1921, Cape Town, Cape Times Limited, Government Printers, 1922, 2.
89. Byrne, *The First Liberal Rheinallt Jones*, 25.
90. Ellen Hellmann, 'Fifty Years of the South African Institute of Race Relations', in *Race Relations in South Africa, 1929–1979*, ed. Ellen Hellmann and Henry Lever (London: Macmillan, 1980), 9.
91. Byrne, *The First Liberal Rheinallt Jones*, 22.
92. Loram News, No. 4, October 1933, Loram Correspondence.
93. Loram News, No. 5, Christmas 1934, 3–4, Loram Correspondence.
94. Ibid; Davis, 'Charles T. Loram', 90.
95. Quoted in 'Rise and Progress of the Negro in America', *Sierra Leone Weekly News*, 15 November 1930, 11.
96. Thomas J. Woofter was a specialist on race relations at the University of North Carolina. Reinhallt Jones became acquainted with Woofter during his tour of the US in 1930. J. D. Rheinhallt Jones to C. T. Loram, 13 April 1933, Loram Correspondence.
97. C. T. Loram to J. D. Rheinhallt Jones, 18 November 1936, Loram Correspondence.
98. C. T. Loram to J. D. Rheinhallt-Jones, 8 May 1934, Loram Correspondence.
99. C. T. Loram to J. D. Reinhallt-Jones, 4 January 1935, Loram Correspondence.
100. Rich, *White Power*, 7.
101. Berman, 'Education in Africa and America: A History of the Phelps-Stokes Fund, 1911–1945', 242–3.
102. Contributions from other sources, mainly Britain, were also received, but were considerably smaller. Rheinhallt-Jones succeeded in obtaining the sum of £1,000 from the Rhodes Trust in England during said period. Byrne, *The First Liberal Rheinallt Jones*, 28.
103. R. D. Heyman, 'C. T. Loram: A South African Liberal in Race Relations', *International Journal of African Historical Studies* 5, no. 1 (1972): 47–8.
104. Notice to Members of the Seminar, H. P. Stokes Series, Schomburg Center for Research in Black Culture, New York Public Library.
105. Berman, 'Education in Africa and America: A History of the Phelps-Stokes Fund, 1911–1945', 243.

Bibliography

ARCHIVAL SOURCES

Archives

Carter-Karis Collection. Microfilm reel 14a, 2:XT8:96/1,2. Archives. Hoover Institution on War, Revolution and Peace, Stanford, California.
Correspondence with African Students Overseas 1933. South African Institute of Race Relations. University of Witwatersrand, Johannesburg, South Africa.
Garvey, Marcus. Papers. African Studies Center, University of California, Los Angeles.
Loram, Charles. Correspondence. South African Institute of Race Relations. University of Witwatersrand, Johannesburg, South Africa. Microfilm CD2459.J6.568r. Hoover Institution Library, Stanford, California.
H. P. Stokes Series. Schomburg Center for Research in Black Culture. New York Public Library, New York.
South Africa: A Collection of Miscellaneous Documents, 1902–1963. Microfilm reel 12. Archives. Hoover Institution on War, Revolution and Peace, Stanford, California.

Published documents

Azikiwe, Nnamdi. *Zik: A Selection from the Speeches of Nnamdi Azikiwe*. London: Cambridge University Press, 1961.
Bracey, John H. Jr., August Meier and Elliott Rudwick, eds. *The Afro-Americans: Selected Documents*. Boston: Allyn and Bacon, 1972.
Hill, Robert A., ed. *The Marcus Garvey and Universal Negro Improvement Association Papers, 27 August 1919–31 August 1920*. Vol. 2. Berkeley: University of California Press, 1983.
Hill, Robert A., ed. *The Marcus Garvey and Universal Negro Improvement Association Papers, 1 September 1921–2 September 1922*. Vol. 4. Berkeley: University of California Press, 1985.
Johns, Sheridan III. *Protest and Hope, 1882–1934*. Vol. 1 of *From Protest to Challenge: A Documentary History of African Politics in South Africa, 1882–1964*. Eds. Thomas Karis and Gwendolyn M. Carter. Stanford: Hoover Institution Press, 1972.
Maugham, R. C. F., British Consul-General in Dakar, Senegal, to George Curzon, Principal Secretary of State for Foreign Affairs of Great Britain. 17 August 1922. As published under the title, 'The Influence of Marcus Garvey on Africa: A British Report of 1922'. *Science and Society* 32, no. 1 (Winter 1968): 321–3.
Report of the Native Affairs Department for the Years 1919 to 1921. Capetown: Cape Times Limited, Government Printers, 1922.

NEWSPAPERS

African Times and Orient Review (London), July 1912.
African World (London), 14 August 1920–30 September 1921.
Baltimore Afro-American, 9 May 1924, p. 1. Archives: African Studies Center, Marcus Garvey Papers, UCLA; File: Touvalou-Houenou.
Central African Times (London), 25 May 1901.
Chicago Tribune, March 1946, clipping in Personal Papers of Dr Alfred Bitini Xuma, 1921–49, Johannesburg.
Colonial and Provincial Reporter (London), 7 August–20 October 1920.
Les Continents (Paris), 1 October 1924.
Depeche Coloniale et Maritime (Paris), 6 September 1921.
Gold Coast Aborigines, 19 November 1898–25 February 1899.
Gold Coast Chronicle, 12 May 1900–5 July 1901.
Gold Coast Leader, 13 January 1906–12 January 1924.
Gold Coast Nation, 6 February 1913.
Gold Coast Times, 16 February 1924.
Lagos Daily News, 30 December 1931.
Lagos Standard, 27 May–28 October 1903.
Lagos Weekly Record, 13 October 1894–27 November 1920.
La Nation Belge (Brussels), 24 September 1921.
Negro World (New York), 21 March 1921–27 October 1928.
Nigerian Pioneer 22 October–17 December 1920.
Outlook, 29 March 1902.
Pretoria News, n.d., press cutting. AD 1433/Cp 9.5 (Joint Council of Africans and Europeans). Catalog Record of the South African Institute of Race Relations, University of Witwatersrand, Johannesburg, South Africa.
Rhodesia Herald, 6 June 1924.
Sierra Leone Weekly News, 12 May 1900–6 May 1939.
Times of Nigeria, 1–8 February 1916–24 May 1920.
West Africa (London), 12 February 1919–8 October 1921.
West Africa Mail and Trade Gazette (London), 24 September 1921.

UNPUBLISHED SOURCES

Achode, Codjo. 'The Negro Renaissance from America Back to Africa: A Study of the Harlem Renaissance as a Black and African Movement'. Ph.D. diss., University of Pennsylvania, 1986.
Assensoh, Akwasi B. 'Kwame Nkrumah of Ghana: His Formative Years and the Shaping of His Nationalism and Pan-Africanism, 1935–1948'. Ph.D. diss., New York University, 1984.
Berman, Edward H. 'Education in Africa and America: A History of the Phelps-Stokes Fund, 1911–1945'. Ed.D. diss., Columbia University, 1970.
Bodie, Charles Alvis. 'The Images of Africa in the Black American Press, 1890–1930'. Ph.D. diss., Indiana University, 1975.
Fierce, Milfred C. 'African-American Interest in Africa and Interaction with West

Africa: The Origins of the Pan-African Idea in the United States, 1900–1919'. Ph.D. diss., Columbia University, 1976.

Harr, Wilber Christian. 'The Negro as an American Protestant Missionary in Africa'. Ph.D. diss., University of Chicago, 1945.

Keto, Clement Tsehloane. 'American Involvement in South Africa, 1870–1915: The Role of Americans in the Creation of Modern South Africa'. Ph.D. diss., Georgetown University, Washington, D.C., 1972.

Marable, William Manning. 'African Nationalist: The Life of John Langalibalele Dube'. Ph.D. diss., University of Maryland, 1976.

Nelson, Carlos I. H. 'Kwame Nkrumah: A Study of his Intellectual Development in the United States, 1935–1945'. Ph.D. diss., Temple University, 1985.

Okonkwo, Rina Lee. 'The Emergence of Nationalism in British West Africa, 1912–1940'. Ph.D. diss., City University of New York, 1980.

Ralston, Richard David. 'A Second Middle Passage: African Student Sojourns in the United States During the Colonial Period and Their Influence upon the Character of African Leadership'. Ph.D. diss., University of California at Los Angeles, 1972.

Ranger, T. O. 'The Myth of the Afro-American in East-Central Africa, 1900–1939'. African Studies Center, University of California, Los Angeles, April 1971. Mimeographed.

Roth, Donald Franklin. '"Grace Not Race" Southern Negro Church Leaders, Black Identity, and Missions to West Africa, 1865–1919'. Ph.D. diss., University of Texas at Austin, 1975.

Scott, Emmett J. 'Tuskegee in Africa and Africa at Tuskegee'. Manuscript in the Washington Papers Container 334, Library of Congress, Washington, D.C., n.d. The author used a photocopy available in Hoover Archives, Hoover Institution, Stanford University.

Scott, William R. 'A Study of Afro-American and Ethiopian Relations, 1896–1941'. Ph.D. diss., Princeton University, 1971.

Shepperson, George. 'The African Abroad or the African Diaspora'. Paper presented at the International African History Conference, Tanzania, 1965.

PUBLISHED SOURCES

Adams, C. C. and Marshall A. Talley. *Negro Baptists and Foreign Missions*. Philadelphia: The Foreign Mission Board of the National Baptist Convention, USA, Inc., 1944.

Afigbo, A. E. 'The Establishment of Colonial Rule, 1900–1918'. In *History of West Africa*. Vol. 2, eds. J. F. A. Ajayi and Michael Crowder, 424–83. London: Longman, 1974.

Agbodeka, Francis. 'The Fanti Confederacy, 1865–1869: An Enquiry Into the Origins, Nature and Extent of an Early West African Protest Movement'. *Transactions of the Historical Society of Ghana* 7 (1964): 82–123.

Andersson, Efraim. *Messianic Popular Movements in the Lower Congo*. Uppsala, Sweden: Studia Ethnographica Upsaliensia. XIV, 1958.

Angell, Stephen Ward. *Bishop Henry McNeal Turner and African-American Religion in the South*. Knoxville: University of Tennessee Press, 1992.

Anthony, David H. 'Max Yergan in South Africa: From Evangelical Pan-Africanist to Revolutionary Socialist'. *African Studies Review* 34, no. 2 (September 1991): 27–55.

Ayandele, E. A. *Holy Johnson: Pioneer of African Nationalism, 1836–1917*. London: Frank Cass, 1970.

———. *The Missionary Impact on Modern Nigeria, 1842–1914: A Political and Social Analysis*. New York: Humanities Press, 1967.

———. *A Visionary of the African Church: Mojola Agbebi, 1860–1917*. Nairobi: East African Publishing House, 1971.

Azikiwe, Nnamdi. *My Odyssey: An Autobiography*. New York: Praeger, 1970.

Barkun, Michael. *Disaster and the Millennium*. Syracuse: Syracuse University Press, 1986.

Bascom, William. 'African Culture and the Missionary'. *Civilisations* 3, no. 4 (1953): 491–502.

Bastide, R. 'Messianism and Social and Economic Development'. In *Social Change: The Colonial Situation*, ed. Immanuel Wallerstein, 467–77. New York: John Wiley and Sons, 1966.

Berman, Edward H. 'Educational Colonialism in Africa: The Role of American Foundations, 1910–1945'. In *Philanthropy and Cultural Imperialism: The Foundations at Home and Abroad*, ed. Robert F. Arnove, 179–202. Boston: G. K. Hall, 1980.

———. 'Tuskegee in Africa'. *Journal of Negro Education* 41, no. 2 (Spring 1972): 99–112.

Blyden, Edward W. 'Africa and the Africans'. In *Readings in African Political Thought*, ed. Gideon-Cyrus M. Mutiso and S. W. Rohio, 10–18. London: Heinemann, 1975.

———. *The African Problem and other Discourses, Delivered in America in 1890*. London: W. B. Whittingham, 1890.

———. 'Ethiopia Stretching Out Her Hands Unto God: or Africa's Service to the World'. In *Readings in African Political Thought*, ed. Gideon-Cyrus M. Mutiso and S. W. Rohio, 3–9. London: Heinemann, 1975.

Boadi-Siaw, S. Y. 'Brazilian Returnees of West Africa'. In *Global Dimensions of the African Diaspora*, ed. Joseph E. Harris, 291–308. Washington, D.C.: Howard University Press, 1982.

Boahen, A. Adu. *African Perspectives on Colonialism*. Baltimore: Johns Hopkins University Press, 1987.

Boone, Clinton Caldwell. *Congo as I Saw It*. New York: J. J. Little and Ives, 1927.

Bovet, Pierre. 'Education as Viewed by the Phelps-Stokes Commissions'. *International Review of Missions* 15, no. 59 (July 1926): 483–92.

Brookes, Edgar H. *The Colour Problems of South Africa: Being the Phelps-Stokes Lectures, 1933, Delivered at the University of Cape Town*. Westport, Conn.: Negro University Press, 1970.

Bruner, Jerome S. 'Myth and Identity'. In *Myth and Mythmaking*, ed. Henry A. Murray, 276–87. Boston: Beacon Press, 1968.

Bundy, Colin. *The Rise and Fall of the South African Peasantry*. London: Heinemann, 1979.

Burkett, Randall K. *Garveyism as a Religious Movement: The Institutionalization of a Black Civil Religion*. Metuchen, N.J.: Scarecrow Press, 1978.

Byrne, Errol. *The First Liberal Rheinallt Jones*. Johannnesburg: Angel Press, 1990.

Cary, Joyce. *The Case For African Freedom and Other Writings on Africa*. Austin: University of Texas Press, 1962.

Cassell, C. Abayomi. *Liberia: History of the First African Republic*. New York: Fountainhead Publishers, 1970.

Cauthen, Baker J. and others, eds. *Advance: A History of Southern Baptist Foreign Missions*. Nashville, Tenn.: Broadman Press, 1970.

Cell, John W. *The Highest Stage of White Supremacy: The Origins of Segregation in South Africa and the American South*. Cambridge: Cambridge University Press, 1982.

Charpin, Henri. 'La question noire'. *La Revue Indigene* 18 (November–December 1922): 275–85.

Chirenje, J. Mutero. 'The Afro American Factor in Southern African Ethiopianism, 1890–1906'. In *Profiles of Self-Determination: African Responses to European Colonialism in Southern Africa, 1652–Present*, ed. David Chanaiwa, 250–80. Northridge: California State University Foundation, 1976.

——. *Ethiopianism and Afro-Americans in Southern Africa, 1883–1916*. Baton Rouge: Louisiana State University Press, 1987.

Clarke, John Henrik. *Africans at the Crossroads: Notes for an African World Revolution*. Trenton, N.J.: Africa World Press, 1991.

Coleman, James S. *Nigeria: Background to Nationalism*. Berkeley: University of California Press, 1958.

Coles, Samuel B. *Preacher with a Plow*. Boston: Houghton Mifflin, 1957.

Cook, Mercer, and Stephen E. Henderson. *The Militant Black Writer in Africa and the United States*. Madison: University of Wisconsin Press, 1969.

Copplestone, J. Tremayne. *History of Methodist Missions*. Vol. 4, *Twentieth-Century Perspectives (The Methodist Episcopal Church, 1896–1939)*. New York: Board of Global Ministries of United Methodist Church, 1973.

Couzens, Tim. '"Moralizing Leisure Time": The Transatlantic Connection and Black Johannesburg, 1918–1936'. In *Industrialisation and Social Change in South Africa: African Class Formation, Culture, and Consciousness, 1870–1930*, ed. Shula Marks and Richard Rathbone, 314–37. New York: Longman, 1982.

Cowan, Laing Gray, James O'Connell and David G. Scanlon, eds. *Education and Nation-Building in Africa*. New York: F. A. Praeger, 1965.

Cronon, E. David. *Black Moses: The Story of Marcus Garvey and the Universal Negro Improvement Association*. Madison: University of Wisconsin Press, 1987.

Cunningham, Adrian, ed. *The Theory of Myth: Six Studies*. London: Sheed and Ward, 1973.

Curtin, Philip. *Death by Migration: Europe's Encounter with the Tropical World in the Nineteenth Century*. Cambridge: Cambridge University Press, 1989.

Curtin, Philip, Steven Feierman, Leonard Thompson and Vansina Jan Thompson. *African History*. London: Longman, 1978.

Daniel, Stephen H. *Myth and Modern Philosophy*. Philadelphia: Temple University Press, 1990.

Davis, Charles T. *Black is the Color of the Cosmos: Essays on Afro-American Literature and Culture, 1942–1981*, ed. Henry Louis Gates Jr. Washington: Howard University Press, 1989.

Davis, R. Hunt Jr. 'The Black American Education Component in African Responses to Colonialism in South Africa: (ca. 1890–1914)'. *Journal of Southern African Affairs* 3, no. 1 (January 1978): 65–83.

——. 'Charles T. Loram and an American Model for African Education in South Africa'. *African Studies Review* 19, no. 2 (September 1976): 87–99.

——. 'John L. Dube: A South African Exponent of Booker T. Washington'. *Journal of African Studies* 2, no. 4 (1975/76): 497–528.

Daye, Pierre. 'Le mouvement pan-negre'. *Le Flambeau* 3 (May–August 1921): 359–75.

Delafosse, Maurice. 'Le Congres Panafricain'. *Bulletin du Comité de l'afrique Francaise* (March–April 1919): supplement 53–9.

Detweiler, Frederick German. *The Negro Press in the United States*. College Park, Md.: McGrath Publishing, 1968.

Dillard, James Hardy, Thomas Jesse Jones, and others. *Twenty Year Report of the Phelps-Stokes Fund, 1911–1931*. New York: Phelps-Stokes Fund, 1932.

Drake, St Clair. '"Hide my Face?" On Pan-Africanism and Negritude'. In *The Making of Black America Essays in Negro Life and History*. Vol. 1, ed. August Meier and Elliott Rudwick, 66–87. New York: Atheneum, 1969.

——. 'Negro Americans and the Africa Interest'. In *The American Negro Reference Book*, ed. John P. Davis, 662–705. Englewood Cliffs, N.J.: Prentice-Hall, 1966.

——. *The Redemption of Africa and Black Religion*. Chicago: Third World Press, 1970.

Dube, John L. 'Are Negroes Better Off in Africa?'. *Missionary Review of the World* 17, no. 8 (August 1904): 583–6.

——. 'Need of Industrial Education in Africa'. *Southern Workman* 27, no. 7 (July 1897): 141–5.

Du Bois, W. E. B. 'Africa and the American Negro Intelligentsia'. *Presence Africaine* 5 (1955–6): 34–51.

——. *Dusk of Dawn: An Essay Toward an Autobiography of a Race Concept*. 1940. New York: Schocken Books, 1968.

——. *The Souls of Black Folk: Essays and Sketches*. New York: Fawcett Publications, 1970.

Edgar, Robert. 'Garveyism in Africa: Dr. Wellington and the American Movement in the Transkei'. *Ufahamah* 6, no. 3 (1976): 31–57.

Egonu, Iheanachor. '"Les Continents and the Francophone" Pan Negro Movement'. *Phylon* 42, no. 3 (Fall 1981): 245–54.

Essien-Udom, E. U. 'The Relationship of Afro-Americans to African Nationalism'. *Freedomways* 2, no. 4 (Fall 1962): 391–407.

Fax, Elton C. *Garvey: The Story of a Pioneer Black Nationalist*. New York: Dodd, Mead, 1972.

Fetter, Bruce, ed. *Colonial Rule in Africa: Readings from Primary Sources*. Madison: University of Wisconsin Press, 1979.

Fierce, Milfred C. *The Pan-African Idea in the United States, 1900–1919: African-American Interest in Africa and Interaction with West Africa*. New York: Garland Publishing, 1993.

Flournoy, Beaulah M. 'The Relationship of the African Methodist Church to Its South African Members, 1896–1906'. *Journal of African Studies* 2, no. 4 (Winter 1975/76): 529–45.

Garvey, Amy Jacques. *Black Power in America: Marcus Garvey's Impact on*

Jamaica and Africa: The Power of the Human Spirit. Kingston, Jam.: Amy Jacques Garvey, 1968.

——. *Garvey and Garveyism.* New York: Octagon Books, 1978.

——. ed. *Philosophy and Opinions of Marcus Garvey: or Africa for the Africans.* 2nd edn, 2 vols. London: Frank Cass, 1967.

Geiss, Imanuel. *The Pan-African Movement: A History of Pan-Africanism in America, Europe and Africa.* Trans. Ann Keep. New York: Africana Publishing, 1974.

Gerhart, G., and T. Karis, eds. *Political Profiles, 1882–1964.* Vol. 4 of *From Protest to Challenge: A Documentary History of African Politics in South Africa, 1882–1964,* ed. T. Karis and G. Carter. Stanford: Hoover Institution Press, 1977.

Gorog-Karady, Veronika. 'Stereotypes ethniques et domination coloniale: l'image du Blanc dans la litterature orale africaine'. *Cahiers d'Etudes Africaines* 15, no. 4 (1975): 635–47.

Gray, Richard. *Black Christians and White Missionaries.* New Haven: Yale University Press, 1990.

——. 'Popular Theologies in Africa: A Report on a Workshop on Small Christian Communities in Southern Africa'. *African Affairs* 85 (January 1986): 49–54.

Gregg, John A. 'Africa and a Way Out'. *AME Church Review* 37, no. 4 (April 1921): 205–13.

Haliburton, G. M. *The Prophet Harris: A Study of an African Prophet and His Mass Movement in the Ivory Coast and the Gold Coast, 1913–1915.* London: Longman, 1971.

Harlan, Louis R. 'Booker T. Washington and the White Man's Burden'. *American Historical Review* 71, no. 2 (January 1966): 441–67.

——. *Booker T. Washington, The Wizard of Tuskegee, 1901–1915.* Vol. 2. New York: Oxford University Press, 1983.

Hayford, Casely. *Ethiopia Unbound: Studies in Race Emancipation.* London: C. M. Phillips, 1911.

——. *The Truth about the West African Land Question.* 1913. Reprint New York: Negro Universities Press, 1969.

Hellmann, Ellen. 'Fifty Years of the South African Institute of Race Relations'. In *Race Relations in South Africa, 1929–1979,* ed. Ellen Hellmann and Henry Lever, 1–27. London: Macmillan, 1980.

Helmreich, William B., ed. *Afro-Americans and Africa: Black Nationalism at the Crossroads.* African Bibliographic Center, new ser., no. 3. Westport, Conn.: Greenwood Press, 1977.

Heward, Christine. 'The Rise of Alice Lenshina'. *New Society* 4, no. 98 (13 August 1964): 6–7.

Heyman, R. D. 'C. T. Loram: A South African Liberal in Race Relations'. *International Journal of African Historical Studies* 5, no. 1 (1972): 41–50.

Hickey, Dennis, and Kenneth C. Wylie. *An Enchanting Darkness: The American Vision of Africa in the Twentieth Century.* East Lansing: Michigan State University Press, 1993.

Hill, Adelaide Cromwell, and Martin Kilson, eds. *Apropos of Africa: Sentiments of Negro American Leaders on Africa from the 1800's to the 1950's.* London: Frank Cass, 1969.

Hodges, Tony. *Jehovah's Witnesses in Africa.* Minority Rights Group, no. 29. London: Minority Rights Group, 1985.

Hodgkin, Thomas. *Nationalism in Colonial Africa*. New York: New York University Press, 1962.

Hooker, James R. *Black Revolutionary: George Padmore's Path from Communism to Pan-Africanism*. New York: Praeger, 1967.

——. 'Witnesses and Watchtower in the Rhodesias and Nyasaland'. *Journal of African History* 6, no. 1 (1965): 91–106.

Horton, Africanus B. *Letters on the Political Condition of the Gold Coast*. 2nd edn. London: Frank Cass, 1970.

Howard, Thomas C. 'Black American Missionary Influence on the Origins of University Education in West Africa'. In *Black Americans and the Missionary Movement in Africa*, ed. Sylvia M. Jacobs, 95–127. Westport, Conn: Greenwood Press, 1982.

Huggins, Nathan Irvin. *Harlem Renaissance*. New York: Oxford University Press, 1971.

Hymans, Jacques Louis. 'French Influences on Leopold Senghor's Theory of Negritude, 1928–48'. *Race: The Journal of the Institute of Race Relations* 7, no. 4 (April 1966): 365–70.

Ikejiani, Okechukwu. 'Nigeria's Made-in-America Revolution'. *Magazine Digest* (January 1946): 57–60.

Ikeotuonye, Vincent C. *Zik of New Africa*. London: Macmillan, 1961.

Isaacs, Harold R. 'Du Bois and Africa'. *Race: The Journal of the Institute of Race Relations* 2, no. 1 (November 1960): 3–22.

Jabavu, D. D. T. 'Booker T. Washington: His Methods Applied to South Africa'. In *The Black Problem: Papers and Addresses on Various Native Problems*. 2nd edn, 25–67. Lovedale: Lovedale Institution Press, 1920.

——. *'Native Disabilities' in South Africa*. Lovedale: Lovedale Institution Press, 1932.

——. 'Native Educational Needs'. In *The Black Problem: Papers and Addresses on Various Native Problems*. 2nd edn, 92–6. Lovedale: Lovedale Institution Press, 1920.

——. 'Native Unrest Its Cause and Cure'. In *The Black Problem: Papers and Addresses on Various Native Problems*. 2nd edn, 1–17. Lovedale: Lovedale Institution Press, 1920.

——. 'Natives and Agriculture'. In *The Black Problem: Papers and Addresses on Various Native Problems*. 2nd edn, 97–107. Lovedale: Lovedale Institution Press, 1920.

Johnson, Walton. 'The Africanization of a Mission Church: The African Methodist Episcopal Church in Zambia'. In *African Christianity: Patterns of Religious Continuity*, ed. George Bond and others, 89–107. New York: Academic Press, 1979.

——. 'The AME Church and Ethiopianism in South Africa'. *Journal of Southern African Affairs* 3, no. 2 (April 1978): 211–24.

——. *Worship and Freedom: A Black American Church in Zambia*. New York: Africana Publishing, 1977.

Johnston, Harry H. *Liberia*. Vol. 2. 1906. Reprint, New York: Negro Universities Press, 1969.

Jones, Thomas Jesse. *Education in Africa: A Study of West, South, and Equatorial Africa by the African Education Commission, under the Auspices of the Phelps-Stokes Fund and Foreign Mission Societies of North America and Europe*. New York: Phelps-Stokes Fund, 1922.

Jones-Quartey, K. A. B. *A Life of Azikiwe.* Baltimore, Md.: Penguin Books, 1965.
———. 'Ghana'. In *As Others See Us: The United States Through Foreign Eyes*, ed. Franz M. Joseph, 240–57. Princeton: Princeton University Press, 1959.
July, Robert W. *The Origins of Modern African Thought: Its Development in West Africa During the Nineteenth and Twentieth Centuries.* London: Faber and Faber, 1968.
———. 'Nineteenth-Century Negritude: Edward W. Blyden'. *Journal of African History* 5, no. 1 (1964): 73–86.
Kake, Ibrahima B. 'The Impact of Afro-Americans on French-Speaking Black-Africans, 1919–1945'. In *Global Dimensions of the African Diaspora*, ed. Joseph E. Harris, 195–209. Washington, D.C.: Howard University Press, 1982.
Kane, Hamidou Cheikh. *L'Aventure Ambigue Recit.* Paris: Union Generale D'editions, 1961.
Keto, Clement T. 'Black Americans and South Africa, 1890–1910'. *A Current Bibliography on African Affairs* 5, no. 6 (1972): 383–406.
Kilson, Martin. 'The Emergent Elites of Black Africa, 1900 to 1960'. In *Colonialism in Africa, 1870–1960.* Vol. 2, ed. L. H. Gann and Peter Duignan, 351–98. Cambridge: Cambridge University Press, 1970.
———. 'The National Congress of British West Africa, 1918–1935'. In *Protest and Power in Black Africa*, ed. Robert I. Rotberg and Ali A. Mazrui, 571–88. New York: Oxford University Press, 1970.
Kimble, David. *A Political History of Ghana: the Rise of Gold Coast Nationalism, 1850–1928.* London: Clarendon Press, 1963.
King, Kenneth J. 'The American Negro as Missionary to East Africa: A Critical Aspect of African Evangelism'. *African Historical Studies* 3, no. 1 (1970): 5–22.
———. 'Early Pan-African Politicians in East Africa'. *Mawazo* 2, no. 1 (June 1969): 2–10.
———. 'James E. K. Aggrey: Collaborator, Nationalist, Pan-African'. *Canadian Journal of African Studies* 3, no. 3 (Fall 1970): 511–30.
———. *Pan-Africanism and Education: A Study of Race, Philanthropy and Education in the Southern States of America and East Africa.* Oxford: Clarendon Press, 1971.
Kirk, Geoffrey Stephen. *Myth: Its Meaning and Functions in Ancient and Other Cultures.* Cambridge: Cambridge University Press, 1970.
Kohn, Hans, and Wallace Sokolsky. *African Nationalism in the Twentieth Century.* Princeton, N. J.: D. Van Nostrand, 1965.
Koinange, Peter Mbiyu. *The People of Kenya Speak for Themselves.* Detroit: Kenya Publication Fund, 1955.
Kolakowski, Leszek. *The Presence of Myth.* Trans. Adam Czerniawski. Chicago: University of Chicago Press, 1989.
Kunnie, J. E. 'Black Churches in the United States and South Africa: Similarities and Differences'. In *Afro-Christianity at the Grassroots: Its Dynamics and Strategies*, ed. G. C. Oosthuizen, M. C. Kitshoff and S. W. D. Dube, 80–94. Leiden: E. J. Brill, 1994.
Lang, Andrew. *Myth, Ritual and Religion.* Vols 1 and 2. 1906. Reprint, New York: AMS Press, 1968.
Langley, J. Ayodele. *Pan-Africanism and Nationalism in West Africa, 1900–1945: A Study in Ideology and Social Classes.* Oxford: Clarendon Press, 1978.

———. 'Pan-Africanism in Paris, 1924–36'. *Journal of Modern African Studies* 7, no. 1 (1969): 69–94.

Lanternari, Vittorio. *The Religions of the Oppressed: A Study of Modern Messianic Cults.* Trans. Lisa Sergio. New York: Alfred A. Knopf, 1963.

Levin, Harry. 'Some Meanings of Myth'. In *Myth and Mythmaking*, ed. Henry A. Murray, 103–14. Boston: Beacon Press, 1968.

Levi-Strauss, Claude. *Structural Anthropology.* 2 vols. New York: Basic Books, 1963.

Lewis, David Levering. *W. E. B. Du Bois: Biography of a Race, 1868–1919.* New York: Henry Holt, 1993.

———. ed. *W. E. B. Du Bois: A Reader.* New York: Henry Holt, 1995.

———. *When Harlem Was in Vogue.* New York: Oxford University Press, 1989.

Linden, Ian, and Jane Linden. *Catholics, Peasants, and Chewa Resistance in Nyasaland, 1889–1939.* Berkeley: University of California Press, 1974.

———. 'John Chilembwe and the New Jerusalem'. *Journal of African History* 12, no. 4 (1971): 629–51.

Lohrentz, Kenneth P. 'Joseph Booth, Charles Domingo, and the Seventh Day Baptists in Northern Nyasaland, 1910–1912'. *Journal of African History* 12, no. 3 (1971): 461–80.

Lynch, Hollis R. 'Edward W. Blyden: Pioneer West African Nationalist'. *Journal of African History* 6, no. 3 (1965): 373–88.

———. 'Pan-African Responses in the United States to British Colonial Rule in Africa in the 1940's'. In *The Transfer of Power in Africa: Decolonization 1940–1960*, ed. Prosser Gifford and William R. Louis, 57–86. New Haven: Yale University Press, 1982.

Macdonald, Roderick J. 'Rev. Dr. Daniel Sharpe Malekebu and the Re-opening of the Providence Industrial Mission, 1926–1939: An Appreciation'. In *From Nyasaland to Malawi: Studies in Colonial History*, 215–33. Nairobi: East African Publishing House, 1975.

Magubane, Bernard. *The American Negro's Conception of Africa: A Study in the Ideology of Pride and Prejudice.* Los Angeles: University of California Press, 1967.

———. *The Ties That Bind: African-American Consciousness of Africa.* Trenton, N.J.: Africa World Press, 1989.

Mahaniah, Kimpianga. 'The Presence of Black Americans in Lower Congo from 1878 to 1921'. In *Global Dimensions of the African Diaspora*, ed. Joseph E. Harris, 268–82. Washington, D.C.: Howard University Press, 1982.

Mali, Joseph. *The Rehabilitation of Myth: Vico's 'New Science'.* Cambridge: Cambridge University Press, 1992.

Mann Bond, Horace. 'Forming African Youth: A Philosophy of Education'. In *Africa Seen by American Negroes*, ed. Presence Africaine, 247–61. New York: Presence Africaine, 1958.

Manoedi, M. Mokete. *Garvey and Africa.* New York: New York Age Press, [192?].

Maquet-Tombu, Jeanne. *Le Siecle marche: Recit Historique.* Brussels: Office de Publicite Anc. Etabliss, J. Lebegue Societe Cooperative, 1936.

Marable, Manning. 'Ambiguous Legacy: Tuskegee's "Missionary" Impulse and Africa During the Moton Administration, 1915–1935'. In *Black Americans and the Missionary Movement in Africa*, ed. Sylvia M. Jacobs, 77–93. Westport, Conn.: Greenwood Press, 1982.

Marcus, John T. 'The World Impact of the West: The Mystique and the Sense of Participation in History'. In *Myth and Mythmaking*, ed. Henry A. Murray, 221–40. Boston: Beacon Press, 1968.

Marks, Shula. 'The Ambiguities of Dependence: John L. Dube of Natal'. *Journal of Southern African Studies* 1, no. 2 (April 1975): 162–80.

Martin, Tony. *The Pan-African Connection: From Slavery to Garvey and Beyond.* New Marcus Garvey Library, no. 6. Dover, Mass.: Majority Press, 1983.

——. *Race First: The Ideological and Organizational Struggles of Marcus Garvey and the Universal Negro Improvement Association.* Westport, Conn.: Greenwood Press, 1976.

Mazrui, Ali A. 'The World Economy and the African/Afro-American Connection'. In *Dynamics of the African/Afro-American Connection: From Dependency to Self-Reliance*, ed. Adélaide M. Cromwell, 36–53. Washington, D.C.: Howard University Press, 1987.

Mbiti, John S. *African Religions and Philosophy.* 2nd edn. London: Heinemann, 1989.

Mboya, Tom. 'Our Revolutionary Tradition: An African View'. *Current History* (Dec. 1956): 343–7.

McCracken, John. *Politics and Christianity in Malawi, 1875–1940: The Impact of the Livingstonia Mission in the Northern Province.* London: Cambridge University Press, 1971.

Medford, Hampton Thomas, *Zion Methodism Abroad: Giving the Rise and Progress of the A.M.E. Zion Church on its Foreign Fields.* Washington D.C.: n.p., 1937.

Merlier, Michel. *Le Congo de la colonisation belge a l'independance.* Paris: Francois Maspero, 1962.

Moikobu, Josephine Moraa, *Blood and Flesh: Black American and African Identifications.* Contributions in Afro-American and African Studies, no. 59. Westport, Conn.: Greenwood Press, 1981.

Moses, Wilson Jeremiah. *Black Messiahs and Uncle Toms: Social and Literary Manipulations of a Religious Myth.* University Park: Pennsylvania State University Press, 1982.

——. *The Golden Age of Black Nationalism, 1850–1925.* Camden, Conn.: Archon Book, 1978; New York: Oxford University Press, 1988.

Mphahlele, Ezekiel, B. Enwonwu, and T. O. Oruwariye. 'Comments on AMSAC Pan-Africanism Conference'. In *Readings in African Political Thought*, ed. Gideon-Cyrus M. Mutiso and S. W. Rohio, 71–4. London: Heinemann, 1975.

Mudimbe, V. Y. *The Invention of Africa: Gnosis, Philosophy, and the Order of Knowledge.* Bloomington: Indiana University Press, 1988.

Mwase, George Simeon. *Strike a Blow and Die: A Narrative of Race Relations in Colonial Africa.* Ed. with an introduction by Robert I. Rotberg. Cambridge, Mass.: Harvard University Press, 1967.

Nkrumah, Kwame. *Ghana: The Autobiography of Kwame Nkrumah.* London: Thomas Nelson and Sons, 1957.

Nyang, Sulayman S. *Islam, Christianity and African Identity.* Brattleboro, Vt.: Amana Books, 1984.

Okonkwo, Rina Lee. 'The Garvey Movement in British West Africa'. *Journal of African History* 21, no. 1 (1980): 105–17.

——. 'Orishatukeh Faduma: A Man of Two Worlds'. *Journal of Negro History* 68, no. 1 (Winter 1983): 24–36.

Okoye, Felix N. *The American Image of Africa: Myth and Reality.* Buffalo: Black Academy Press, 1971.

Ottley, Roi. *No Green Pastures.* New York: Charles Scribner's Sons, 1951.

Pachai, Bridglal. *Malawi: The History of the Nation.* London: Longman Group, 1973.

Padmore, George. *Pan-Africanism or Communism.* London, 1956; London: Doubleday, 1971.

Pettazzoni, Raffaele. 'The Truth of Myth'. In *Sacred Narrative: Readings in the Theory of Myth,* ed. Alan Dundes, 98–136. Berkeley: University of California Press, 1984.

Phiri, Kings M. 'Afro-American Influence in Colonial Malawi, 1891–1945: A Case Study of the Interaction between Africa and Africans of the Diaspora'. In *Global Dimensions of the African Diaspora,* ed. Joseph E. Harris, 250–67. Washington, D.C.: Howard University Press, 1982.

Presence Africaine. *Africa Seen by American Negroes.* New York: Presence Africaine, 1958.

Priestley, Margaret. *West African Trade and Coast Society: A Family Study.* London: Oxford University Press, 1969.

Quick, Griffith. 'Some Aspects of the African Watch Tower Movement in Northern Rhodesia'. *International Review of Missions* 29, no. 114 (April 1940): 216–26.

Ralston, Richard D. 'American Episodes in the Making of an African Leader: A Case Study of Alfred B. Xuma (1893–1962)'. *International Journal of African Historical Studies* 6, no. 1 (1973): 72–93.

———. 'Political Change in Colonial African Leadership (ca. 1914–ca. 1945): American and Afro-American Influences'. *Ufahamu* 4, no. 1 (Spring 1973): 78–110.

Ranger, T. O. *The African Voice in Southern Rhodesia, 1898–1930.* Evanston, Ill.: Northwestern University Press, 1970.

———. 'The "Ethiopian" Episode in Barotseland, 1900–1905'. *Rhodes-Livingstone Journal* 37 (June 1965): 26–41.

———. 'The Mwana Lesa Movement of 1925'. In *Themes in the Christian History of Central Africa,* ed. T. O. Ranger and John Weller, 45–75. Berkeley: University of California Press, 1975.

Redkey, Edwin S. *Black Exodus: Black Nationalist and Back-to-Africa Movements, 1890–1910.* New Haven: Yale University Press, 1969.

———. 'The Flowering of Black Nationalism: Henry McNeal Turner and Marcus Garvey'. In *Key Issues in the Afro-American Experience.* Vol. 2, ed. Nathan I. Huggins, Martin Kilson and Daniel M. Fox, 107–24. New York: Harcourt, Brace, Jovanovich, 1971.

Rich, Paul B. *White Power and the Liberal Conscience: Racial Segregation and South African Liberalism, 1921–1960.* Manchester: Manchester University Press, 1984.

———. 'The Appeals of Tuskegee: James Henderson, Lovedale, and the Fortunes of South African Liberalism, 1906–1930'. *International Journal of African Historical Studies* 20, no. 2 (1987): 271–91.

Roberts, Andrew D. 'The Lumpa Church of Alice Lenshina'. In *Protest and Power in Black Africa,* ed. Robert I. Rotberg and Ali A. Mazrui, 513–68. New York: Oxford University Press, 1970.

Robinson, Pearl T., and Elliott P. Skinner, eds. *Transformation and Resiliency in*

Africa as Seen by Afro-American Scholars. Washington, D.C.: Howard University Press, 1983.

Rohdie, Samuel. 'The Gold Coast Aborigines Abroad'. *Journal of African History* 6, no. 3, (1965): 389–411.

Roosevelt, Theodore. *American Ideals and Other Essays, Social and Political.* London: G. P. Putnam's Sons, 1897; New York: Knickerbocker Press, 1970.

Rotberg, Robert I. 'Psychological Stress and the Question of Identity: Chilembwe's Revolt Reconsidered'. In *Protest and Power in Black Africa*, ed. Robert I. Rotberg and Ali A. Mazrui, 337–76. New York: Oxford University Press, 1970.

——. *The Rise of Nationalism in Central Africa: The Making of Malawi and Zambia, 1873–1964.* Cambridge, Mass.: Harvard University Press, 1965.

Rudwick, Elliott M. *W. E. B. Du Bois: Propagandist of the Negro Protest.* New York: Atheneum, 1968.

Runcie, John. 'The Influence of Marcus Garvey and the Universal Negro Improvement Association in Sierra Leone'. *Africana Research Bulletin* 12, no. 3. (June 1983): 3–42.

Sachs, Wulf. *Black Anger: The Mind of an African Negro Revealed by Psychoanalysis.* 2nd edn. New York: Greenwood Press, 1968.

Scanlon, David G., ed. *Church, State, and Education in Africa.* New York: Teacher's College Press, 1966.

Schorer, Mark. 'The Necessity of Myth'. In *Myth and Mythmaking*, ed. Henry A. Murray, 354–8. Boston: Beacon Press, 1968.

Senghor, L. S. 'What is Negritude?' In *Readings in African Political Thought*, ed. Gideon-Cyrus M. Mutiso and S. W. Rohio, 83–4. London: Heinemann, 1975.

Shepperson, George A. 'Abolitionism and African Political Thought'. *Transition* 3, no. 12 (1964): 22–6.

——. 'Ethiopianism and African Nationalism'. *Phylon* 14, no. 1 (1953): 9–18.

——. 'External Factors in the Development of African Nationalism, with Particular Reference to British Central Africa'. In *African Politics and Society: Basic Issues and Problems of Government and Development*, ed. Irving Leonard Markovitz, 179–98. New York: Free Press, 1970.

——. *Myth and Reality in Malawi.* The Fourth Melville J. Herskovits Memorial Lecture. Evanston, Ill.: Northwestern University Press, 1966.

——. 'Notes on Negro American Influences on the Emergence of African Nationalism'. *Journal of African History* 1, no. 2 (1960): 299–312.

——. 'Nyasaland and the Millennium'. In *Black Africa, Its Peoples and Their Cultures Today*, ed. John Middleton, 234–47. London: Macmillan, 1970.

——. 'Pan-Africanism and "Pan-Africanism": Some Historical Notes'. *Phylon* 23, no. 4 (Winter 1962): 346–57.

——. 'The Place of John Chilembwe in Malawi Historiography'. In *The Early History of Malawi*, ed. Bridglal Pachai, 405–28. Evanston, Ill.: Northwestern University Press, 1972.

Shepperson, George, and Thomas Price. *Independent African: John Chilembwe and the Origins, Setting and Significance of the Nyasaland Native Rising of 1915.* Edinburgh: Edinburgh University Press, 1958.

Simons, H. J., and R. E. Simons. *Class and Colour in South Africa, 1850–1950.* Middlesex: Penguin Books, 1969.

Skinner, Elliott P. *Afro-Americans and Africa: The Continuing Dialectic.* New York: Columbia University Press, 1973.

———. *African Americans and U.S. Policy Toward Africa, 1850–1924: In Defense of Black Nationality.* Washington, D.C.: Howard University Press, 1992.

———. 'Personal Networks and Institutional Linkages in the Global System'. In *Dynamics of the African/Afro-American Connection: From Dependency to Self-Reliance,* ed. Adelaide M. Cromwell, 15–31. Washington, D.C.: Howard University Press, 1987.

Smith, Edwin W. *Aggrey of Africa: A Study in Black and White.* New York: Doubleday, Doran, 1929.

Smith, Ken. *The Changing Past: Trends in South African Historical Writing.* Athens: Ohio University Press, 1988.

Sowell, Thomas. *Ethnic America: A History.* New York: Basic Books, 1981.

Spitzer, Leo. *The Creoles of Sierra Leone: Responses to Colonialism, 1870–1945.* Madison: University of Wisconsin Press, 1974.

Stroup, Herbert Hewitt. *The Jehovah's Witnesses 1945.* New York: Russell and Russell, 1967.

Suret-Canale, J. 'Un pionnier meconnu du mouvement democratique et national en Afrique'. *Etudes Dahomeennes,* no. 3 (December 1964): 5–28.

Taylor, John V., and Dorothea A. Lehmann. *Christians of the Copperbelt: The Growth of the Church in Northern Rhodesia.* London: SCM Press, 1961.

Thwaite, Daniel. *The Seething African Pot: A Study of Black Nationalism, 1882–1935.* London: Constable, 1936.

Turner, Bishop H. M. 'The American Negro and the Fatherland'. In *Africa and the American Negro: Addresses and Proceedings of the Congress on Africa . . . December 13–15, 1895,* ed. John Wesley Bowen, 195–8. Miami: Mnemosyne Publishing, 1969.

Uya, Okon Edet, ed. *Black Brotherhood: Afro-Americans and Africa.* Lexington, Mass.: D. C. Heath, 1971.

Walker, F. Deaville. *The Day of the Harvest in the White Fields of West Africa.* London: Cargate Press, n.d.

Walls, William J. *The African Methodist Episcopal Zion Church: Reality of the Black Church.* Charlotte, N.C.: A.M.E. Zion Publishing House, 1974.

Walshe, A. P. 'Black American Thought and African Political Attitudes in South Africa'. *Review of Politics* 32 (Jan. 1970): 51–77.

Walters, Alexander. *My Life and Work.* New York: Fleming H. Revell, 1917.

Walters, Ronald W. *Pan Africanism in the African Diaspora: An Analysis of Modern Afrocentric Political Movements.* Detroit: Wayne State University Press, 1993.

Washington, Booker T. *Up From Slavery: An Autobiography.* Garden City, N.Y.: Doubleday, 1901; Williamstown: Corner House Publishers, 1971.

Webster, J. B. 'Political Activity in British West Africa, 1900–1940'. In *History of West Africa.* Vol. 2, ed. J. F. A. Ajayi and Michael Crowder, 568–95. London: Longman, 1974.

White, Amos Jerome, and Luella White. *Dawn in Bantuland: An African Experiment, or an Account of Missionary Experiences and Observations in South Africa.* Boston: Christopher Publishing, 1953.

Whyte, Quintin. 'Interracial Cooperation'. In *Handbook on Race Relations in South Africa,* ed. Ellen Hellmann, 651–68. Capetown: Oxford University Press, 1949.

Wilcox, W. C. 'John L. Dube: the Booker T. Washington of the Zulus'. *Missionary Review of the World* 22, no. 12 (Dec. 1909): 915–19.

Williams, Walter L. *Black Americans and the Evangelization of Africa, 1877–1900*. Madison: University of Wisconsin Press, 1982.

Wintz, Cary D. *Black Culture and the Harlem Renaissance*. Houston, Texas: Rice University Press, 1988.

Wright, Richard R. Jr. *Eighty-seven Years Behind the Black Curtain: An Autobiography*. Philadelphia: Rare Book, 1965.

Wyse, Akintola J. G. 'The Sierra Leone Krios: A Reappraisal from the Perspective of the African Diaspora'. In *Global Dimensions of the African Diaspora*, ed. Joseph E. Harris, 309–37. Washington, D.C.: Howard University Press, 1982.

Index

Index